((((

Democratic Breakdown
and the
Russian Army

Library of Congress Cataloging-in-Publication Data

Barany, Zoltan D.
Democratic breakdown and the decline of the
Russian military / Zoltan Barany.
p.   cm.
Includes bibliographical references and index.
ISBN-13: 978-0-691-12896-2 (hardcover : alk. paper)
ISBN-10: 0-691-12896-0 (hardcover : alk. paper)
1. Russia (Federation). Russkaia Armiia—Reorganization. 2. Russia (Federation).
Russkaia Armiia—Political activity. 3. Civil-military relations—Russia (Federation).
4. Russia (Federation)—Politics and government—1991– I. Title.
UA772.B275 2007
322′.50947—dc22
2006033996

British Library Cataloging-in-Publication Data is available

A University Co-operative Society Subvention Grant awarded by
the University of Texas as Austin aided the marketing of this book, and is
gratefully acknowledged by Princeton University Press.

This book has been composed in Sabon with Insignia display

Printed on acid-free paper. ∞

press.princeton.edu

Printed in the United States of America

1   3   5   7   9   10   8   6   4   2

(((

CONTENTS

《《《

*To my beloved little daughter,
Catherine*

((((

ACKNOWLEDGMENTS

One of the first undergraduate term papers I wrote in the Soviet and East European Studies program at Carleton University in the mid 1980s analyzed Admiral Sergei Gorshkov's drive to establish a global Soviet navy. Although since then I have occasionally wandered far in my research and writing from Soviet-Russian military issues, they have never left my peripheral vision. Since the late 1990s—starting with a symposium on Russian politics I organized and the subsequent book my colleague Robert Moser and I edited—Russian civil-military relations returned to my professional life as one of my primary preoccupations. This book is the culmination of my work in this field.

I am happy to recognize colleagues who took the time to read parts of the manuscript in its various incarnations and provided me with constructive criticism: Mark Beissinger, Michael Dennis, Roger Haydon, Dale Herspring, Patricia Maclachlan, Jennifer Mathers, Thomas Nichols, Scott Parrish, Anna Seleny, and Brian Taylor. I want to record my special appreciation to Dale, Tom, and Brian for their own first-rate scholarship on the core issues of this book and their careful and straightforward comments that improved my study. I presented the theoretical argument to the Comparative Politics/Democratization Workshop in my department, and its members—Henry Dietz, Wendy Hunter, Raúl Madrid, Rob Moser, and Ami Pedahzur—rewarded me with sage advice. The talented group of graduate students in my spring 2006 "Soldiers and Politics" seminar read the entire manuscript and gave me excellent feedback.

I am grateful to the many friends and colleagues—in addition to those mentioned above—who facilitated introductions, wrote letters on my behalf, answered queries, sent materials, talked with me about the project, or invited me to talk about it: Pavel Baev, A. David Baker III, Archie Brown, Valerie Bunce, Daniel Chirot, Joseph Derdzinski, Vladimir Gel'-man, Aleksandr Golts, Lionel Ponsard, and David Yost. There are many others, mostly in Russia, whose positions would make it most imprudent to thank them publicly. They know who they are and how much I value their assistance. Two visiting fellowships—at the Centre for International Relations at the University of Oxford in 2003 and at the East-West Center in Honolulu in 2006—provided pleasant and stimulating work environments for the beginning and the completion of the project. I tried out different parts of the argument at the U.S. Air Force Academy, the University of Texas, Texas A&M University, the University of Wisconsin, the NATO Defense College in Rome, the East-West Center, and St. Antony's College at Oxford, and the questions and comments from these audiences had proved to be very helpful.

The project received a good deal of financial support from various sources in my ever-generous home institution, including a Faculty Research Assignment that freed me from teaching responsibilities for the fall 2004 semester. The Frank C. Erwin, Jr., Centennial Professorship I have been privileged to hold paid for some of the travel and research expenses. I was honored to receive yet another award from the International Research and Exchange Board for a research trip to Moscow in 2005. I declined the grant, with IREX's full understanding and support, because by this time doing fieldwork on "sensitive subjects" in Russia had become dangerous both for researchers—who, like me, refuse to mislead the Russian authorities about what they are interested in studying—and, even more so, for those willing to talk to them.

Portions of my earlier work on Russian military politics and related subjects found their way into the book in a much revised form. I thank the editors and publishers of these publications for permitting me to cite myself.

"Controlling the [Russian] Military: A Partial Success," *Journal of Democracy* 10:2 (April 1999): 54–67.

"Politics and the Russian Armed Forces," in Zoltan Barany and Robert G. Moser, eds., *Russian Politics: Challenges of Democratization* (New York: Cambridge University Press, 2001), 174–214.

The Future of NATO Expansion (New York: Cambridge University Press, 2003).

"The Tragedy of the *Kursk*: Crisis Management in Putin's Russia," *Government and Opposition* 39:3 (summer 2004): 476–503.

"The Politics of Russia's Elusive Defense Reform," *Political Science Quarterly* 121:4 (winter 2006–7): 597–627.

I want to thank Chuck Myers at Princeton University Press for his interest in and enthusiasm for this study and attentive involvement in the publication process. The book is better because of his efforts and those of others at the press with whom it was a pleasure to work: Jack Rummel and Deborah Tegarden.

Finally, a word of thanks to my "girls": My wife, Patricia Maclachlan, a fellow social scientist, urged me to write this book because she knew that I would enjoy researching and writing it and I did, for the most part. We broke with our long-standing tradition of not discussing each other's work as I asked her to read some of the manuscript. Patti brought to this task her uncompromising standards and made some terrific suggestions. Our little daughter, Catherine, is far less interested in my scholarly pursuits than in maximizing the time we spend together. I am old enough to have my priorities in order and have tried to make sure that my work does not encroach on our family life. I am confident that I more or less succeeded but just in case she is not entirely satisfied, I dedicate this book to Catherine as paternal settlement. I doubt that she will ever read it but I know she will be delighted to see her name on the dedication page.

Zoltan Barany
September 2006
Austin, Texas

((((

Democratic Breakdown
and the
Russian Army

((((

INTRODUCTION

The fifteen years since the founding of the new, post-Communist Russian Army have been marked by the unprecedented deterioration of the once-proud Soviet military. Unprecedented, that is, because there is no similar case in world history of a dominant armed force so rapidly and so thoroughly deteriorating without being defeated in battle. As a perceptive 2001 article noted, "Russia's fall from military superpower Number Two to a country whose army can be neutralized by bands of irregulars fighting with little more than the weapons on their backs" was one of the most spectacular elements of the Soviet Union's collapse.[1] The army's decline had actually begun during the late-Brezhnev era in the early 1980s and then had gathered momentum in the late 1980s under President Mikhail Gorbachev. The rule of Russia's first president, Boris Yeltsin, however, was synonymous with a virtual free-fall of the military's effectiveness and overall standards.

A plethora of articles and books published in Russia and abroad have depicted the shocking conditions in the armed forces brought about by the years of neglect, financial constraints, and competing priorities for state attention. In the 1990s officers left the service in droves to escape poor pay, lack of adequate housing, insufficient training, and plummeting social prestige. Soldiers were often compelled to feed themselves by foraging in forests and fields, their commanders rented them out as laborers, and the physical abuse they were subjected to by fellow conscripts and commanders alike frequently drove them to desertion or suicide. In the meantime, a seemingly endless string of major accidents and defeat at the hands of a ragtag guerrilla force added to the army's public humiliation.

In some respects—particularly regarding the armed forces' material conditions—matters have improved since the ascension of Vladimir Putin to the presidency in 2000. Most important, defense expenditures have been steadily and significantly boosted under his tenure for two reasons. First, the president apparently recognized the magnitude of the army's problems, particularly after the tragedy of the *Kursk* nuclear submarine in August 2000. Second, owing to the substantial and long-term increases in the world market price of Russia's main sources of export, crude oil and natural gas, more money has become available for defense spending. Nonetheless, many of the underlying causes of the armed forces' predicament have not been seriously addressed let alone eliminated, and the military has not undergone the fundamental reforms it needs. To be sure, radically transforming a huge organization like the Soviet military establishment is anything but easy. Still, I contend, little has been done and much of whatever *has* been done has been often ill-conceived and in many ways seemingly directed at re-creating the Soviet Army. That fighting force was appropriate to counter the challenges of the 1970s and even 1980s but not those of the early twenty-first century.

Why has meaningful defense reform been absent in Russia fifteen years after the USSR's demise? After all, the Kremlin—particularly since the emergence of Putin—has clamored for a leadership role in world affairs, it has been the beneficiary of a financial boon owing to increasing world commodity prices, and it has a long and proud military tradition upheld by millions of veterans who demand a rapid reversal of their army's fading fortunes. Pursuing this puzzle points to the very essence of Russia's increasingly authoritarian political system, and it can be largely explained by two major and closely interrelated factors.

First, since the mid 1980s Soviet-Russian military elites have gradually acquired a political presence that is unacceptable even by the most generous definition of democratic civil-military relations, which is, in itself, an important indicator of the degree of democratization. In recent years, as Michael McFaul and his colleagues note in a fresh appraisal of the contemporary Russian polity, the "military's influence on political decisions has grown significantly."[2] This is all the more surprising because the increasing political role of Russian generals has occurred simultaneously with the remarkable decline of the strength and effectiveness of their forces. The most detrimental way in which the top brass have exploited their political clout has been their steadfast and successful opposition to substantive defense reform, which they view as a threat to their own interests. Although efforts to transform the military in line with shifting political and strategic realities originated in the mid 1980s, other than a significant reduction of manpower in the 1990s and the introduction of contract service in recent years, no radical changes have taken place. As a result, the Russian army remains out of tune with the times and, if current reform concepts survive, will remain so in the foreseeable future. Its standards in practically all important respects have fallen far behind those of even middle-rank European military powers, not to mention those of the United States or Great Britain.

Second, in the final analysis, the blame for the absence of major defense reform and the growing political presence of the military should be laid at the doorstep of the Russian president. Since 1993 Russia has become a state characterized by "superpresidentialism," a term that depicts inordinately extensive executive powers. A parallel development has been the declining importance of the Russian legislature and judiciary as independent institutions. By definition, democratic civilian control over the armed forces is balanced between the executive and legislative branches of the state. In Russia—as in many other authoritarian states—however, civilian oversight has become synonymous with presidential domination. In essence, as long as the president does not feel compelled to rein in the armed forces, the latter will be able to promote their corporate interests though they may counteract those of the nation.

The Russian armed forces and their relationship to the post-Communist state and society is an important subject for several reasons. First, Russia remains a pivotal state, a major player in contemporary world politics keenly interested in the restoration of its great power status even if the United States alone can claim to be a superpower or, as former French foreign minister Hubert Vedrine would have it, "hyperpower." Second, Russia does control massive stockpiles of nuclear and other weapons of mass destruction. The security of those weapons—which depends primarily on the military—is an important concern to both Russians and others in the world around them. Third, in Washington, at least, Moscow is viewed as America's partner in the fight against international terrorism and nuclear proliferation, it has been the recipient of substantial Western security-strategic aid, and its military bases are located in some instances only miles away from U.S. installations in the Caucasus and Central Asia. The evolution of Russia's army is, therefore, something U.S. policy makers, defense professionals, and the American public should be concerned with. Finally, as I noted above, because the state of civil-military relations is a gauge of democratization, Russian military politics ought to provide a telling commentary about the country's fifteen-year-long post-Communist path.

THE THEORETICAL FRAMEWORK

The main purpose of this book is to explain three related phenomena and their causes in the post-Communist Russian context: the elusive nature of major defense reform, the political role of generals and senior officers, and the institutional arrangements of civilian control over the armed forces. I will make three interrelated arguments:

The fundamental reason for the absence of substantial defense reform is the military elites' opposition to it. The armed forces leadership is against the sort of reform Russia needs—the army's transformation to a more mobile, flexible, and smaller force with a higher proportion of professional soldiers rather than draftees—because it directly contradicts its interests in several respects. Cuts in manpower would require reducing the bloated Russian officer corps. Decreasing the ratio of conscripts—let alone abolishing the draft—would rob officers of the easily intimidated labor force they have been able to exploit for their own purposes. More-over, many generals continue to believe that the army should prepare for a large-scale war and, therefore, it must be capable of mobilizing hun-dreds of thousands or even millions of soldiers, which would necessitate the retention—and given Russia's demographic predicament, even exten-sion—of the conscription system.

Russian military elites have acquired a political role that is incompati-ble with democratic politics. Although the army was politically influential in the Communist period, its *independent* political role was very limited. This has changed in the past fifteen years. Hundreds of active-duty officers have run for political office because there are no legal regulations that forbid it. During the Yeltsin era leading generals often publicly criticized the state and its policies, thwarted policy implementation, and refused to carry out orders, more or less with impunity. Under Putin the frequency of such behavior has drastically declined, owing to increasing state strength and more direct executive supervision—principally through De-fense Minister Sergei Ivanov. Still, although the political participation of the armed forces leadership has appreciably diminished, Putin has actually reinforced the notion of the military's legitimate political presence by appointing generals—along with many more security services personnel—to influential political positions.

The ultimate explanation for the military's political role and the absence of meaningful defense reform points to the Russian polity, in which, since 1993, power has gradually shifted toward the executive branch, more precisely, to the president. As a result, in contemporary Russia the legislature is nearly as powerless as it was in late-Soviet times. Civilian control over the armed forces, far from a balance of oversight responsibilities between the legislature and the executive, has come to mean, in practice, presidential authority. It would be irrational for the president to prohibit the political activities of military personnel or to aggressively push defense reform. In fact, he has a stake in appointing more officers to powerful political posts because they—and, more generally, the military-security establishment—have comprised an unwavering support base for him. There are a number of other equally important and rational grounds for Putin's reluctance to consider defense reform a top priority: political consensus about the nature of reform is lacking, there are several competing and arguably more pressing items on his agenda, financial resources remain finite, and many in the political establishment still think of defense spending as a "non-productive expenditure" particularly when the country's nuclear arsenal provides a sturdy deterrent to large-scale foreign aggression.

My objective in this book is to explain and support these arguments. What theoretical approaches can be summoned to enrich, complement, and illuminate the story and explain the Russian military's political influence? Although the civil-military relations literature is an obvious candidate to help us out, we can use some of the key ideas of the new institutionalism approach even more profitably.

INSTITUTIONALISM AND INSTITUTIONAL DECAY

The various strands of new institutionalism have not produced a universally accepted definition of institutions, but the one provided by Douglass North—institutions as "a set of rules, compliance procedures, and moral and ethical behavioral norms designed to constrain the behavior of individuals in the interest of maximizing the wealth or utility of principals"—is a common point of reference and, for the purposes at hand, a good starting point.[3] Institutionalist approaches tend to focus on the "regularities in repetitive interactions, . . . customs and rules that provide a set of incentives and disincentives for individuals."[4] The chief end-function of institutions, after all, is "to regularize the behavior of the individuals who operate within them."[5]

Indeed, institutionalist approaches are at their strongest when called on to explain the workings of institutions in a stable environment. They are less successful in dealing with institutions in flux. Writing about rational choice institutionalism, Robert Bates and his coauthors acknowledge that "political transitions seem to defy rational forms of analysis."[6] There is broad agreement, however, that once institutions get established they tend to perpetuate themselves and become resistant to change, especially sudden change. Institutional change, "a shift in the rules and enforcement procedures so that different behaviors are constrained or encouraged," is ordinarily incremental.[7] Still, as North argues, "Wars, revolutions, conquest, and natural disasters are sources of discontinuous institutional change," that is, radical change in the formal rules of the game.[8]

For institutionalists—especially historical institutionalists—change is path dependent, that is, when a policy is being formulated or an institution is established, certain choices are made that are usually self-perpetuating. As Margaret Weir has argued, "Decisions at one point in time can restrict future possibilities by sending policy off onto particular tracks, along which ideas and interests develop and institutions and strategies adapt."[9] In other words, events at Time A set institutions on a particular historical or political trajectory that becomes difficult to reverse at Time B because the costs of change outweigh the benefits. The importance of path dependence is that it focuses our attention on the "formative moments" or "critical junctures" for institutions and organizations when the path is set, confirmed, or changed.[10] As North put it, "Path dependence means that history matters."[11] I concur with Paul Pierson, who argues that there is institutional change even after path dependence sets the course. Nonetheless, his strong emphasis on "self-reinforcing or positive feedback processes in the political system"[12] seems to prevent him from considering even the potentiality of *negative* institutional change. In this study I demonstrate that this is a mistake: protracted negative institutional change— a phenomenon I call "institutional decay"—once a path is settled on is an equally possible outcome, although the new institutionalism approach has not provided a helpful way of accounting for it.

Students of comparative politics have utilized the concept of institutional decay in various ways. For example, Minxin Pei notes that contemporary Chinese political institutions deteriorate for many reasons (including "the weakening ideological appeal of a political doctrine" that defines an institution's missions and upholds its norms) and that decay may take several forms (e.g., massive abuse of power by the ruling elite and deterioration of organizational cohesion). This sort of decay in turn leads to declining organizational effectiveness.[13] In his study of Soviet rural transformation Neil Melvin argues that broadening the participation of policy debates to include specialists and professionals in the 1980s led to the decay and eventual fragmentation of policy-making institutions.[14] Neither scholar, however, define institutional decay, and their usage for the concept of institutions is limited to formal structures. In his work on Sri Lankan ethnic conflict, Neil Devotta does provide a definition for the concept—"institutional decay, especially in a poly-ethnic setting, ensues whenever the state's rule-making, -applying, -adjudicating, and -enforcing institutions eschew dispassionate interactions with all constituencies and groups and instead resort to particularistic interventions"[15]—but this is far too imprecise and context driven to be of more general utility.

I define institutional decay as *a process marked by the erosion and breakdown of previously accepted and observed rules and norms governing organizational behavior.* Along with institutionalists, I consider rules as formal institutions that are codified (such as laws and regulations). Norms, on the other hand, are informal institutions that are culturally based and accepted behavioral standards or customs reflected and reinforced by the organization's history. Ordinarily, institutional breakdown has much to do with the erosion of norms that, in fact, support rules. Institutional decay usually begins with the wearing away of previously robust informal institutions due to destabilizing influences that then provoke degenerative changes in formal institutions. For instance, behaviors that were initially considered objectionable and illegal may be accommodated by changing legal regulations. In some instances, however, the reverse can also occur, meaning, that the revision of formal institutions (rules) can lead to and advance the decay of informal institutions (norms).

Let me relate the concepts of institutional decay and path dependence to Russian civil-military relations and show how they help us account for the Russian army's changing political role. For decades, firm and clearly defined institutional standards and procedures had regulated and were integral characteristics of Soviet civil-military relations. These basic rules (formal institutions) included the army's protection and promotion of the party-state's interests, its obedience to military superiors and civilian authorities, and its careful management of state assets. Among the essential norms (informal institutions) were the officers' unquestioned loyalty to the Communist Party of the Soviet Union (CPSU), their avoidance of active political interference and criticism of politicians, and their rejection of using subordinates for private gain. Soviet officers were thoroughly indoctrinated with these norms and socialized to accept them unquestioningly. Few experts would dispute that these rules and norms no longer define contemporary Russian civil-military relations though they may still exert some influence on the military establishment. The concepts of path dependence and institutional decay help to explain why.

I contend that there are three formative moments or critical junctures that have determined the course of Soviet and then Russian civil-military relations in the past two decades. These three moments have reinforced the institutional decay, which, in turn, is manifested in the political presence of Russian military elites. They are (1) Gorbachev's *invitation* to officers to actively participate in politics; (2) Yeltsin's *acquiescence* to a new institutional environment that did not deny the military's political role; and (3) Putin's *confirmation* of this role through the appointment of generals to important political posts and his reluctance to enforce the implementation of state policies (such as radical defense reform) in the armed forces.

These formative moments have been critical to the specific path and institutional decay of civil-military relations. The end result of this negative change has been that the active political presence of generals has gradually become an acceptable feature of Russian politics. The three Soviet-Russian presidents share the primary responsibility for this outcome because their actions defined these critical junctures. Gorbachev's action set into motion precisely the kind of "revolution" North identified, a drastic change in the rules of the game as it was theretofore played. He set civil-military relations on a new path that his successors in the Kremlin further strengthened as they expanded their own powers. In contemporary Russia the president enjoys virtually unbridled political authority to initiate policy and enforce its implementation without any authentic legislative or judicial opposition. Instead of establishing civilian control over the military shared by the president, the government, and the parliament, Yeltsin and Putin equated civilian control with presidential oversight. They not only failed to promote legal instruments that barred soldiers and officers from holding elected positions but passively allowed (Yeltsin) or actively encouraged (Putin) their political participation.

There are also some notable differences between Russia's two presidents. Yeltsin's state was relatively weak and competing priorities and lacking interest prevented him from rerouting civil-military relations onto a democratic course, which would have been a thankless political task in any case. His neglect of the military not only practically ensured the army's failure to obtain desperately needed resources from the state, but it also allowed military elites to increase their autonomy and to continue to get away with unacceptable behavior as long as they did not directly challenge Yeltsin's prerogatives. Under Putin, by way of contrast, the security-military apparatus has become the regime's essential support base. At the same time, owing in part to Putin's vigorous restoration of state power and to better treatment from the Kremlin, army leaders have moderated their overt opposition to state policy. To be sure, at no time have Russian presidents been impotent appeasers of the army. Rather, the point is that, for a number of reasons, establishing democratic civil-military relations in an increasingly authoritarian polity not only has not been a priority, it has not been an objective.

This sort of executive role, in turn, has fostered the institutional decay in Russian civil-military relations. The key markers of this decay have been military officers' independent participation in elections and in elected political bodies; open encouragement of their subordinates to run for elected office; the existence of often unpunished acts of insubordination; public criticism of and/or opposition to state officials and/or state policy; threat of resignation to elicit policy modification; willingness to purposefully mislead politicians and withhold information from them; and spread of large-scale corruption and criminal behavior that includes the mistreatment and neglect of subordinates and materials under their supervision. The most important outcome of the top brass' increased political role has been its spirited, long-term, and ultimately successful opposition to radical defense reform.

The obvious competing explanation for the absence of substantial defense reform is that its cause has been not the military's opposition and, ultimately, the polity dominated by executive power that tolerates that opposition, but the resource-poor environment in which the Russian armed forces have existed since their inception. This argument does not stand up under scrutiny for several reasons. First, Russian governments, particularly Putin's, have been able to push through and allocate money for high-priority projects such as the new tax and land codes. Second, not all aspects of military reforms would cost money, moreover, the reforms that are needed to establish the kind of armed forces that Russia needs might well save money even in the short term. Third, since 2000 the Russian state has been the beneficiary of a spectacular windfall, owing to significant increases in oil revenue, yet that has made little difference in the realization of substantive defense reform. Finally, the real cost of defense reform is not financial but political in terms of political capital and the cost of not paying attention to higher-priority issues.

The Civil-Military Relations Approach

Although the institutionalist approach provides the most useful theoretical handle for our puzzle, we should not overlook some key insights of the civil-military relations literature that will strengthen our explanation. The field of civil-military relations has not produced a grand theory that can account for divergent cases and patterns.[16] There is a notable theoretical literature on the timing, strategy, planning, and execution of coups, for instance, and on the conditions that motivate military personnel to overthrow their governments.[17] But the armed forces' political activism can take much more nuanced forms than coups d'état or the lack thereof and ought to be viewed as taking place along a continuum of multiple factors such as scale, means, and organizational prerogatives. "Military influence," the range of institutional behavior that falls somewhere between the extremes of violent coup d'état and the army's full compliance with its civilian masters, has proven more difficult to theorize about, even though it is perhaps the most important concern of civil-military relations scholars. One of the key problems is that accurately measuring the gradations between the two end-points of the coup/no-coup spectrum is extraordinarily difficult given the complexity of cases, the number of potential explanations, and their varying importance relative to one another. Having said that, what contributions to the civil-military literature are *useful* for our inquiry?

Two scholars, in particular, succeeded in shedding light on the progressive stages of military influence. Timothy Colton identified four broad policy domains in which military elites are generally interested in expressing their preferences (internal, institutional, intermediate, and societal) and four methods they use to exert their influence (official prerogative, expert advice, political bargaining, and force).[18] Alfred Stepan, on the other hand, listed eleven "military prerogatives," spheres—such as the army's constitutionally sanctioned role in the political system; its relationship to the chief executive, the government, and the legislature; and its role in intelligence, police, state enterprises, and the legal system—where the military as an institution assumes the right, formal or informal, to exercise control over its own internal governance and to play a role in extramilitary jurisdictions within the state apparatus that are germane to its interests.[19] Though these tools are imperfect—Colton's construct would be hard pressed to account for behind-the-scenes influence and Stepan's "low-moderate-high" gauge does not permit the accurate appraisal of military influence—they are helpful in thinking analytically about military participation in politics in general and, more specifically, in pinpointing the changes in the political presence of the Soviet-Russian military elites through time.[20]

Understanding the concept of military influence in contemporary Russia is especially important because coup theories provide no useful guide to this case where generals have not staged a successful coup d'tat in over two centuries. The absence of coups is in itself perplexing in view of Russia's tumultuous history. Brian Taylor contends that organizational culture theory offers the most persuasive explanation to this conundrum because it emphasizes "the unique experiences in the life of an organization as an explanation for subsequent behavior."[21] Studying the Russian army from the organizational culture perspective accentuates the officer corps' view that armed intervention against the country's civilian leaders is fundamentally wrong. Organizational culture theory goes far in explaining the absence of military coups but not the lack of balanced civilian control over, nor even more important, the political role of, Russian military elites.

When looking for additional insights to advance our understanding of civil-military relations in democratizing states, it is necessary to distinguish postpraetorian (such as numerous Iberian and Latin American polities) from post-Communist regimes. In the former, where generals were the de facto state rulers, the *demilitarization of politics* was the objective of prodemocracy reformers. In the latter, where the military was an institutional servant of the Communist Party, the goal has been the *depoliticization of the military.*[22] Democratization theorists tend to agree that civil-military relations is one area in which the post-Communist past is beneficial rather than detrimental for democratizing states.[23] In the ancien rgime, the reasoning goes, the armed forces were under firm civilian (i.e., Communist Party) oversight and kept in check by the internal security forces and other control mechanisms. In short, there were no major problems that endangered civilian oversight, and this fact, as conventional wisdom would have it, must bode well for the democratic era. This argument is entirely sensible when related to post-Communist regimes in general but its validity for the post-Soviet case is negated by two important qualifications.

The first qualification relates directly to what Thomas Nichols has called the "constitutional complication," the notion that although legal regulations governing civil-military relations in the USSR (and in other Communist states) existed, they meant little owing to the predominant position of the CPSU over state institutions, including the judiciary.[24] This complication is significant because, given that constitutional and legal norms were more or less inconsequential, the shifting power dynamics in the late 1980s allowed different interpretations of loyalty. Put more concretely, a very real dilemma was bound to arise: should officers be loyal to the party tenets they had been indoctrinated with or should they try to follow the unpredictable political signals emanating from Gorbachev's Kremlin?

The second qualification has to do with the fundamental changes that took place in civil-military relations at the end of the Soviet era. Gorbachev encouraged internal debate not only in the Communist Party but also in the ranks of the military by, as I mentioned above, actually *inviting* serving officers to voice their views and otherwise participate in politics. Officers turned out to be most responsive: they soon began to publicly criticize Gorbachev and his policies and stood for election to the Supreme Soviet (the legislature). In sum, the USSR's last president expunged the positive influence Communist-era civil-military relations might have had in the post-Soviet era by reversing the solid control of civilians over the armed forces.

All in all, theoretical contributions to the civil-military relations field help explain the areas and stages of the Russian generals' political influence and their aversion to toppling the regime. In addition, empirical and normative contributions to the literature shed light on the gap between the ideals of democratic consolidation and the actual conditions in contemporary Russia.[25] They are especially useful in evaluating the issue of civilian control when complemented by recent works that describe the evolution of the Russian polity's presidential domination.[26] But these insights are secondary to understanding the puzzle of the Russian generals' enlarged political role: they merely complement the robust explanation provided by the institutionalist approach.

CONCEPTS AND CAVEATS

To appreciate the broader context in which I view Russian civil-military relations requires some understanding of three key basic concepts: defense reform, military strategy, and military doctrine. I include "defense reform" among the concepts to be explained because "reform" is often taken to suggest simply change. I take "reform" to mean "to amend or improve by change of form or removal of faults or abuses"[27] and understand "defense reform" as change that *improves* the armed forces in *substantive, meaningful* ways. Although this book is about neither military strategy nor doctrine, it is not possible to appreciate the necessity of defense reform if one does not know the given country's needs based on its strategy and doctrine. In other words, we cannot know the type of army Russia ought to have if we do not know the tasks assigned to it in the military doctrine. Like other basic social science concepts (such as institutions, civil society, nationalism, and empire) there is not one universally accepted definition of strategy or doctrine; in fact, at times they are confused with one another.[28] Therefore, it seems useful to explain the way I employ them.

The word *strategy* comes from the Greek "strategia" which essentially means "generalship." Consequently, it does have a particular military denotation—specifically the deploying of forces before the enemy is engaged—although "strategy" is extensively used in other areas, notably in the business world. In security and military affairs "strategy" has been used to describe two different notions, one indicating a narrower concept pertaining to military techniques and the other referring to a significantly broader idea closer to the contemporary conception of "national security." An example of the first usage is the critical study by the eminent international relations scholar, B. H. Liddell Hart, of the two classical Prussian strategic thinkers, Carl von Clausewitz and Helmuth von Moltke. Liddell Hart defined strategy as "the art of distributing and applying military means to fulfill the ends of policy."[29] The alternative, best described by the term "grand strategy," is ordinarily used to encompass the management of the resources of the entire state in the conduct of warfare. Barry Posen defined it as the "collection of military, economic, and political means and ends with which a state attempts to achieve security."[30] Unless otherwise noted, in this book "strategy" is used in this second, "grand strategy" sense.

Military doctrine, in principle, exists to support military strategy. Doctrine may be thought of as a form of military planning that is between the more general strategy and the more specific (often unit-level) tactics. Military doctrine offers a way of thinking about military problems, issues, and challenges but not a means of how to solve them. Doctrine should be considered as a guide—rooted in a broadly accepted way of thinking—rather than a direction. It certainly does not prescribe specific steps to be taken by commanders in any given contingency. Military doctrines may be shared by various branch services of a national defense force and even by different states (often belonging to the same alliance). Substantively, the military doctrine appears in doctrinal documents that ordinarily outline a nation's (or service branch's or alliance's) military objectives; its overall mission; a general plan of how it should achieve its objectives; various concerns it should be aware of while carrying out its mission; and occasionally even historical examples. Military doctrine changes along with the evolving nature of warfare and the shifts in the threat environments in which the nation or armed service exists.

Although the focus of this study is the Russian armed forces proper, I shall be careful not to lump the military together with the various security forces. The leaders of the latter are more closely allied with Putin and the security agencies, most of them originating from the KGB where he had spent much of his career. The relationship between these structures—whose weight in the state bureaucracy began to increase under Yeltsin—and the contemporary Russian presidency is closer than between the armed forces and the executive branch. Clearly, the security services constitute the first-line of Putin's support, their chiefs are the type of individuals the president knows best and trusts most.

A few words need to be said about terminology to prevent potential confusion. Throughout the book I use the term *Russian army* to denote the entire armed forces (including army, navy, air force, strategic rocket forces) unless otherwise specified. For stylistic reasons, I shall use "army," "armed forces" and "military" interchangeably and "the top brass," "the generals," the "military elites," and "the armed forces leadership" in a similar manner. Furthermore, by "general" or "the generals," unless otherwise specified, I mean individuals in the armed forces proper and not in the employ of any of the numerous security services and armed formations under the aegis of the fourteen militarized ministries (themselves often referred to as "power ministries" and their personnel as the "men of power" or *siloviki*). Finally, in keeping with the vocabulary of the institutionalist approach, I take "institutions" to denote behavioral roles and norms rather than conventional organizations.

To avoid potential misunderstandings, I want to lay out clearly what this book is and is not about. At the risk of repeating myself, the focus of this study is the evolution of civil-military relations in post-Communist Russia and the way it explains the continued lack of substantial defense reform. I am particularly interested in understanding why the relationship between the armed forces and the state leaves so much to be desired from the perspective of democratic standards. I contend that Russia gradually turned away from its democratization experiment beginning in 1993, following the bloody conflict between the president and the legislature. This, in my mind, was *the* major turning point in both Russia's democratization experiment and in the executive's relationship to the armed forces. The move toward authoritarianism gained momentum and accelerated in 2000, however, once Putin moved to the helm. I suggest that the changes in Russia's civil-military relations reflect the steady breakdown in its democratization process.

This book does not offer a detailed analysis of Russian foreign policy and addresses the Commonwealth of Independent States and other former Soviet republics only from the viewpoint of civil-military relations and defense reform. Neither do I intend to provide a blow-by-blow account of the Chechen Wars. Many scholars and journalists have already done so, and I see no need to duplicate their efforts here. I will devote close attention to the Russian army's performance in the Caucasus and to aspects of that conflict directly germane to civil-military relations, however. Furthermore, this book does not deal with Russia's defense industries and their conversion, and it does not offer technical analyses of the country's new or existing weapons systems. I do not offer an exhaustive survey of Russia's nuclear arsenal or analyze Moscow's policies regarding nuclear proliferation. I do, nonetheless, engage the issue of nuclear weapons in connection with Moscow's military doctrine and insofar as the safety of those arms concerns the world beyond Russia and, especially, the United States.

A Roadmap to the Book

The bulk of this book is comprised of five chapters. Chapter 1 sets the scene with a case study of the August 2000 tragedy of the nuclear submarine *Kursk* that focused worldwide attention on the problems of the Russian armed forces and the country's democratization process. I portray the accident as a metaphor for the many problems of Russia's armed forces, civil-military relations, and "façade-democracy." Starting with a brief description of the accident, I examine the reaction of the military leadership, the government, the legislature, and the president to the tragedy. How did they manage the crisis? Who took responsibility for the mistakes that were made? What did their actions say about the admirals and the political leaders? Then I look at the investigation and its findings, the causes of the accident and its treatment by the media, and what they reveal about the state of Russia's armed forces and its democratization process. Finally, I entertain the question of what lessons have been learned by Russian politicians and military leaders from this tragedy.

The concept of "decay" possesses an important temporal element, and we can only appreciate the magnitude of decay if we view it in its proper chronological framework. The purpose of chapter 2 is to lay the groundwork and offer the reader an assessment of the Soviet/Russian military's decline through a structured comparison of some key security-defense issues approximately two decades apart: around 1985—the year Gorbachev took office—and at present (September 2006), approximately at the middle of Putin's second presidential term. The key issues to be contrasted are (a) strategy and doctrine; (b) the state of the armed forces (budget, manpower, training, and equipment); (c) social issues such as prestige, privileges, and the life of ordinary officers and soldiers. In the final section of the chapter, I will briefly compare the performance of the Soviet/Russian army on the battlefields of Afghanistan and Chechnya. To be sure, given major contextual differences, this is not an exercise from which far-reaching generalizations could be extracted. Still, such a comparison will help pinpoint the actual strengths and weaknesses of the armed forces.

Chapter 3 is primarily concerned with explaining the biggest change in post-Communist civil-military relations: the growing political activism of the military elite. The underlying argument here is that in the new Russia the army was "departified" rather than "depoliticized." In fact, the officer corps has become more politicized in the post-Soviet era, a phenomenon that is, in itself, a manifestation of the failure of Russia's democratization project. The top brass' active political presence is a significant issue from at least two important angles. First, it goes directly against the fundamental principles of democratic civil-military relations. Second, the military's political clout is crucial when the government weighs its traditional concerns, such as foreign affairs, as well as social issues and financial matters germane to the defense and security establishments. The chapter is divided into three sections, which focus on the electoral participation of armed forces personnel, the political careers of a group of influential generals, and the public opposition of some high-ranking officers to state policy. I relate these substantive issues to the three formative moments that set the path of Russian civil-military relations.

No other policy domain illustrates the state of current Russian civil-military relations more accurately than that of defense reform. More than fifteen years after the proclamation of the new Russian state, several formidable obstacles, from inadequate resources to poorly prepared conscripts, continue to hinder substantive reform. The most important impediment, however, is neither economic nor social but political, rooted in the army's opposition to the reform and the president's reluctance to enforce its implementation. The main objective of chapter 4 is to explain why. After an appraisal of the military reforms that *have* been implemented I outline the type of defense reform Russia actually needs to successfully face current geostrategic challenges. I evaluate the reform proposals of political parties and the Ministry of Defense and then explain why Russian presidents have not forced the top brass to implement necessary defense reform. The last section briefly chronicles the long-standing feud between the Defense Ministry and the General Staff and its implications to the army's reform.

Chapter 5 highlights the "civil" part of the civil-military relations equation. There *is* civilian control of the armed forces in Russia, and my goal here is to show how the military is overseen and managed in a superpresidential and increasingly authoritarian system. First, I look at the methods through which Yeltsin could maintain the military on a shoestring budget and still sustain the support of its leaders. Next I turn to the "power ministries" and their role in Russian politics and civil-military relations. I continue by examining the legislature as an agent of civilian oversight and assess its progressively weakening impact on the armed forces as a law-making and budget-passing body. In the rest of this chapter the focus shifts to Putin and his record of leadership pertaining to military-security matters, his rapport with the top brass, and his approach to defense reform.

In the Conclusion I address two major issues. First, I consider Russia's democratization experience and look at how civil-military relations fit into the country's broad political framework. Second, I briefly examine the relationship between Russia on the one hand and NATO and the United States on the other, with special attention to nuclear weapons, NATO's ongoing expansion, and the conflicting interests of Moscow and Washington in the post-Soviet world. I end with a few words about U.S. policy toward Russia.

((((

CHAPTER 1

The Tragedy and Symbolism of the *Kursk*

The individual is nonsense, the individual is zero.
—*Vladimir Mayakovski, 1921*

Human life still costs nothing here.
—*Leonid Radzikhovski, 2000*

The sinking of the nuclear submarine *Kursk* on 12 August 2000—the first major accident of the Russian Navy since the end of the Soviet Union—is enlightening for students of contemporary Russia for several reasons. First, predicaments of this sort tend to reveal the instinctive reactions of political leaders to potential emergencies and afford a rare glimpse into how they might manage subsequent crises. In other words, the handling of this incident can help us understand Russia's political elite in general and its head of state in particular. The tragedy of the *Kursk* was the first unrehearsed, unscripted event to test the country's newly minted president, Vladimir Putin. It was an opportunity for Putin to prove his mettle and for the world to take his measure according to his response to the crisis.

Second, the accident also provided a chance to gauge whatever changes might have taken place in the organizational behavior and institutional culture of Russia's armed forces. After operating in a post-Communist political framework for nearly a decade, what would be the admirals' reaction to the crisis, how would they share its specifics with the public, and how would they fulfill their responsibilities? Finally, the disaster also presented a challenge for the Russian media and its overseers and an occasion to appraise journalistic freedom in the country. In short, the sinking of the *Kursk,* and far more so, the manner in which the ensuing crisis was managed by political and military elites and portrayed by the media, reveals a good deal about Russian politics and society.

An analysis of the *Kursk* disaster and its aftermath fittingly sets the scene for a comprehensive study of Russian military politics. Learning about this case helps us understand the ways in which politicians and military leaders operate, their attitudes toward their colleagues and the public, and offers telling details about the morale and discipline of the armed forces and the condition and maintenance of their equipment. A case study of the *Kursk* accident underpins the central arguments of this study: it shows the clout military leaders had acquired by 2000; it demonstrates the consequences of the absent defense reform, the resilience of the old Communist-era mentality, and the top brass' ways of thinking; and it lays bare the reluctance and hesitance of their commander-in-chief to directly confront them. The disaster occurred only a short time after Putin took office but the ways in which he dealt with the crisis and the lessons he seems to have learned from it foreshadowed some key aspects of his rule. Finally, this case also provides an opportunity to ponder the changes—in political and military attitudes, crisis management techniques, and the overall conditions of the armed forces—that have taken place since the accident.

The purpose of this chapter, then, is to reconstruct both the *Kursk* incident and the reaction to it by Russian military and political authorities. I am especially interested in learning what this case tells us about decision-making in contemporary Russia. To be sure, I am not suggesting that broad generalizations can be based on decision-making processes in response to major crises. Still, I would submit that the way in which emergencies are handled does divulge a great deal about the fundamental political impulses, "knee-jerk reactions" as it were, of top decision makers. The main argument of this chapter is that the way Russian political and military elites managed this crisis did not differ significantly from the manner in which their predecessors did—for instance, the nuclear accident in Chernobyl in 1986—in the late Soviet period. The Kremlin's handling of the October 2002 Moscow hostage crisis and several others since support this contention.

I proceed as follows: after a brief account of the disaster, its cause, and the initial rescue efforts, I examine the response of the political and military authorities with special attention to President Putin. In the following section I analyze the investigation, its findings, and its recommendations.

I continue by assessing the media's record of informing the public about the crisis and its aftermath. Finally, I conclude this chapter with some reflections on the lessons that could be learned from and the symbolism of the sinking of the *Kursk*.

THE ACCIDENT

On 10 August 2000, the Northern Fleet of the Russian Navy commenced its largest exercise in more than a decade. The scenario to be played out was similar to those of Soviet-era maneuvers, the end of the Cold War and of the USSR notwithstanding: a clash between two large naval groups with the participation of more than 7,800 seamen and 22 submarines and warships—including the *Piotr Velikii* heavy cruiser and Russia's only aircraft carrier, the *Admiral Kuznetsov*.[1] The exercise had several objectives. First, it was designed to be a show of muscle by Russia's elite naval units. The admirals wanted to demonstrate the navy's capabilities and importance to President Putin, especially in view of the ongoing interservice rivalry and power struggle between Defense Minister Igor Sergeev and Chief of the General Staff Anatolii Kvashnin rooted in their disagreement over spending priorities and, more broadly, on their vision of Russia's military stature. Second, political conservatives—and this category included most of the armed forces elite—who still believed in the fundamental Western threat to Russia, intended to drive home the point that the navy had not lost its teeth. And third, the conventional purpose of maneuvers of this magnitude was to teach naval leaders the control of large formations, officers the management of their sailors and vessels, and crews the use of communications and weapon systems.

One of the war game's star participants was the navy's pride, the nuclear-powered submarine *Kursk*. It was the newest of the eleven Project 949A ("Antei") submarines (designated Oscar-II class by NATO) commissioned by the Russian Navy between 1986 and 1995. Powered by two nuclear reactors with a regulation crew of 130 and underwater displacement of 18,300 tons, these submarines—measuring 154 meters (508 feet) in length and 18.2 meters (60 feet) at the beam—are true man-made behemoths of the sea. Their arsenals may include up to 24 SS-N-19 ("Granit") missiles, antisubmarine weapons (that can be equipped with nuclear warheads), and a battery of torpedoes.[2] The Antei design represents the height of Soviet nuclear submarine technology but it is a remnant of the past.

These reputedly unsinkable vessels were built to fight U.S. aircraft carriers and supplied with enough firepower to destroy an entire carrier group. In a war with the West the assignment of the *Kursk* and its siblings—the largest attack submarines ever built—would have been to cut NATO in half by severing the transatlantic link.

At around 7:30 AM GMT on Saturday, 12 August, seismic monitoring stations near and far detected two explosions 135 seconds apart in the vicinity of the Russian naval exercise. The blasts occurred aboard the *Kursk*, located at approximately 140 kilometers (85 miles) off the Murmansk coast in the Barents Sea. The first detonation in the torpedo bay at the front of the submarine wrought serious damage and sparked an unquenchable fire; the second, 45 to 50 times larger with the explosive power of nearly two tons of TNT, in effect demolished the submarine's bow (front section).[3] As a number of Russian and foreign experts immediately suggested and the two-year long official investigation eventually confirmed, the blasts and thus the sinking of the *Kursk* were caused by the spontaneous discharge of a practice torpedo in the vessel's first compartment.

The submarine's entire crew of 118 perished. The first explosion killed the personnel in the torpedo bay; the second, which ripped through the front of the ship, ended the life of most of the crew. There were 23 survivors who were either on duty in the ninth compartment (at the rear) or managed to make their way there during the little over two minutes between the explosions. How long they stayed alive before they succumbed to carbon-monoxide poisoning has been the source of a major controversy—like much else surrounding the accident—in which opinions ranged from a few minutes to many hours. Once the bodies were recovered forensic experts found evidence suggesting that they may well have lived for up to five days.[4]

Admiral Viacheslav Popov, commander of the Northern Fleet, was on the *Piotr Velikii* directing the maneuvers. The warship was close to the *Kursk* when it went down and recorded the blasts, yet Popov ignored the signals, steered his ship away from the area, and ordered a search only nine hours later. It took thirty-one hours after the explosion to locate the *Kursk* on the seabed in part because its emergency systems (including the buoy that was supposed automatically to surface in case of distress) failed to work. While Russian authorities refused to accept any foreign aid, their rescue teams spent days in futile attempts to open the submarine's escape hatch. Norwegian and British divers, who were permitted to take part in the rescue effort after much delay, accomplished this task in a few hours but for those aboard the *Kursk* it was too late.

THE REACTION

A number of Russian and foreign publications have described the authorities' response to the *Kursk* crisis as "a massive cover-up," likening it to the official treatment of the Chernobyl nuclear disaster more than fourteen years before. The days-long silence of the heads of state (it took Mikhail Gorbachev nine days to publicly respond to Chernobyl, "only" four for Putin), the often conflicting lies, the refusal of outside aid in the critical first days following the accident, the fixation on secrecy, and the disregard for human life all support this view.[5]

The Military Leadership

The Russian high command took more than two days to announce on Monday, 14 August, that the *Kursk* was in "serious trouble," and even then it deliberately misled the public by stating that the accident occurred on Sunday, not on Saturday morning. (On Sunday, in fact, Admiral Popov told the media that the exercise had been a resounding success and both sailors and their equipment had performed their functions flawlessly.) A torrent of intentional misinformation followed. The rumors, half-truths, and lies that the navy employed to shift blame and dodge responsibility created false hopes and obstructed rescue efforts.

The navy leadership never revealed why the alarm was sounded only twelve hours after the explosions on the *Kursk* were registered by seismological and acoustics equipment and why it took thirty-one hours to locate the submarine.[6] Nor did it explain the reason for keeping the accident a secret for more than fifty hours. On 14 August naval authorities admitted that the vessel "descended to the ocean floor" (the word "sink" was not to be used) but they insisted that the entire crew was alive, that they were connected with them "with the help of prearranged signals," and that "air and power are being pumped from the surface into the ship."[7] All of these statements were untrue.

Admiral Vladimir Kuroedov, the commander-in-chief of the Russian Navy, repeatedly proclaimed that rescue workers did everything possible to save the submariners even though it was clear that they were ill-prepared and did not have access to the tools necessary for their mission. Even in the face of incontrovertible evidence to the contrary, Kuroedov maintained in an interview a year after the disaster that rescue crews were well equipped but their "effectiveness was reduced to zero by the submarine's disastrous condition."[8] He failed to explain the reasons for the foreign divers' rapid success, however. Naval spokesmen blamed the failure of the rescue operations on poor weather, although according to meteorologists conditions in the area were generally fine.

Admiral Gennadii Verich told the government and the crew members' relatives that the key reason for the abortive rescue effort was that the navy had never possessed the special equipment or the personnel to help people get out of a stranded submarine. This, too, was a lie. Actually, it was Verich himself who described the Northern Fleet's emergency diving service as "redundant" in the mid 1990s. The unique rescue apparatus was subsequently sold off (some as scrap metal on vague grounds) to private firms or sunk in the Barents Sea.[9] The fleet command simply had to know that they did not possess the proper equipment but preferred to stall—possibly causing the death of their comrades—rather than to get help from abroad.[10] More generally, both the Ministry of Defense and the navy blamed their impotent rescue attempts on the penniless plight of the armed forces.[11]

Popov and Kuroedov (along with other admirals) were especially eager to appear guiltless because they were candidates for promotions—the former for the post of chief of the Navy General Staff and the latter as a possible successor to the aging defense minister Sergeev—and indications of their culpability would have been damaging to their careers.[12] In their position the only "acceptable" offender was an alien ship, preferably belonging to a NATO member state. Consequently, from the beginning of the crisis the navy and the Ministry of Defense accused a foreign intruder of causing the accident. Even though no evidence has ever been found to substantiate this charge and everything to refute it, they would consider no other theory, and some of them have continued to adhere to it long after the official investigation ruled it out.[13]

On 18 August 2000, the Northern Fleet held its first-ever press conference, albeit reluctantly. Steeped in Soviet-style secrecy, the admirals were merely responding to the mounting public outcry—and particularly to the growing outrage of "*Kursk*-relatives"—and the media's discontent with the lack of reliable information. Until 21 August—that is nine days after the tragedy—the navy command repeated that there were survivors in the submarine. Only then, when NATO rescue teams were hours away, did the Northern Fleet finally issue a statement recognizing the loss of the entire crew. At the same news conference Admiral Popov declared that, if need be, he would spend the rest of his days finding out who "organized" the sinking of the *Kursk*.[14] Later, in a memorable piece of theatrics, Popov snatched off his cap and begged for forgiveness on prime-time television, crying "forgive me for not saving your sailors."[15] At the same time, the navy had refused to release the names of the stricken submariners, leaving their anxious families in the dark (journalists eventually obtained them by bribing officers).

Nearly a month after the accident the Defense Ministry got the chance to redeem itself when the armed forces' daily *Krasnaia Zvezda* conducted a lengthy interview with the senior deputy chief of the General Staff, Colonel General Valerii Manilov. Instead of setting the record straight, Manilov furnished more lies: that the *Piotr Velikii* was in an area far from the *Kursk* when the disaster struck; that the fleet was perfectly prepared for any contingency; that it had no censorship policy in place; and that "absolutely all information on the accident and the conditions on site was made available to foreign specialists." For the military's inept crisis management the general faulted "persistent journalists" and traitorous officers (whom he described as "scum") who sold information to the media. He disclosed neither the reasons why the media were forced to buy information nor why the Northern Fleet banned its officers from discussing the tragedy if, indeed, there was no censorship.[16]

In sum, the navy's reaction to the tragedy might have been very similar if the accident had occurred fifteen or twenty years before. Some of their responses were, nonetheless, understandable. For instance, it was hardly surprising that military leaders were reluctant to discuss the technical details of the *Kursk*'s design or wanted to limit the information given to foreign rescue crews to the data indispensable for their work. At the same time, the obsessive secrecy surrounding innocuous information, the commanders' aversion to passing on bad news to their superiors, the refusal to recognize responsibility, the unjustified delays in taking action, the unnecessary and often contradictory lies to the public, and most important, the little apparent concern with the lives of potential survivors and their families all hark back to Soviet times.

The Government, the Legislature, and Foreign Aid

It is perhaps ironic that Russia's Security Council met just days before the disaster and decided on sweeping cuts to the entire armed forces with the intention to bring military spending in line with the country's financial means. Moreover, the council also resolved to further reduce allocations to the strategic nuclear force in order to fund other branches of the armed forces. The latter decision was a clear victory for Kvashnin who had been engaged in an intense public debate with Sergeev about spending priorities.

Ten days after the tragedy, former prime minister Yevgenii Primakov, leader of the Fatherland-All Russia faction in the Duma (the legislature's lower house), announced that the sinking of the submarine "illuminated the situation in the country, the state of our armed forces, and the situation in the navy." According to Primakov, the military's decline could only be reversed by raising military expenditures, increasing the legislative control over the military budget, and reestablishing order in the Ministry of Defense.[17]

In mid September, a number of Duma members posed hostile questions to Deputy Prime Minister Ilia Klebanov, charging the authorities with deliberately misleading the public. Klebanov, who headed the governmental commission investigating the incident and was reputedly also in the running to head the Defense Ministry, responded that he knew about statements that "were not spreading disinformation, but on occasion they appeared like disinformation."[18] Members of the legislature appealed to President Putin to include Duma representatives in the investigating commission but rejected a proposal by several parties and formations (the Union of Rightist Forces, Fatherland-All Russia, and Russian Regions) to form an independent parliamentary commission. Given that the Russian Constitution does not make provisions for parliamentary inquiries, even if delegates were to set up their commission they were unlikely to obtain access to classified information connected to the disaster, and witnesses or experts were not obligated to attend its deliberations. The Duma passed several resolutions pertaining to, among other things, financial support for the victims' families and their own willingness to participate in the deliberations of the governmental commission. Aleksei Mitrofanov, a Liberal Democrat deputy, proposed requesting U.S. president Bill Clinton and British prime minister Tony Blair to allow Duma members to inspect American and British submarines that were allegedly implicated in the accident. His motion was rejected by Duma speaker Gennadii Seleznev.[19]

Not surprisingly, politicians on all sides used the sinking of the *Kursk* to promote their causes. Supporters of the military elites (and Russia's great power ambitions) blamed inadequate defense outlays for the tragedy and argued for drastically increased state defense expenditures. Those favoring robust nuclear forces demanded that rather than maintaining large, expensive, but still poorly funded conventional forces, spending should be focused on nuclear weapons to prevent another *Kursk* fiasco. Politicians like Prime Minister Mikhail Kasianov, who advocated more prudent military budgets (and more modest strategic aspirations), contended that Russia had to scale back its defense spending to fiscally realistic levels, and it neither needed nor could afford costly single-purpose weapons like the *Kursk*.

One of the most controversial features of the reaction of governmental and military authorities to the crisis was their failure to request and/or accept foreign assistance until after it was too late to help potential survivors. On 14 August, a few hours after the military leadership announced that something was amiss with the *Kursk*, a number of foreign governments offered whatever help Moscow deemed necessary. Britain, for example, immediately volunteered its sophisticated LR-5 deep-sea rescue vehicle and Norway its superbly trained emergency diving teams and equipment.

Nonetheless, Russian authorities for five days declined to welcome assistance from abroad, in part owing to false hopes that domestic personnel and gear could do the job, their anxiety that military secrets might be revealed during the rescue operation, and their humiliation over their own helplessness in handling the crisis. In the words of *New York Times* columnist Thomas Friedman, they refused help because "they feared it would sully the honor of Mother Russia's army and puncture Russia's pretense to still being a superpower" and because saving lives was not one of their prime concerns.[20] Only on 17 August—that is, five days after the accident—did the navy's second-in-command, Vice-Admiral Aleksandr Pobozy, go to Brussels to consult with NATO representatives. Some Russian and foreign observers—and 85 percent of respondents to a local poll—regarded Moscow's delay in asking for foreign help "criminal" and maintained that it may well have contributed to the death of the survivors aboard the *Kursk*.[21]

To make matters worse, once they grudgingly accepted assistance, Russian naval authorities provided the British and Norwegian rescue teams with inaccurate information (e.g., that the submarine's escape hatch was irreparably damaged; that it opened counterclockwise rather than clockwise), forced further holdups, and limited their choice of action. A Russian expert likened the navy's attitude toward the foreign rescuers to "open sabotage."[22] Still, on 21 August, the latter managed to open the escape hatch of the completely flooded vessel. Norwegian admiral Einar Skorgen who directed the operation was furious at his Russian hosts for concealing indispensable data and thereby risking the lives of his crew.[23] Russian naval officials maintained the same sense of overzealous secrecy during the salvage operations in the summer of 2001, also performed with the assistance of West European companies and personnel. They prohibited foreign divers from going near the front of the *Kursk* (where the damage to the vessel left its inside exposed), leaving the diving bell, and doing any drilling.

The President

The disaster occurred when Vladimir Putin had been in office for only seven months. A mid-level KGB officer prior to his meteoric rise in the political hierarchy, nothing prepared him for handling this sort of crisis.[24] His decision to continue vacationing for days after the accident was perhaps the most fiercely criticized detail of the official reaction to the disaster. Many thought that Putin should have immediately interrupted his holiday to take charge of the situation because only he could have cut through the red tape and forced the admirals to do their utmost to save the survivors.

Due to his passivity and aloofness in the early days of the crisis, Putin was viewed by many Russians as an emotionless, cynical bureaucrat (a *gosudarstvennik*), whose vacation was more important than the lives of his troops. Until this point in his tenure he had profited from comparisons with Boris Yeltsin who was widely regarded as an undignified drunk and an embarrassment to the country. In the days of the *Kursk* crisis, however, people recalled Yeltsin's impulsive warmth with nostalgia. To be sure, in August 2000 Putin was enjoying the first few days of vacation with his family since he had become president. More important, at this point he was entirely inexperienced in managing crises and later admitted that he "just did not think about it [public relations]."[25] While Yeltsin surrounded himself with a coterie of advisors who managed his elections and public appearances, Putin kept close counsel with the only people he would trust: former colleagues from the KGB/FSB (the FSB, the Federal Security Service, is the KGB's post-Soviet incarnation) and the St. Petersburg city administration. Image-making was not the forte of these individuals. Putin's Kremlin advisors—principally Aleksandr Voloshin and Gleb Pavlovsky—those whose job it was "to sell the president to the people," were reportedly apprehensive of military leaders and their contempt for political reformers. In the end, they did not offer advice to the president on what they perceived as a military issue.[26]

Independent politicians like Gorbachev took Putin to task for "missing out on things" while opposition leaders such as Boris Nemtsov called his inaction "immoral."[27] In his defense, the president said that he was closely following events but he thought a presidential visit to the accident site would have been disruptive and would have diverted attention from rescue efforts. Unlike Gorbachev, who never assumed culpability for the handling of the Chernobyl accident,[28] Putin publicly and from early on took full responsibility for the *Kursk*. He should not be condemned for repeating the admirals' lies at press conferences in Russia and abroad because whatever direct information he had came from the military.[29] The president must be faulted, however, for defending the admirals' decision to delay informing the public by saying that two days were necessary for the navy "to find out what was happening."[30] He also erred for doing nothing to discourage the military elite's persistent but groundless charges that the disaster was caused by a British or an American vessel. In the aftermath of the crisis Putin realized that navy leaders consistently misled him in order to undermine his policy of improving relations with Britain and the United States by insisting on the collision theory.[31]

Unlike Gorbachev, who used the May 1987 Red Square-landing of a West German teenager piloting his Cessna airplane as a convenient pretext to fire troublesome generals—replacing a higher proportion of the military leadership than Stalin did in 1937–38—in the days following the *Kursk* accident Putin did not give in to whatever temptation he might have felt to purge the top brass.[32] In fact, he refused to accept the resignation letters dutifully submitted by Sergeev, Kuroedov, and Popov, insisting that no blame should be assigned until the full details of the tragedy were established. Instead, Putin used the occasion to denounce his political enemies like Boris Berezovsky, Vladimir Gusinsky—who controlled some of the media outlets so critical of him—and other tycoons "who had assisted in the destruction of the army, the fleet, and the state," people with "villas in Spain and the south of France."[33]

On 23 August Putin finally made the journey to Vidaevo, the desolate navy town where the submariners' families lived. In a three-hour meeting held at the local House of Culture, the president tried to console the relatives and reassure them that they would be taken care of. In Vidaevo, Putin made two important but controversial public gestures. The first concerned an unprecedentedly generous state-provided compensation package for the relatives. Each victim's immediate family was promised a new apartment and received 720,000 rubles (about $26,000). The city of Kursk, which gave its name to and sponsored the crew of the submarine, granted free electricity, telephone services, and public transportation to family members. (Sixteen widows announced their intention to move there from Vidaevo in the days following the disaster.) Furthermore, all crew members were posthumously decorated with the Order of Valor while the commander of the *Kursk*, Captain Gennadii Lyachin—who, incidentally, earned less than a Kursk trolleybus driver—was awarded the title of Hero of Russia. (In an act of commemoration that borders on the bizarre, the *Kursk* itself was also awarded a posthumous prize, "For the Best Shot at a Naval Target.")[34] In addition, private donors and numerous Russian and foreign enterprises and governments had contributed to charities to help the victims' relatives.[35]

The state's unexpected magnanimity and the huge disparity between the compensation extended to the survivors of the *Kursk*'s crew and that provided to the families of Russia's other military casualties did not fail to arise suspicion. As one family member said, "We get a lot more than the Chechen widows, ten times more. The Russian government doesn't give out money like that for nothing; I think they bought us off. There must be something they are trying to hide. They must be feeling guilty."[36]

In 2000, the standard payment for the death of a contract soldier was 3,600 rubles ($130, i.e., 1/200th or 0.5 percent of the payment to the *Kursk* families) plus 750 rubles for each immediate family member.[37] Moreover, aside from the insultingly paltry financial restitution, in recent times Soviet/Russian war dead were surrounded by official indifference or worse. In many cases soldiers who fell in Afghanistan in the 1980s or in the Chechen campaigns a decade later, frequently went unburied for years and their families were informed that they died of illness or in traffic accidents. The coffins of combat dead have been routinely distributed around ordinary graveyards without reference to the place and cause of death in order to conceal the extent of the carnage.[38] As Veronika Marchenko, the head of the Mothers' Rights Foundation asked, did the authorities consider it "more honorable to die underwater then in a burning tank in Grozny?"[39]

The second gesture was the president's pledge to bring up the *Kursk* from the bottom of the sea and return the remains of the crew to their relatives regardless of cost. Well-aware of the importance of death rites in Russian tradition and Orthodox religious ritual, Putin vowed to grant the families the chance of a proper burial.[40] He delivered on his promise in October 2001, after numerous delays. Some admirals and pundits criticized the effort, however, charging that the lifting of the *Kursk*, in effect, became the test of Putin's word and the mark of his resolve at enormous public expense. Military leaders had openly wondered whether the approximately $130 million—the operation's price-tag and almost twice the entire annual budget for running Russia's fleet of submarines—might not have been better spent elsewhere.[41] These funds would have gone far to provide advanced training for emergency service personnel and to equip the navy with up-to-date rescue equipment. Notwithstanding the financial and opportunity costs, keeping his promise had fueled the president's post-*Kursk* domestic standing.

The popular reaction to his management of the crisis signified the first serious public opposition Putin had faced in his entire career. Still, maybe the political apathy of the Russian electorate can explain that even though a large majority (73 percent according to one poll) thought that Putin should have been at the site of the accident providing help and moral support, nearly 60 percent said that their views of the president did not change and only 27.8 percent professed their diminished esteem for him.[42] In the end, Putin—who in June 2001 called the *Kursk* fiasco the worst experience of his presidency—suffered surprisingly little damage to his popularity from his handling of the crisis.[43]

THE INVESTIGATION

Given the magnitude of the tragedy and the publicity surrounding it, identifying its cause assumed paramount importance. The main investigation was headed by the prosecutor general of the Russian Federation, Vladimir Ustinov. A governmental commission led by Deputy Prime Minister Klebanov and the FSB conducted separate inquiries. There were several early signs that these were not going to be impartial investigations. For instance, nearly half of Klebanov's commission was comprised of officials—himself as well as high-ranking naval officers including Kuroedov—with a stake in blocking certain angles of the investigation. At the same time, independent experts were not asked to participate in the inquiry. President Putin assigned the FSB to find out whether or not there were grounds for preparing a criminal case. Nonetheless, legislation regulated the investigational activities of the special services and, strictly speaking, the FSB's involvement in the case was illegal.[44] One objective circumstance, however, greatly contributed to the thoroughness of the investigation. The fact that the *Kursk* sank in relatively shallow waters (about 100 meters [330 feet]) permitted its lifting and careful inspection.

The Theories

Most experts quickly agreed that the direct cause of the sinking was the detonation of a practice torpedo in the *Kursk*'s bow. The key question that remained, therefore, was what caused the explosion of that weapon. Throughout the course of the investigation two theories were favored to explain the accident. The leading cause entertained by the majority of the investigators was an underwater collision of the *Kursk* with a foreign vessel that, in turn set off a torpedo. Military leaders (who presented it as actual fact on 14 August 2000),[45] conservative and right-wing politicians, and generally those who had a vested interest in poor relations between Russia and the West endorsed this scenario. There was some circumstantial evidence to advance their position: three foreign submarines, the USS *Memphis* and the USS *Toledo* of the United States and the British HMS *Splendid* were monitoring the Russian naval exercise in the Barents Sea, although nowhere near the vicinity of the maneuvers. Both London and Washington categorically denied their vessels' involvement, and there was no indication of foul play. Still, a number of state and military leaders—including Klebanov, Kuroedov, and some Duma members—continued to maintain that the only true cause for the sinking of the *Kursk* was its collision with a foreign submarine with no evidence to support their contention.[46]

The second plausible source of the tragedy was the spontaneous detonation of the practice torpedo (that is, it was the direct and not the indirect cause of the accident). The investigation eventually concluded that this was the mishap's direct cause. The Russian media offered logical and conclusive explanations why this could be the only reason for the accident as early as January 2001, although military leaders vehemently opposed this interpretation.[47] What actually happened was that a practice torpedo fueled with an extremely unstable and combustible substance (hydrogen-peroxide) exploded and set off the other weapons in the torpedo bay.

Numerous additional hypotheses were also publicly contemplated, often by individuals who were far from objective observers. One of these was the purported Muslim or terrorist connection, which suggested that the two Daghestani weapons specialists aboard the *Kursk* to oversee torpedo tests were, in fact, Chechen terrorists. The confirmation of this hypothesis by the Supreme Military Council of the Chechen *mujaheddin* did not ease its debunking.[48] Evidently some investigators were "absolutely clear" six months after the accident that the *Kursk* did not collide with a foreign submarine but was actually the victim of a torpedo attack by the USS *Memphis*.[49] Prominent articles in German and British magazines and newspapers (*Der Spiegel, Berliner Zeitung, Sunday Times*)—as well as in Russian publications such as *Zhizn'* and *Novaya Gazeta*—claimed to have been in possession of documents indicating that the *Kursk* was disabled by an underwater torpedo accidentally launched by the *Piotr Velikii*.[50] Navy spokesman Captain Igor Dygalo described these suggestions as "invention and provocation."[51]

Other sources suggested that a collision with another Russian vessel (possibly a supply ship) was responsible for the *Kursk*'s demise.[52] Even the extremely remote chance that a mutiny broke out aboard the *Kursk* received some attention fueled by rumors and misinformation.[53] Finally, investigators also considered the possibility of the submarine's collision with an underwater mine, possibly left behind as long ago as World War II. Nonetheless, it was difficult to comprehend that any naval mine could have produced the kind of damage the *Kursk* sustained.

Findings and Repercussions

In August 2002 Prosecutor General Ustinov submitted a 133-volume top secret final report concluding his investigation into the *Kursk* disaster. Within a few days, the government published a four-page summary of Ustinov's findings in the daily *Rossiiskaia Gazeta*.[54] The report blamed the tragedy on a practice torpedo leaking its volatile hydrogen-peroxide fuel in the torpedo bay. More generally, it uncovered a shocking level of negligence on all levels of the command; stunning breaches of discipline; and shoddy, obsolete, and poorly maintained equipment.

In 1955, after a fatal accident on the HMS *Sidon*, the British Admiralty banned the use of the high-test peroxide (or hydrogen-peroxide) for torpedo propulsion.[55] Nearly half a century later the *Kursk*'s torpedoes were still fueled by this volatile substance, which permitted higher speed and range than conventional propellants. Still, Rear Admiral Valerii Dorogin—a Duma deputy who was involved in the investigation as an expert—agreed with Ustinov's verdict that the equipment was not to be blamed for the mishap. Dorogin insisted that there was nothing wrong with the torpedo on the *Kursk*, and it boasted with a 99.99 percent reliability rating.[56] In view of his statement one wonders why the Russian Navy withdrew from service all hydrogen-peroxide propelled torpedoes following the disaster.

On 1 December 2001, President Putin, after listening to Ustinov's interim report on the investigation fired twelve high-ranking officers of the Northern Fleet for "serious flaws in the organization of service." Fleet commander Admiral Popov and his chief-of-staff, Rear Admiral Mikhail Motsak, were demoted. (True to Russian tradition, however, both admirals soon obtained positions no lower than their military posts: Popov as representative of the Murmansk region in the Federation Council [the legislature's upper house] and Motsak as deputy presidential envoy for the North-Western Federal District.)[57] In a statement that can only be described as peculiar, however, Putin and Chief of the General Staff Kvashnin insisted that dismissing the entire command of the fleet had nothing to do with the accident even though almost all of the officers punished were directly involved with the submarine, the organization of the exercise, or the rescue services.[58] In February 2002 the president demoted Klebanov—who was just as ardent a supporter of the collision theory as the top brass—to head the Ministry for Industry, Science, and Technology.

It may be the final strange twist to this tragedy that in the end, at least as far as the authorities were concerned, no one was to blame and no one could be held responsible.

Broader Causes: Shortcomings of Training and Discipline

The accident was surprising in terms of the drama it inadvertently provided but, considering the state of Russia's armed forces, should not have been unexpected. Many of the military's problems have been generated by Russia's gross negligence of its armed forces in the 1990s. Other weaknesses are the result of subjective but related factors such as low morale and professionalism.

In its five-year life-span the *Kursk* completed only one mission—a sustained deployment to the Mediterranean Sea in 1999—due to lack of funds for fuel.[59] Indeed, many of its sailors and junior officers had seldom or never been at sea. Most of the submarine's crew was inexperienced, mainly because there were no exercises held in which they could attain or maintain, much less improve their skills. They were hardly prepared to assume responsibility for two dozen live torpedoes. The Prosecutor General's report indicated that crew members had never handled the type of torpedoes the *Kursk* was outfitted with prior to the fateful maneuvers. Furthermore, investigators found that the submarine's logbook—which could have held clues to many specific questions of the inquiry—was forged.[60] The primary cause of many of the frequent accidents in the armed forces is, in the words of the respected military expert, Pavel Felgenhauer, "poor training, bad morale, and nonexistent discipline."[61]

The torpedoes on the *Kursk* were described as "being ancient" (having been standard naval equipment since 1957) but, experts claimed, they were not replaced because they were both expensive and extremely powerful weapons.[62] According to several sources it was widely known that one of the practice torpedoes was dropped during transport—the impact likely produced the cracks for the fuel to leak—but it was loaded anyway.[63] Removing the damaged weapon from the *Kursk* was apparently not simple because the unloading cranes at the submarine base had long been out of order.[64] An investigative report published by *Moskovskii Komsomolets* revealed that the navy, the Duma, the Federation Council, and the government had been exchanging letters as early as 1999 pertaining to repairs of the cranes used to unload missiles from nuclear submarines but the defense order was never implemented.[65]

Inspections of submarine torpedoes in 2000 and 2001 turned up corrosion in some weapons and many tattered rubber gaskets that allowed fuel to leak.[66] These gaskets required frequent replacement but investigators rarely found reliable data on their age. The rescue submersibles that were supposed to save the sailors were not equipped properly, their indispensable batteries had not been replaced (which was one reason why they had to switch off power to prolong search time), and their crew had never practiced on nuclear submarines.[67] Sailors deliberately deactivated the *Kursk*'s emergency buoy—presumably to prevent self-activation—though it was functional even after the explosions. Russian military prosecutors contended that if all the requisite security regulations had been adhered to prior to the *Kursk*'s leaving its port and during the exercise itself, the sunken submarine would have been found in less than an hour.[68]

Sloppiness and poor discipline characterize not just infantry and tank regiments but also the elite units of the armed forces that deal with nuclear weapons. There is much dereliction of duty even at the highest levels. For example, Admiral Popov did not order the mandatory rescue exercises that would have prepared the fleet for emergencies similar to the disaster. One explanation of the idleness during the many hours of absent radio contact between the *Piotr Velikii* and the *Kursk* was that the Fleet Command was used to constant failures of equipment. According to Adolf Meshuiev, head of Russia's Explosion Resistance Scientific Center and a retired naval officer, damaged torpedoes are not rare aboard ships thanks to "traditional Russian negligence."[69] Investigators also confirmed that many sensitive parts on the *Kursk* remained in use long after their recommended service life.

The Media and the Public

The *Kursk* accident quickly became a test of media freedom in Russia. Media outlets pursued the story with vigor and some of them unleashed a barrage of criticism at the president, the armed forces, and state authorities. Some intrepid journalists were determined to bring to the public the reality behind the deliberately misleading official statements.[70] *Izvestia*, a newspaper ordinarily sympathetic toward the Kremlin ran the front-page headline, "The Price of National Pride: Human Lives," while the more independent *Novaya Gazeta* countered with "Our State Is Not Weak: It Is Irresponsible."[71] NTV, an independent television channel and its radio counterpart, *Ekho Moskvy*, provided painstaking analyses of official statements and their contradictions.

The media's most sensational coup was describing how Nadezhda Tylik, the distraught mother of one of the *Kursk* crew members, was forcibly injected with a sedative while haranguing Deputy Prime Minister Klebanov at a meeting between family members and the authorities at the Vidaevo Naval Base.[72] The incident was filmed by a brave cameraman and was televised in the West but not in Russia. Both this inexcusable assault on human dignity and the official response to it ("the solicitous administration of needed tranquilizers") were stark reminders of Soviet times.[73]

Even fearless journalists could only do so much given their restricted access to reliable information and the persistent misinformation emanating from the military and the government. Northern Fleet officials adamantly refused to release even the names of the victims. After employees of the tabloid daily, *Komsomolskaia Pravda*, obtained that information by bribing an officer (with eighteen thousand rubles), the authorities attempted to ban journalists from contacting the relatives of the stricken submariners.[74] In spite of their easier access to the authorities, none of the television networks under government supervision distinguished themselves by offering objective coverage. Only the crew of the state-controlled RTR television network was allowed to be present at Putin's tense visit with the relatives in Vidaevo; all others were kept away. RTR only broadcast a heavily edited version of the meeting (although unofficial transcripts—complete with Putin's tirades against those who brought ruin to Russia—were later published). A Norwegian airplane that flew over the rescue site was blamed by Russian authorities for interference until it was discovered that it was chartered by Russian journalists desperate for solid material.[75] The dearth of credible information undoubtedly contributed to the many absurd conspiracy theories independent newspapers featured after the sinking of the submarine.

The attitude of Russian politicians toward the media during the crisis was hardly surprising, though Mikhail Gorbachev, usually a strong supporter of Putin's regime, did concede that "people felt that the authorities were making fools of them, and the press could get no information."[76] More typical was the reaction of Communist Party leader Gennadii Zhuganov, who called for new controls on the media to end "anti-state propaganda."[77] Overlooking the possibility that the press might have actually worked in the public interest, President Putin was infuriated by some of the media's denunciation of his and the government's handling of the crisis. In front of the relatives in Vidaevo the president lamented that "unfortunately we cannot order them [the media] to stop although that would be the right thing to do."[78]

The same survivors of the victims whom the president intended to comfort were routinely lied to and treated with callous insensitivity by the navy. In fact, they found out about the tragedy not from the navy but by happenstance (some of them ran into members of the rescue team on the street). No wonder that they openly complained that "of course the navy is doing everything it can to hide the truth from us" and "why should we expect anything but more lies?" [79] The authorities' management of the crisis did little to reverse the traditional skepticism with which ordinary

Russians had regarded them. In September 2000, for instance, 79 percent of those polled thought that the government was "hiding the reasons for the tragedy" and only 11 percent felt that it was telling the truth.[80] A year after the accident—with investigators still a long time away from releasing their conclusions—45 percent of survey respondents believed that its cause had long been established but withheld from the public.[81]

A handful of Russian nongovernmental organizations extended prompt assistance of various kinds to the victims' families; their activities constitute one of the few bright aspects of the crisis. The Mothers' Rights Foundation provided legal aid to mothers of the servicemen killed on duty who demanded the punishment of those responsible for the accident. Veronika Marchenko, MRF's outspoken leader, wondered, in an oft-quoted written statement, "what to do to make the government value citizens' lives more than oil, military secrets, or its own prestige."[82] The St. Petersburg-based Submarine Seamen's Club was closely involved in the efforts of the victims' families to find out what really happened on the *Kursk*. It was the club's head, Captain Igor Kudrin (Ret.), who discovered that a large number of torpedoes coming from the same lot as the one that caused the tragedy were discarded throughout the 1990s due to microcracks in the welding seams.[83] These NGOs were the first to start collecting cash for the families and help fund their trips to Northern Fleet Headquarters in Severomorsk.

IMPACT, LESSONS, SYMBOLISM

Although the impact of the *Kursk* fiasco on the Russian military was not inconsequential, it should not be overestimated. The navy pulled the torpedoes using the volatile hydrogen-peroxide fuel from service, reorganized the Northern Fleet, found the money to purchase some modern deep-sea rescue equipment, and succeeded in negotiating a framework agreement with NATO to cooperate on saving stricken submarines.[84] Paradoxically, the military scored an important victory: its budgets have substantially increased since 2000, in part because the accident focused attention on its privations. The tragedy also highlighted how far out of synch Moscow's international ambitions, its military expenditure, and the state of its armed forces were with reality. Since August 2000—indeed, since 1991—the president and other high-ranking politicians have made many official declarations regarding the critical need to drastically reform the military establishment; as of the summer of 2006, the objective has not been accomplished.

And, accidents continue to occur with troubling frequency. In August 2002, 119 of the 156 people aboard a Mi-26 transport helicopter were killed when it was hit by a surface-to-air missile in Chechnya. The number of fatalities would have been considerably lower if repeated Defense Ministry directives that the helicopters not be used to carry personnel beyond their seating capacity had been followed: the Mi-26 has fixed seating for only 80 passengers.[85] In August 2003, less than a week after two helicopter gunships collided in midair over Siberia, a K-159 decommissioned nuclear submarine sank in the Barents Sea as it was being towed to a scrapyard. Nine of the ten sailors on board perished as a result of negligence and lack of professionalism.[86] Defense Minister Sergei Ivanov himself blamed the national trait of carelessness and a "frivolous Russian reliance on chance" for the sinking of the submarine.[87] A host of other recent accidents since then—such as the September 2006 fire on a nuclear submarine caused by poor training and maintenance that left two sailors dead—indicate that the years after the *Kursk*'s misfortune have not brought a new appreciation of safety and discipline to Russia's armed forces.[88]

Only some of the lessons drawn from the *Kursk* fiasco have been absorbed by Russian politicians. Perhaps most important, President Putin learned to appreciate the media's power to shape public opinion and that the stinging criticism he received could only be checked by controlling the press. In a remarkably short period of time the government succeeded in doing just that. Within about eighteen months, the Kremlin had gained control of the three major television networks that reproached the president and the cabinet during the crisis and had engineered the closure of the fourth. The same fate had befallen numerous broadcast, print, and electronic media outlets.[89] In December 2002, Yuri Shchekochikhin, deputy chairman of the State Duma Security Committee contended that "any official can now go to court against a newspaper" and collect a "completely abnormal sum in compensation" and thereby assure the publication's demise. Shchekochikhin, who represented the pro-western Yabloko party in the legislature and was an editor of the investigative journal *Novaya Gazeta*, added that in terms of expected conformity to the official line, Russia had "returned again to the period at the end of the 1970s and early 1980s" and that it ranked second after Algeria in terms of the number of journalists killed.[90] The following summer Shchekochikhin died—

doctors involved in the case were convinced that he was poisoned—while researching an article on fraud and corruption in the FSB.[91] Actually, during President Putin's tenure—as of early September 2006—at least twenty-three journalists have been killed.[92] In its 2004 world press freedom ranking, the international organization Reporters without Borders placed Russia 147th on a list of 167 countries.[93] A 2005 Human Rights Watch report concluded that Putin had gradually established his control over the media that blatantly promoted the Kremlin while vilifying the remaining opposition.[94]

The Russian president strongly disagrees with these assessments of media freedom, however. In a 2000 interview with the American television station, CNN, Putin said that there was no difference in the Kremlin's approach to private and government-controlled mass media.[95] Four years later he insisted in another interview that "we broadcast everything objectively and we will continue to do so."[96] In a 23 December 2004 press conference he contended that the Russian media were "as free as any other."[97]

Some observers suggested that Putin and the Russian political elite might learn from the *Kursk* crisis that it was "best to react quickly and publicly to criticism" and that the Russian people would not tolerate indifference and deceit from their leaders.[98] This hopeful conjecture seemed to be confirmed by the government's handling of yet another calamity, the July 2001 crash of a Tu-154 airliner near Irkutsk in which all 145 on board perished. The authorities quickly disclosed all relevant facts and conducted a swift but thorough investigation.[99] The Kremlin's management of the November 2002 Moscow hostage crisis when Chechen terrorists took some eight hundred hostages in a Moscow theater, however, once again lent support to those who remained wary of Putin's regime. Although following the crisis the president congratulated himself and his government on a "successful operation," it is unlikely that his jubilant public addresses convinced the families of the dozens of dead hostages. Their number has been variously put at 129 and 136, with 75 people who were thought to have been in the theater at the time still missing, all but three of them the casualties of the special forces' botched assault. The authorities steadfastly refused to identify the toxic gas they used that actually killed the hostages, thereby clearly adding to the number of casualties. The treatment of the sick by emergency workers was crude and incompetent. The authorities charged with responding to the emergencies were unprepared for the medical care of the victims, even though the imminent demand for their services must have seemed all but certain after several days of the hostage crisis. The government forces' heavy-handed approach was well illustrated also by their take-no-prisoners mentality: they shot all 41 terrorists, many of them while they were unconscious.[100] The obsession with secrecy, the disregard for human life, and the negligent planning of the rescue operation suggested that little had changed since the sinking of the *Kursk*.[101]

Lamentably, in August 2005 an even more appropriate occasion arose to contemplate how much the Russian navy had changed in five years' time. On 4 August a 13-meter (40-foot) AS-28 ("Priz") minisubmarine with seven crewmen aboard got stuck on the floor of the Pacific Ocean in 190-meter (630 feet) deep waters about 70 kilometers (44 miles) off the shores of the Kamchatka Peninsula. After all of the navy's salvation plans had failed, the authorities requested help from abroad, which was quickly rendered by the United Kingdom, the United States, and Japan. In the end, an unmanned remote-controlled rescue submersible of the Royal Navy—airlifted to the site from a naval base in Scotland—quickly cut the cables that had snarled the vessel and its propeller. All crewmembers survived unharmed.

Let us see what has changed. The obvious positive change, the officials' appeal for help from abroad, is somewhat negated by the fact that the AS-28 carried no secrets and its design—unlike that of the *Kursk*—had no mysteries about it. Even so, a number of naval leaders, most prominently retired admiral Eduard Baltin, strongly criticized the appeal for foreign involvement because "this region is stuffed with [Russian military] secrets."[102] Moreover, the navy waited for more than twenty-four hours after the first distress signals were sent out by the submarine's crew, and according to several sources, it might have taken even longer if an anonymous caller—presumed to be the wife of one of the sailors—had not alerted a local radio station.[103] Officials did little to diminish the confusion either about what incapacitated the Priz's propeller—fishing nets? synthetic and steel communications cables? top secret underwater antenna system?—or concerning the reason why the navy's own rescue service was unable to perform. According to retired admiral Popov, since 2000 the navy had spent tens of millions of dollars on modern rescue equipment but, others noted, it still did not have specially equipped ships from which divers could have gone that deep.[104] Yet other officials said that the navy *did* possess the proper equipment, but its operators were on holiday or that the Russian rescue submersibles were stationed at the Northern Fleet and could not be disassembled and transported to the Pacific on time.[105]

Another thing that did not change was President Putin's inaction during the tense days of the emergency. His critics have identified a pattern of presidential silence during calamitous events—also evident, for example, during the *Kursk* accident and the Beslan hostage crisis in 2004—and explained it by the administration's obsession with projecting strength and its fear that it might be associated with or blamed for potential trage-dies.[106] The Kremlin's spin doctor, Gleb Pavlovsky, has, in fact, attributed Putin's enduring popularity to the fact that he has always been seen as being above the social crises and terrorist attacks of recent years.[107] It is also not clear whether the firing of navy commander Admiral Kuroedov—whose resignation, as I noted, was tendered but not accepted in 2000—after the 2005 incident constitutes a change in Putin's behavior. After all, the president waited for a month after the accident, Kuroedov was known to be ill, and the date of his dismissal—or was it really scheduled retire-ment?—coincided with his sixty-first birthday. His successor, Admiral Vladimir Masorin—previously the navy's chief of staff—blamed the acci-dent on the navy's own sloppiness and broken-down rescue equipment. According to him the Russian Navy had a more advanced rescue subma-rine than the vessel used by the Royal Navy but negligence in handling it made it inoperable. Moreover, Masorin added, "the fear of assuming responsibility is the main problem in the Russian military."[108] Following the accident, the government friendly daily, *Izvestia*, wrote that the navy's rescue services "improved but almost imperceptibly" in the five years since the *Kursk* tragedy.[109]

CONCLUSION

It is hard to escape the multifaceted symbolism conjured by the tragedy of the *Kursk* and its aftermath. The accident aptly illustrated the long-term decay of Russia's once-proud armed forces. That the extravagant investments in sophisticated weaponry are not coupled with a concern or resources for their maintenance is a legacy of the Soviet era. The ill-pre-pared, large-scale exercise without the proper support of emergency equipment illustrates the hazards of attempting to preserve superpower status on a shoestring budget. The carelessness in the navy decried by many commentators has not been eliminated. The floating capsule that was never tested on the *Kursk* and had thus failed to facilitate the twenty-three initial survivors' escape was likewise not tested more recently on the *Gepard* nuclear submarine. The latter vessel was commissioned by President Putin in December 2001, and in both instances, "orders from the very top" effectively rushed the submarines into service without proper testing to meet deadlines, a practice also typical of the Soviet era.[110]

The *Kursk* accident also reveals that continuity rather than change describes the Russian military's institutional culture, and accountability remains a foreign concept. Military elites must have known the cause of the submarine's sinking a few weeks after it occurred but they kept deceiving the public because no one would take the blame. The prosecutor general's decision to hold no one culpable for the death 118 sailors and the loss of the submarine symbolizes the political elite's own aversion to embrace the notion of individual responsibility. At the same time, the *Kursk* accident also demonstrates some changes in civil-military relations brought about by the institutional decay of the armed forces. More specifically, this incident well illustrates the top brass' willingness to deliberately mislead and to withhold vital information from the president and other politicians. Furthermore, one could wish for no clearer confirmation of the military elites' criminal neglect of their subordinates and the weapons entrusted to them than the tragedy the *Kursk* provided.

Aside from these differences—as well as the inspired work of some journalists and NGOs, the generous (though inequitable) compensation package, and President Putin's assumption of culpability—one could argue that Russia's new political and military elites dealt with the emergency pretty much the way their forerunners would have done fifteen or twenty years earlier. Most important, the tragedy of the *Kursk* suggests that, like their predecessors, the country's current leaders, and especially its military elites, are more or less indifferent to the value of ordinary human life.[111] Between the individual and the state, in Russia—as in the Soviet Union—the latter continues to triumph.

《《《

CHAPTER 2

Assessing Decay

THE SOVIET/RUSSIAN MILITARY, 1985–2006

The Russian Army is never as strong as it describes itself,
but never as weak as it seems from the outside.
—Old Russian adage, cited in Dmitri Trenin and
Aleksei Malashenko, *Russia's Restless Frontier*

The Army is a copy of society and suffers from all its
diseases, usually at a higher temperature.
—Leon Trotsky, *The Revolution Betrayed*

Although the objective of the foregoing chapter was to examine how a major defense-related crisis was handled in the early days of Vladimir Putin's presidency, I also sought to offer some insight into the policies of the Russian state and especially, the predicaments of its army. Why and how have conditions in the not-long-ago proud and mighty force deteriorated to this extent? How are Russia's officers and soldiers trained and equipped to respond to the challenges they face? How have their everyday lives changed? What does their performance in the battlefields of Chechnya tell us about the Russian Army? The framework of chapter 1 did not allow the analysis of these and other pertinent issues. Nonetheless, understanding the contemporary Russian military and the political and socioeconomic environment in which it operates requires answers to these questions. This chapter, then, has two main tasks: first, to show the disparities between the armed forces of the late-Communist period and of the present; and second, to lay out the empirical background on which the next three chapters—mostly concerned with civil-military relations—can be built.

The underlying argument of this chapter is that the Russian armed forces suffer from a two-decade long institutional decay. In order to appreciate their current plight one needs to look at the military at an earlier point in time. The date 1985 seems like a logical point of departure. Although it is not the year that marks the zenith of Soviet military might—that distinction would probably belong somewhere in the latter stages of Leonid Brezhnev's rule (1964–82)—it was still a point when signs of the army's deterioration might have been impending but were not yet apparent. This, of course, was also the year Mikhail Gorbachev won the USSR's top job, an event justly considered "the beginning of the end" of the Soviet Union. Using 1985 as the starting point also makes sense because Soviet civil-military relations and the Soviet army had not yet been jolted by the massive changes they would experience during the Gorbachev era. The endpoint of the comparison is the present (September 2006), the sixth year of Putin's presidency and the fifteenth after the fall of the USSR.

This chapter is divided into four parts, all focusing on different facets of Soviet/Russian security and military issues though, given my primary emphasis on post-Soviet affairs, the sections pertaining to contemporary Russia do receive priority treatment. First, I examine Soviet and Russian strategy and doctrine in 1985 and 2006. Then I assess the state of the armed forces with special attention to their budget, manpower, training, and equipment. In the third part the attention shifts to social issues that matter to military personnel, such as prestige, privileges, and material well-being. In each of these sections the objective is to offer a concise review of salient questions and identify the changes that have occurred since 1985. One sensible way to evaluate a military force is to appraise its performance in combat. I attempt to do just that in the last section as I briefly contrast the Soviet/Russian army's record in Afghanistan in the 1980s and in Chechnya in the 1990s and beyond.

STRATEGY AND DOCTRINE

The Soviet state's official ideology required that its military strategy be rationalized with the "objective laws" of Marxist-Leninist thought.[1] These imperatives, along with practical ones that reflected Russia's age-old imperial expansionist ambitions, made up much of Soviet strategy. Interestingly, in Soviet strategic writing the concepts of doctrine and strategy are often confused, used interchangeably, or conflated. For instance, in *Soviet Military Strategy*, a massive tome edited by Chief of the General

Staff Vasilii D. Sokolovskii in 1962, doctrinal matters—such as various methods of preparing offensive maneuvers—are often discussed as if they were strategic ones.[2] Nonetheless, this work had remained an influential statement on Soviet strategy until the early 1980s. A crucial point that emerged from *Soviet Military Strategy* was a strategic perspective that reflected a shift from past preoccupation with land warfare toward an expanded focus on global strategic war.

By the early 1980s many Western specialists had considered the USSR no longer so much as Lenin's creation but a great military empire in the classical tradition.[3] According to this view, Soviet leaders were expected to continue to convert available economic resources into military strength to serve the overall objective of increasing territory under Soviet or Communist control. At the same time, while the goal of enlarging the real estate ruled by Marxist-Leninist parties remained constant, Moscow had become more prudent in pursuing that goal in contrast to the occasionally reckless actions of the Khrushchev era. By this time, also, the Kremlin was able to reap the rewards of the decades-long program of building a quantitatively and qualitatively superior air force capable of offensive actions in faraway strategic theaters.

As the mid 1980s rolled around, Soviet strategists had few reasons for optimism, however. The economy, partly as a result of enormous defense outlays, was exhausted and nothing indicated that it could be revived without fundamental reforms. Even before Gorbachev took office, a number of leading Soviet strategic thinkers had advocated the need for major economic restructuring in order to assure that resources needed by the military would be available.[4] In the USSR's overall population the proportion of non-Russian nationalities had continued to grow while those of Russians and, more generally, Slavs, had started to decline precipitously. Moreover, despite the massive infusions of resources into the military-industrial complex, the Soviet Union had not only lagged behind that of the United States but the technology gap between the two superpowers had begun to widen. These factors had led many strategists to emphasize the importance of the country's extant and relatively inexpensive strategic nuclear deterrent, increasingly at the expense of its conventional military capabilities.

In his report to the Twenty-seventh Congress of the Communist Party of the Soviet Union (CPSU) in 1986, Gorbachev announced that a world war was not inevitable and major states should lower their military potential to a level of "reasonable sufficiency."[5] He also pledged that his country would not be the first to use nuclear arms in a military conflict. Actually, little of this was new. Brezhnev had publicly renounced the first-use of nuclear weapons in 1982. This policy was predicated on the theses that (a) no country could win a nuclear war and (b) it was not possible to carry out a preemptive strike on the USSR because of the high level of combat readiness of Moscow's nuclear forces.[6] Subsequently, no-first-use of nuclear weapons became a cornerstone of Soviet military doctrine.

Marshal Nikolai Ogarkov, one of the most important Soviet military leaders in the 1970s and early 1980s, wrote that "the political mission of war must fully correspond to the military potential of the state, the combat resources of the armed forces, and the methods of conducting military actions."[7] What Ogarkov advocated—in effect, the diminished role of military strategy in the larger context of grand strategy—was realized during the Gorbachev years. Consequently, the Soviet Army had come to be viewed in the West as a less threatening force. This was also the result of a seemingly genuine concern in the Kremlin that directly linked the need to reduce military spending to the worsening economic conditions.[8]

"Seemingly" genuine, because some army leaders have subsequently questioned the credibility of Soviet policy. For instance, General Matvei Burlakov, who supervised the Soviet withdrawal from East Germany and Hungary in the early 1990s and was deputy defense minister in the middle of that decade, admitted in 2005 that the Soviet General Staff in the 1980s was fully prepared for the first-use of nuclear weapons in a contingency.[9] Andrei Karaganov, a director of the Russian Academy of Sciences, wrote that Gorbachev's speeches on strategic matters were seldom taken seriously because "Moscow often kept voicing contradictory statements" and "implementing entirely different policies."[10] To make matters worse, Gorbachev was wont to float ideas, such as that nuclear powers should scrap their entire arsenals, which both Soviet and Western experts considered preposterous. In 1985 Marshal Ogarkov defined Soviet military doctrine as

> a system of guiding principles and scientifically based views of the CPSU and the Soviet Government on the essence, nature, and methods of waging war which may be unleashed by the imperialists against the Soviet Union, as well as on military construction and the preparation of the Armed Forces and the country to destroy the aggressor.[11]

Unlike defense doctrines in the Western sense—which ordinarily are little more than collections of widely shared norms and standards pertaining to the use of armed forces in combat—the Soviet doctrine comprised concerns far beyond the military and included issues having to do with patriotic education, the location of strategic industries, and matters germane to foreign relations. Furthermore, although high-ranking military officers did participate in the formulation of the USSR's military doctrine, it was first and foremost the distillation of the CPSU's security policy. As several Western specialists noted, the Soviet Union had two separate doctrines: a so-called "declaratory" or "propaganda" doctrine devised for foreign consumption and an "operational" or "real" doctrine for the purposes of internal usage.[12] This distinction is important because although the essence of Soviet military doctrine (i.e., the "operational" one) had changed little through the years, it was repeatedly modified. One such amendment was the 1974 assertion that military support for national liberation movements was a "sacred duty of the Soviet people." The "declaratory doctrine," on the other hand, was quite sensitive to and had more or less accurately reflected the changes in the international political climate and particularly in superpower relations.

Since Khrushchev's time Kremlin leaders had insisted that Moscow's military doctrine was unequivocally defensive. Interestingly, both Brezhnev and Gorbachev made announcements to this effect with great fanfare as if they had been the first to do so. Even so, the Soviet military's distribution of forces, armaments, and training principles had continued to maintain a purely offensive posture, consistent with long-standing Russian military tradition.[13] Moscow's historical commitment to the offensive reflected not only tradition but also its conviction that victory could only be achieved through offensive maneuvers.[14] In essence, the USSR's military doctrine supported the basic tenets of its grand strategy, which is to say, the expansion of Communist influence beyond the Soviet Union's borders in order to accelerate, as Marxist-Leninist theory posited, the inevitable collapse of imperialism. After 1987, once Gorbachev's "New Thinking" gained a foothold in the defense establishment, doctrinal writings had begun to reflect the changes prescribed. Around this time military thinkers started to underscore that the quintessential objective of Soviet military doctrine was the prevention of nuclear *and* conventional war.[15] Nonetheless, the most original and insightful arguments on doctrinal innovation came not from the uniformed ranks but from a small but vocal group of civilian commentators in strategic and international affairs.[16]

In the wake of the Cold War the post-Soviet military establishment had lost its traditional external mission along with a significant portion of its arsenal located in what became the member states of the Commonwealth of Independent States (CIS). The presence of nearly 25 million ethnic Russians outside the Russian Federation's borders was an additional stimulus in the adoption of a new military doctrine. In 2006, fifteen years after the collapse of the Soviet state, Russian strategic and doctrinal affairs are fraught with contradiction, incongruity, disconnectedness. Nonetheless, "continuity" might best characterize the mindsets of Soviet/Russian military elites. Let us see how things have changed in two decades.

The numerous conflicting public statements of political and military leaders and the inconsistencies of the official documents they issue concerning strategic and doctrinal issues indicate that Russia and its armed forces have yet to find their place in the post–Cold War world. In November 1993, after studying the newly released Russian military doctrine, air force commander and Deputy Defense Minister Marshal Yevgenii Shaposhnikov publicly complained that "we still do not know what we are, where we are going, and what our ultimate goals are. . . . Our blueprint for national security should follow from a blueprint for the development of the Russian state."[17] As the director of the Ministry of Defense's official think-tank on strategic policy, Vladimir Dvorkin, opined ten years (!) later: "How can we reform our Army when we have not defined the threats it must deal with? We must first identify our national interests, then we'll know who our enemies might be."[18] Little has changed since then.

Perhaps the most important change that *has* occurred since the end of the Cold War is that the relevance of Marxist-Leninist thought to military strategy was fully and formally rejected by political and military elites around 1990. Subsequently, Russian strategists have become more attuned to traditional geopolitical approaches and concepts such as balance of power and spheres of influence. In addition, they began to study strategic issues like demographic change, the availability of raw materials and other resources, and current and future trends in economic development.

Assessing Russia's military doctrine is a difficult proposition owing to its many inherent contradictions. In its short post-Soviet history the country has had three different defense doctrines and many other formal statements (strategic concepts, white papers, and the like) that share remarkably little in the way of overarching themes or a consistent framework. Many of these documents, in fact, were forgotten soon after their ceremonial unveiling without any apparent efforts to update or reevaluate them. Let us briefly consider the three incarnations of Russia's military doctrine and their paradoxical nature that underscore the country's strategic affairs. The 1993 doctrine, devised entirely by the General Staff, toughened Russia's position on the first-use of nuclear weapons and called for their use if conventional arms were not sufficient.[19] It permitted the armed forces' deployment in several well-specified internal political scenarios (e.g., threats to Russia's territorial integrity and constitutional order), in essence retroactively approved their use during the October 1993 storming of the White House, the legislature's seat. Moreover, this document also justified the wholesale liquidation of unlawful paramilitary units in Chechnya and elsewhere.

The next doctrine, approved by a Presidential Decree in April 2000, was notable for its anti-Western tone and made no effort to take into account the changes in Russia's security environment. It identified the global hegemony of the United States and NATO as the clearest threat to Russian national security even though by this time Moscow was involved in a brutal war against Chechen separatists on its own territory. The document called on the Ministry of Defense to make plans for future global military confrontations and, among other things, suggested that the navy build fifteen aircraft carriers to challenge the United States on the open seas.[20] The 2000 doctrine's framers were apparently unaware that Russian politicians—including President Putin and Defense Minister Sergeev—had repeatedly emphasized that Moscow had no strategic enemy, that no large-scale aggression posed a threat to the country, and that global hazards to Russian security were created not by the United States or NATO but by "regional crises and international terrorism." Only after 11 September 2001, did battling terrorism receive a privileged position on the list of Russia's strategic concerns, but it did not necessarily stay at the top of the list. Furthermore, this doctrine suggested *both* that Russia should lower the nuclear threshold *and* that it ought to rely more on nuclear weapons as its armed forces grew weaker.

The most recent, so-called "Ivanov Doctrine" (after Defense Minister Sergei Ivanov) was prepared jointly by the Ministry of Defense and the General Staff and released in October 2003. It is fraught with similar internal contradictions as its predecessors and faithfully reflects the power struggle between the two entities at the time. The political-conceptual threat analysis—elaborated by the ministry—maintains that there is no major threat to Russian security at present, names no strategic enemy, and identifies fundamentalism, armed separatism, terrorism, and smuggling as the key challenges to Russia's national interest. This part of the doctrine explicitly lowers the threat posed by NATO and recommends that the Russian Army should prepare for new types of conflicts, especially local and regional ones, and prescribes that Russia should be able to fight two local wars at the same time.[21] More specifically, the document calls for the creation of a rapid-reaction force to be operational by 2007 and complemented by an army based largely on volunteer contract soldiers.

Nevertheless, the portions of the doctrine dealing with military operational issues and actual force structure—that is, the parts worked out by the General Staff—predict a global nuclear threat as well as the possibility of a large-scale conventional war against NATO.[22] This part specifies NATO as the main enemy and requires preparations for an all-out attack from the West.[23] As Aleksandr Golts, one of the few independent Russian defense experts wrote at the time, "My reading of all these contradictions is that Russian generals badly need some big enemy, some big adversary, in order to keep these Soviet-type armed forces."[24]

At times, especially if circumstances so require, the very same politicians can explicitly or implicitly suggest that the main enemy of Russia remains the U.S.-dominated NATO. For instance, following the tragedy at the Beslan school in 2004, Putin hinted that Russia's real enemies were not the notorious Chechen separatists but the United States, NATO, and, more generally, the West.[25] In a sense, these inconsistencies emanating from the political leadership allow the top brass to rationalize, justify, and maintain their own outdated perspectives on doctrinal matters. To be sure, a number of factors such as the eastward expansion of NATO, its wars in Bosnia and against Serbia, the establishment of American military bases in Central Asia, and the continued rapid technological development of the U.S. armed forces have played into the hands of those Russian defense officials who have not been divested of their Cold War attitudes. Thus, even though the probability of an all-out war between Russia and NATO is virtually nil in the foreseeable future, for the past fifteen years Russia's generals have been preparing to fight the United States in just such a war. In short, there is much continuity, especially in terms of strategic and conceptual legacies, in contemporary Russian strategy and doctrine. The military leadership is dead set against preparing for low-intensity conflicts for which their army—still very much the mass-mobilization army of the Soviet era—remains completely unsuited.[26]

In essence, Russia's political and military elites have failed "to appropriately adjust military strategy and policy to new realities."[27] Many of the strategic concepts and other documents have been based on Soviet-era fears and an obsolete view of the world and have focused on contingencies that are unrealistic and unnecessary. Since the fall of the Soviet Union, Russian generals have engaged in "strategic camouflage nominally accepting the absence of enemies while keeping the overall strategic matrix essentially intact."[28] A somber assessment in early 2006 concluded that Russian generals were still "making preparations for an abortive war against NATO" and that the "Soviet Army has remained almost intact" in the last decade-and-a-half.[29]

BUDGET, MANPOWER, TRAINING, EQUIPMENT

There *are* important differences between the Soviet Army of 1985 and the Russian Army of 2005, and they are most apparent in the four categories discussed in this section. In absolute and relative terms the military's manpower and budget have become a lot smaller. The thorough training Soviet officers, soldiers, sailors, and airmen had received for decades has been replaced by instruction that fails to prepare their successors for likely present and future challenges. Similarly, the contemporary Russian armed forces do not possess the quality and quantity of equipment and weaponry they need to fight the battles they can plausibly expect to fight.

"Soviet statistics" may be deemed an oxymoron as hard data pertaining to most aspects of political, social, and economic activity or condition originating from the USSR was unreliable. Not surprisingly, this was especially so for information regarding defense- and security-related issues. Trying to make sense of the incomplete, disparate, and false data released by the USSR's propaganda agencies had occupied many Western experts and spawned an entire intelligence-gathering industry of electronic detection facilities, satellites, and other data collection techniques.[30] Despite the astonishing sophistication of some of these methods, American and other intelligence and security agencies had still occasionally provided information that was imprecise or subject to misinterpretation or manipulation.

Defense Expenditures

In time, the overall accuracy of American estimates of Soviet defense spending and other military-security issues had undoubtedly improved, though still remained imperfect. In 1985 the Soviet Union's military budget was by far the largest in the world in terms of its share of the gross national product (GNP) and second only to the United States in absolute numbers. The ratio of Soviet defense spending to the GNP, however, had decreased after the early 1950s (it was 24.2 percent in 1951, 23.4 percent in 1952, and 19.4 percent in 1953, the year Stalin died) and settled into the 15–16 percent range for much of the rest of the Cold War.[31] In 1985 it was 14.9 percent at 1982 prices and 15.9 percent at current prices. Under Gorbachev's tenure the defense spending to GNP ratio peaked in 1987 (at 15.7 percent at 1982 prices 17.6 percent at current prices) and then began to decline.

Although data on defense-related issues emanating from Moscow have become more credible since 1991, they still do not fully stand up to scrutiny. Under Yeltsin, military expenditures plummeted in real terms, although the precise numbers differ depending on who is doing the counting and when the counting occurred. For this reason, no two yearbooks of the respected Stockholm International Peace Research Institute provide the same figure for Russian defense expenditures of a given year. Yeltsin had decreed that defense spending be kept under 3.5 percent of the GNP (for the regular armed forces and the paramilitary organizations combined). This objective, according to SIPRI data, was achieved only in 1998. It is important to consider that even at 8 percent Moscow's defense outlays would have been similar to that of Britain with an army one-seventh as large.[32] When considering the burden of military expenditures on the Russian economy, the fact that in 1997–98 it was slightly smaller than that of the Netherlands should also be kept in mind.

There were several major problems with military budgets during the Yeltsin years. First and most obvious, the funds earmarked for defense were inadequate considering the size of the armed forces they were supposed to maintain. Second, in the late 1990s, given the partial meltdown of the Russian economy and subsequent additional budget cuts, in some years the government allocated as little as 50 percent of the funds requested by the Ministry of Defense. Third, in most years, actual disbursements to the military were significantly lower than the budget figure because—due to the shortfall of funds, the Defense Ministry's relatively low priority, its large debts to the state budget, and political reasons—the Ministry of Finance refused to transfer the money. (For example, in 1997 the Finance Ministry sent only 77.4 percent and in 1998 only 69.3 percent of the money promised to the Ministry of Defense.)[33] Fourth, a sizable share of the resources that *were* distributed was not spent on their intended purpose—e.g., salaries, food, and uniforms for personnel; payments to utility companies—owing to large-scale corruption and embezzlement. Finally, aside from the money squandered as a result of criminal activities, a large proportion was wasted because of poor management and procurement decisions. Until 2001 the Defense Ministry had incurred major debts to the point that for months it was unable to pay its utility bills, occasionally prompting electricity companies to cut service to defense installations.[34]

Since the low point of 1998, Russian military budgets have steadily increased. This trend has accelerated in recent years as defense expenditures have risen at an average rate of more than 10 percent since 2000. Still, while the last Soviet defense budget of 1991—far smaller than military expenditures in the 1970s and 1980s—was $155 billion, in 2003, even with supplemental increases, the Russian military budget barely reached $15.5 billion.[35] For 2004 the rate of increase slowed down to 4 percent. In that year the Defense Ministry's budget was 411 billion rubles ($14.6 billion), and the total military expenditure (including spending on paramilitary forces and military research and development [R&D]) reached 632 billion rubles ($21.6 billion). The budget increases have meant that funds for R&D and the procurement of new equipment could also start to increase in 2001.

In the 2005 defense budget of about $18 billion rubles (up by 28 percent from 2004 but still less than 5 percent of U.S. defense outlays), the largest sums were earmarked for information and command systems, computer systems, and surveillance and navigation systems, including space projects.[36] The projected defense budget for 2006 (about $20 billion) signified an increase of about 20 percent, although it is still less than Saudi Arabia's military expenditures. In May 2006 defense officials announced that the 2007 budget allocated a 27 percent increase in military expenditures compared to 2006; three months later Defense Minister Ivanov revised that figure to 29 percent.[37] That Moscow's defense budget is several times greater than its appropriations for health-care and education combined puts Russian military outlays in yet another perspective. The new budget continues to devote relatively small amounts to combat training and personnel maintenance. The Defense Ministry wants its budget evenly split between maintenance and development by 2011, and by 2017 this ratio should 30 percent to 70 percent, respectively, that is, precisely the reverse of the 2001 spending pattern.[38] As I will explain in chapter 4, given the absence of real civilian oversight, how monies are actually spent remains a mystery to all but a few individuals in the Ministry of Defense.

Officials in Moscow are eager to point out that, despite the major increases in defense outlays, Russia spends comparatively little on the armed forces. According to their own data, from 1991 to 2006 Russia's military expenditures had decreased by 87 percent compared with 31 percent in the United States and 27 percent in Germany and the United Kingdom. Moreover, in 2006 defense spending in Russia amounted to $3,800 per soldier, while in the United States the figure was $190,000, in Great Britain $170,000, in Germany $94,000, and in Turkey $12,700.[39] Nonetheless, if the basis for comparison is 2000 to 2006, then Russia's military spending has grown by more than 350 percent. Moreover, if the 2007 state budget is approved—as widely expected—then defense and security outlays will have increased by almost 500 percent during Putin's presidency.[40]

The Size of the Armed Forces

At the time Gorbachev became the USSR's leader, the Soviet army was comprised of 5.3 million men, half of whom were draftees. There were an additional 6.3 million reservists with conscript service within the previous five years. Most units—particularly those stationed in the east and west of the Soviet Union and in Eastern Europe—received rigorous training appropriate to their missions. Although Marxist-Leninist political indoctrination took up a considerable share of instruction—both for conscripts and professional soldiers—by 1985 this training component had become less methodical and exacting than earlier.[41] After the end of the Cold War, Soviet troops were withdrawn from Europe and the former Soviet republics according to logistical instead of strategic considerations. Consequently, Russian forces are still concentrated in the west and east—where bases and garrisons had already been available—rather than in the south where existing threats are.

Since the fall of the USSR, when roughly 3 million men had worn its uniform—including 575,000 officers and 280,000 ensigns—the military's manpower has shrunk drastically.[42] Although the exact size of the armed forces may not be known to anyone—commanders have a strong incentive to exaggerate the number of their troops—it has hovered around 1.1–1.2 million uniformed personnel and 875,000 civilians for the past several years, despite repeated announcements of further reductions. Manpower continues to be based on conscription, although a sizable proportion of soldiers and noncommissioned officers (NCOs) are now volunteers. According to Defense Minister Ivanov, in March 2006 there were 60,000

contract soldiers on active duty and with an additional 25,000 slated to
join them during the year; his ministry expects to have 144,000 volunteers
in 2008 when they will presumably form the core of the NCO ranks.[43]
The army has suffered not only from the exodus of qualified officers but
also from the absence of well-trained NCOs. The shortage of officers is so
acute that in many regiments 40 percent of platoon leaders are so-called
dvukhgodichniki, reserve officers with little practical military training.[44]

Notwithstanding President Yeltsin's 1996 electoral pledge to abolish
conscription by 2000, there are no such plans in the works. Actually,
Yeltsin's 1992 decision to reduce the length of service from twenty-four
months to eighteen months had to be reversed in 1995 owing to manpower shortages. In fact, due to extremely unfavorable demographic
trends, a larger proportion of young men will have to be drafted than in
the past decade and a half. As of July 2006 Russia's population was 142.4
million, 348,000 less than at the beginning of the year, and more than 6
million less than in 1992 despite a net influx of more than 5.5 million
migrants.[45] Prominent demographers predict that by 2050 the country's
population will decline to between 122.6 million and 77.2 million.[46]
There are numerous interconnected reasons for the continued shrinking
of Russia's population by about 750,000 annually. Birthrates are low: for
simple reproduction 215 births/100 women are necessary, the actual rate
in Russia is 151/100.[47]

Russia's birthrate of about 9.95 per 1,000 people is low compared to
14/1000 in the United States but not when weighed against the German
figure of 8.3/1000. But the critical statistic is that while in the United
States the death rate per 1,000 people is 8.2 and in Germany 10.6, the
Russian figure is an alarming 14.65.[48] Standards of public health remain
abysmal; Russians continue to have the shortest life-expectancy in Europe
(58 years for men, 72 for women).[49] In 2004 the state spent $120 per
capita on health-care, less than 10 percent of Greece's outlays.[50] In his
2006 State of the Nation speech President Putin identified the demographic crisis as the most serious problem facing Russia.[51]

Not surprisingly, in recent years the Ministry of Defense has made a
concerted effort to attract to the armed forces a large and hitherto mostly
untapped pool of potential recruits: women. In 2005 there were approximately ninety thousand women in uniform, including five thousand officers (among them four colonels but no generals).[52] The collapse of the
Soviet Union more or less eliminated concerns regarding the ethnic hetero-
geneity of the troops; the vast majority of professional soldiers are ethnic

Russians. The army is characterized by an unusually high officer-to-soldier ratio. This is partly the result of the Defense Ministry leadership that is loath to enforce any major downsizing of the central apparatus causing the "multiple duplication of redundant functions."[53] There are more than fifteen hundred generals (about two hundred in the Ministry of Defense central staff alone) who often remain in rank even after their positions are reclassified to colonel grade.[54] In June 2006, a Defense Ministry spokesman indicated that the armed forces planned to eliminate more than three hundred general officer posts by the end of the year, but skepticism about the execution of the plan is hardly misplaced when considering similar past proposals. Although the Russian military is nearly 20 percent smaller than the U.S. armed forces, it employs twice as many officers (about 450,000).[55]

Training and Arsenal

Since 1985 three out of every four military colleges and academies have been abolished owing to the army's reduced size, lack of funding, streamlining of specialized schools, and dearth of qualified instructors and officer candidates. In 2005 the Ministry of Defense maintained fifty-seven such organizations (ten academies, nine universities, and thirty-eight institutes) in which the standards of officer-training have greatly deteriorated across the board in the last two decades.[56] This is especially so in specialties for which schooling is expensive. Foremost among these, of course, is pilot training. According to Defense Minister Ivanov, in 2003 air force pilots flew just 12 to 44 hours a year, several times less than the regulation 160 to 180 hours (allotted to their Indian and Chinese colleagues); little wonder that pilot errors caused seven of the eight aviation accidents in the first ten months of that year.[57] Another problem is that the bulk of flight hours are taken by relatively experienced majors and lieutenant colonels while young air force lieutenants hardly get any training at all. Consequently, most top pilots are now forty-one to forty-three years old in a system with a mandatory retirement age of forty-five.[58]

Defense officials, including Ivanov, like to insist that combat readiness has improved in recent years. In April 2005 he went so far as to declare that "[Russian] conventional forces are on par with the leading armed forces of the world,"[59] but clearly, there is a long, long way to go. As a result of poor objective conditions, morale, and discipline, the capabilities of most units are so low that, in 2002, Chief of the General Staff Kvashnin publicly said that the officer corps was "mired in theft and corruption" and the decline in combat readiness could "become irreversible."[60] Defense reforms call for the formation of "permanent combat-ready" units but the side effect is often the further weakening of others. Russia's capacity to project conventional military power beyond its borders is very limited. Moreover, whatever training most units do receive is largely irrelevant to the kind of challenges they can anticipate facing in the foreseeable future. In the last several years Russian units have participated in a growing number of exercises—some of them with foreign partners—but their true performance is hard to gauge from the glowing and uncritical reports echoing Soviet-era accounts.

It is similarly difficult to judge the usefulness of these maneuvers given the aforementioned tendency of Russian leaders to contradict themselves. In May 2005 Ivanov lauded the "Mobility 2004" exercises that "enabled us to test our ability to airlift permanent combat readiness units from western Russia, for example, to the Russian Far East and vice versa."[61] A few months earlier, however, when he was still working on discrediting Kvashnin, Ivanov publicly ridiculed the need for the very same exercises, likening them to "rehearse hitting a mosquito with a hammer."[62] Like most information provided by Russian political-military leaders, one is well advised to take the number of maneuvers Russian troops participate in with a grain of salt. In a January 2006 *Wall Street Journal* article, Ivanov boasted that "the number and level of large-scale exercises has grown to more than 50" in 2005.[63] In fact, only thirty-one of these were held at the regimental level and just one involved an entire division even though the Russian military contains more than twenty divisions and hundreds of regiments.[64]

The Russian Army inherited the bulk of the Soviet Army's formidable arsenal, made up of thousands of missiles and aircraft and tens of thousands of tanks and artillery pieces.[65] An enormous, technologically sophisticated, and resource-rich armaments industry served the needs of the country's vast military machine. It possesses 635 intercontinental ballistic missiles (ICBMs), 22,800 main battle tanks, 30,000 artillery pieces, 14 strategic and 37 tactical submarines, 600 bombers, and 900 fighter jets among other equipment.[66] It also has about 7,700 operational nuclear warheads (4,279 strategic warheads and 3,400 tactical nuclear weapons) and 927 nuclear weapons delivery systems.[67] Although supplying the military with new weapons systems was not a priority for the Kremlin in the

1990s, the army has been able to complement its arsenal in recent years when spending on new weapons has drastically increased (by 50 percent more in 2006 than the year before, for instance). The most important acquisitions by the strategic missile troops are 36 SS-27 (Topol-M2) ICBMs, each with six to ten launches; several diesel submarines and anti-submarine ships by the navy; the new Iskander tactical theater missile system by the army; and the recently developed Mi-28N ("Night Hunter) helicopter by the air force. There are a whole range of ships under construction and new nuclear-powered submarines will soon join the navy, armed with Bulava (SS-NX-30) ballistic missile systems.[68] From 2006 to 2011, Putin recently said, "we must significantly increase the procurement of modern aircraft, submarines, and strategic missiles."[69]

A new, even longer term (2007–2015) armament program announced in June 2006 earmarks 5 trillion rubles ($185 billion) for weapon procurement.[70] This could mean a major improvement in Russia's arsenal but there are profound problems regarding the kind of weapons that have been and are to be purchased by the Defense Ministry. The primary cause of these shortcomings is rooted in the aforementioned confusion about the type of challenges Russia faces and will face. The idea behind the new program is that Russia should be able to fight one global war, one regional war, and several localized wars simultaneously.[71] There are internal contradictions in this notion—for instance, fighting a global war requires colossal mobilization while local wars demand mobile professional forces—that are not addressed quite apart from the fact that if Russia has had a difficult time defeating Chechen separatists it is hard to foresee it fielding an army that could even come close to meeting these challenges in the near future.

At a time when the leading militaries of the world—namely those of the United States and Great Britain—are increasingly relying on unmanned vehicles, airplanes, and robotics preparing for noncontact wars, the Russian defense industry continues to produce upgraded versions of weapons that were designed in the 1970s and 1980s and are unsuited for future wars.[72] About 3 trillion rubles—that is, 60 percent of the new program—are to be spent on the purchases of fourteen hundred tanks, thousands of infantry vehicles, and heavy artillery pieces.[73] These weapons might be in line with the preferences of the generals who anticipate fighting World War III but are hardly going to be useful in localized conflicts or antiterrorist operations. In an April 2006 article, a presidential aide, Aleksandr Burutin, was quoted of saying that "the share of modern armaments and military hardware is only 10–20 percent [of the total]," that the armed forces possessed "over 40,000 weapons that [can] hardly ever be used and whose storage costs a lot," and that "the number of useless weapons still exceeds the number of new weapons commissioned by the government." Incidentally, Burutin squarely contradicted Defense Minister Ivanov who only a few days before portrayed the state of weapons procurement and modernization in glowing terms.[74] Nonetheless, Ivanov—who is known to tailor his stated views according to the occasion and audience—himself slammed the Russian electronics industry in September 2006 for "still using models from 1980–85" and possessing the technical standards "of yesterday or before."[75] He appealed to the business community to invest in electronics programs for the military.

The vast majority of the army's weapons are obsolete and poorly maintained. For instance, the tank and aircraft inventory remains mostly unchanged since the Afghan war. Owing to inadequate funds for maintenance and due to sheer negligence, many easily salvageable weapons just rust away. Submarines sink because of corrosion (as in 1997 and 1999), vehicles and machines leak dangerous fuels, and personnel are forced to cannibalize weapons for spare parts unavailable elsewhere. According to the Defense Ministry's official statistics released in 2005, 60 percent of deployed ICBMs are past the service life planned for them, about half the tanks require major repairs and only 20 percent meet modern requirements, and no more than 30 percent of fighter planes are combat ready.[76]

The most troubling area is weapons safety. A 2002 report of the Russian State Atomic Inspection Agency (RSAIA) divulged that 190 nuclear submarines decommissioned from the navy because of their "miserable safety conditions" posed a serious threat to the population and the environment. Because they are considered "military objects," the army does not let the RSAIA inspect them.[77] In a 2002 interview on the NBC News program *Meet the Press* Ivanov responded with a categorical "No" when asked about reports of weapons-grade and weapons-usable nuclear materials having been stolen in Russia.[78] Nonetheless, there are good reasons for the lingering qualms about weapons safety. For example, on two separate occasions in one week in 2002, battle-ready T-72 tanks, complete with multiple-launch rocket systems, were discovered in warehouses near Moscow.[79] Environmental protection has not been a serious concern in the military, and it has caused innumerable cases of air, soil, and water pollution. Perhaps none of them is more astounding than the lake of fuel oil covering more than 45,000 square meters and containing some 18,000 tons of oil at a military base in Kirov Oblast. "Lake Fuel Oil," as it is referred to on military maps and in documents, appeared sometime in the 1970s from the leakage of storage units and pipelines and has yet to be cleaned up.[80]

Social Issues: Living Standards, Conscription, Corruption

Throughout much of the Communist era the military was the second most privileged Soviet institution after the Communist Party. Members of the armed forces elite who survived the extensive purges under Stalin and Khrushchev's ill-advised reorganization schemes with their lives and jobs intact lived surrounded by relative luxury and privilege. By the mid 1980s the military had enjoyed nearly two decades of continuous prosperity, political tranquility, and elevated social status. Brezhnev's long tenure was the Soviet army's "golden age."

In 1985 the military occupation was one of the most highly rewarding careers in the Soviet Union. The state took good care of its officers and NCOs whose living standards were higher than those of others with similar levels of education. The perquisites included heavily subsidized housing, transportation, and vacations; relatively high salaries; medical care at special hospitals; and preferential admission to educational institutions for the children. Officers enjoyed considerable social standing, they were entrusted with sophisticated weapons, and were viewed as the past, present, and future guarantors of the USSR's peace and security. Many members of the armed forces had the opportunity—rare for the average citizen—to live in foreign countries where they were deployed as occupation forces, military advisors, or security personnel. Indeed, one of the main attractions of the military career was the opportunity to escape the drabness of ordinary life.[81]

The situation of conscripts, however, was altogether a different matter. In 1985 young males were conscripted for two years in all branches of the armed forces except for the navy where they served for a three-year period. Fresh draftees were not told in advance where they would be stationed and often ended up several time zones away from their homes. Ordinarily, their living quarters were crowded and poorly kept and their provisions were of inferior quality. They were permitted to buy their own

food at the base cafeteria or kiosk if they could afford it, which was unlikely (without their parents' financial assistance) because their salaries
were extremely low, about five dollars a month.[82] According to official
sources, the draftees' physical condition and "ideological awareness"—
that is, level of Marxist-Leninist indoctrination—were satisfactory.[83] As
several studies have pointed out, ethnic discrimination against non-Rus-
sians, and especially non-Slavs, was not unusual though it was officially
discouraged.[84] Hazing, the abuse of junior conscripts by senior soldiers,
was already a cause for concern but not yet the widespread phenomenon
that it has become.[85] It was only in connection with the war in Afghanistan
that social ills in the army started to be discussed in the Soviet press. Drug
addiction received much of the attention as it had gradually become a
serious problem, especially among soldiers along the USSR's southern
borders. By 1989, crime in the armed forces was rising by 14.5 percent
and weapons theft by 50 percent annually.[86]

The deterioration in the army personnel's socioeconomic conditions
between 1985 and 2006 is, quite simply, shocking. It is the result of a
combination of diverse and often related factors. The end of the Cold War
brought with it the collapse of the Soviet empire and greatly diminished
functions for the military, while state policy manifested itself most plainly
in the long years of meager defense outlays. Finally, the proliferation of
more attractive career opportunities in the new economy drew talent that
once might have considered a military career into the private sector.

The military profession's social status started to decline under Gorbachev. Journalists began to write about widespread problems in the military, such as the poor discipline in the units fighting in Afghanistan, as
well as specific shortcomings such as the breakdown of the air defense
service that allowed a German teenager to land his airplane on Moscow's
Red Square in May 1987. These events for the first time also affected the
general population's attitude about the armed forces. Though for decades
the army was the "sacred cow" in Russia's culture, its increasingly obvious problems suggested that the major economic sacrifices average Russians made for the military might have been in vain.

At the same time, one should not underestimate the effect on the military establishment produced by the frequent humiliations it has suffered
in the last quarter century. In 1979 a string of calamities began with the
invasion of Afghanistan, followed by the ill-conceived and counterproductive policies of the Gorbachev-era, including the repeated deployments
of army units against unarmed civilians that shook the public's traditional

confidence in the military. This streak of misfortunes only continued with the loss of the Soviet Union's external and then internal empire, the collapse of the state itself, crippling budget cuts, and the mismanaged wars in Chechnya. These tribulations have generated a profound negative shift in the military's organizational psychology, undermining its confidence and contributing to its pervasive malaise. A closely related development has been the military's plummeting social prestige owing to—among other things—its active involvement in the August 1991 coup attempt, the October 1993 shelling of the White House in Moscow, the widespread corruption that accompanied the withdrawal from Eastern Europe and the CIS, the weak performance in the Caucasus, and a multitude of avoidable accidents that claimed many hundreds of lives annually.

Not surprisingly, then, by 1996 high school students rated "army officer" as the least prestigious on a long list of occupations.[87] In an interview in late 2004, Chief of the General Staff Yuri Baluyevskii identified raising the prestige of the military profession as one of his top priorities.[88] Opinion polls show that a gradually decreasing proportion of officers are proud of wearing the Russian Army's uniform; in 2005 this figure was only 40 percent.[89] In early 2006 pollsters of the prominent Levada Center asked what kind of emotions people felt when thinking of the armed forces. The top answer was "pity."[90]

The societal reputation of the military as an effective institution has been at a low point for years, although public trust in the army, a very different issue, remains fairly high (48 percent in 1997 and 60 percent in 2003).[91] During the 1990s, when the Russian media was still relatively free, reports on the armed forces tended to be negative, although, in all fairness, there were few success stories to tell. Military leaders frequently decried the "biased" and "unpatriotic" media attitudes toward the army.[92] As I indicated in the previous chapter, Putin's rule has been synonymous with the growing limitations on media freedoms and the persecution of courageous journalists. Defense Ministry personnel are not allowed to give interviews without special permission, and only loyal and trusted journalists are invited to attend military events and receive "the measured-out and weighed-out information."[93] Consequently, the military's press coverage has become more favorable in recent years in part because mishaps such as accidents and failed missile launches are now seldom reported in the mainstream, Kremlin-controlled press.[94] Even so, the public remains skeptical about the army's effectiveness. A 2002 public

opinion survey found that 49 percent of the respondents judged the ministry's work disapprovingly.[95]

Opinion polls also show overwhelming public opposition to conscription (64 percent in 2002), especially when the respondent's close relative is the putative draftee (74 percent in 2002, 77 percent in 2004, 69
percent in 2006).[96] In 2003, 86 percent of those surveyed thought that
Russia needed a professional army.[97] In fact, the mandatory military service has become something to avoid at all cost. In 1995 27 percent, in
2002 13 percent, and in 2005 only 9 percent of youths subject to the draft
actually entered military service.[98] Until April 2006, when—in order to
boost the number of conscripts—the legislature passed a bill cutting military service deferments to sixteen, there were twenty-five legal grounds to
avoid the draft based mostly on medical, social, and occupational status.
Those who cannot get deferments usually bribe the authorities. About
forty thousand (that is, a sufficient number to staff three-and-a-half divisions) a year simply dodge the draft. The military ends up with the least
desirable men of their cohort. Data on the spring 2005 conscription cycle
show that 70 percent of the young men called up for service were medi-
cally unfit, 45 percent had never held a job or studied at the postsecondary
level, 5 percent had criminal records, 25 percent had not finished high
school, nearly one-ninth were alcoholics and/or regular drug users, and
some were illiterate.[99] The top brass have made one concession to regional
officials in exchange for their support of local garrisons: conscripts are
now usually allowed to serve near their homes.[100]

The conditions for ordinary draftees are appalling. As recently as 2003
the budget assigned for the conscripts' food supply was sufficient only for
two-thirds of them.[101] Throughout the 1990s and in the early 2000s soldiers often were sent mushrooming and berry-picking in order to stave
off hunger. The 2006 budget stipulated the cost of food ration per soldier
at a level of 63.6 rubles per day, which, as Russian analysts noted, was
"not much but not starving either." The biggest problem draftees face
once in the armed forces is not the inadequate food, clothing, or equipment, however, but the treatment they are subjected to by their commanders and fellow conscripts. The widespread and brutal hazing (*dedovshchina*) is essentially a system of sadistic treatment of soldiers by NCOs and
longer-serving conscripts. The noted Polish writer, Ryszard Kapuściński,
called it "one of the malignant tumors eating away at the Red Army" in
1994.[102] More than a decade later, Russia's human rights ombudsman

Vladimir Lukin identified hazing as the country's "most painful and dismal human rights problem" that drives thousands to desertion, suicide, or violent crime annually.[103]

In a New Year's Eve 2005 hazing incident in Chelyabinsk, a nineteen-year-old draftee, Andrei Sychyov was so severely abused that his legs and genitals had to be amputated. As usual, the first impulse of Defense Minister Ivanov (and the local commanders) was to try to cover up the incident, the second to evade responsibility, and the third to blame "irresponsible news coverage" and threaten media organizations that publicized the case with "investigation."[104] Even so, public outcry this time could not be prevented and it included protests calling for Ivanov's resignation—ten thousand signatures were collected toward that end—and rhetorical questions in some courageous newspapers, such as "How many more lives will have to be sacrificed to further Sergei Ivanov's career?"[105] Ivanov's response—he said to the press that "I think *nothing serious happened* otherwise I would have certainly known about it"[106]—was actually not surprising; after all, in 2005 alone hazing was the direct cause of six thousand injuries requiring hospitalization and sixteen deaths in the army.[107] On 4 August 2006, Russia's new prosecutor-general, Yuri Chaika, revealed that in the first seven months of the year there had been thirty-five hundred reports of conscript abuse and a death toll of seventeen soldiers.[108] The day after Chaika's announcement a soldier was beaten so ruthlessly by his captain in Lukhovitsy, near Moscow, that he died of his injuries a few day's later.[109]

There are also disturbing reports of commanders selling their conscripts into virtual slavery to local farmers and businessmen or forcing them into prostitution. The military prosecutor of the city of Ivanovo, northeast of Moscow, reported in 2001 that his office alone launched two to three cases concerning such slavery every year.[110] In December 2005 Ivanov finally suspended General Yevgenii Veselov, deputy commander of the Moscow Military District, for using soldiers to build houses without compensation. This case against the nicknamed "Dacha General" was the first major disciplinary action since Ivanov's order to stop the misuse of conscript labor in October 2005.[111] In February 2006 a Novosibirsk military court fined a deputy division commander $2,100—but did not relieve him of duty—for renting out soldiers to local businesses as laborers.[112]

Low morale breeds poor discipline, which, in turn, causes frequent mishaps. Nongovernmental organizations claim that approximately 10 soldiers a day die in accidents and noncombat related activity; the Ministry of Defense admits 1,200 noncombat deaths in 2002, and 1,000 for 2004.[113] According to the ministry's figures—vigorously disputed by human rights NGOs—1,064 soldiers died of noncombat causes in 2005, 276 of them committed suicide.[114] In the summer of 2005 several political organizations formed a League for Abolishing the Draft with the sole purpose of calling a nationwide referendum to end conscription. The most important NGO in support of conscripts' interests is the Soldiers' Mothers Union—itself comprised of numerous Committees of Soldiers' Mothers from across the country—founded in 1989. It has fought over the Defense Ministry's suspicious data regarding the mistreatment of conscripts and has achieved an international reputation as a fearless fighter for draftees' rights, even in the face of frequent harassment by the authorities.[115] In November 2004 the association—once described by the Russian high command as "deranged shrews"[116]—had formally become a political party to oppose the Chechen War, promote defense reform, and advocate more humane behavior in the armed forces.

Problems also plague the corps of noncommissioned officers who should be the backbone of the armed forces. Unlike in western armies, where NCOs constitute a cadre of highly trained and effective middle-managers, they remain the most underutilized human resource in the Russian military. They seldom receive specialized training—at present less than 25 percent of the NCOs have professional qualifications; most are ordinary conscripts, not volunteers[117]—possess minimal independent decision-making powers, and command little respect from officers and soldiers alike. Owing to paltry wages and miserable living conditions tens of thousands of NCO positions are unfilled.[118] The shortage of qualified sergeants is partly responsible for many of the conscripts' problems, given commanders' practice of assigning authority to unfit senior soldiers elevated to NCO ranks who then terrorize their subordinates.

The officer corps' morale leaves a lot to be desired. Since 1991 nearly 500,000 officers have quit the military. Most of those who possessed in-demand skills have left the army long ago; inevitably, those who stay do not represent Russia's best and brightest. About 40 percent of young officers graduating from military academies retire from service after two or three years. Salaries, though repeatedly raised under Putin, are still low but much higher than in the 1990s when full colonels were often paid less than city bus drivers. Even in June 2002 an army general made 9,306 rubles ($300) a month, a lieutenant serving as a platoon commander

2,369 rubles ($76). A major pay raise in the following month "boosted" their earnings to 13,198 rubles ($426) and 4,288 rubles ($138), respectively.[119] Nonetheless, in 2006 platoon or company commanders—ranking from senior lieutenant to captain—are still paid less than escalator attendants in Moscow (8,000 rubles [around $285]). The monthly wage of a Moscow streetcar driver (18,000 rubles) is said to be beyond their dreams.[120] At the same time, since 2000 officers have received their pay more or less on time in stark contrast with the practice of the Yeltsin years. The high command is committed to further increase salaries to make the profession more attractive. The 2006 state budget plans to boost salaries by an average of 15 percent and double-digit raises are envisioned by the Defense Ministry for the next three years.[121]

Nevertheless, as a result of inflation and the taxation of military incomes (introduced in 2001) living standards have improved far less than officers had hoped.[122] The government's policy to eliminate some benefits in 2005 has been even more harmful because now members of the armed forces must pay in full for public transportation (rather than the previous 25 percent), pay taxes on their pensions, forgo preferential household loans, and get along without in-kind food rations. An additional reason for the bleak prospects of many military families is that the majority of military wives do not work because they cannot find employment in most posts their husbands are assigned to.[123] According to the Defense Ministry, in 2005, 34 percent of officers' families lived below the poverty line and 20 percent were ready to resign their commissions; these figures actually indicated an improvement from 2003 when they stood at "more than a third" and "fewer than half," respectively.[124] Although, owing to various assistance programs, the housing situation of professional soldiers has improved since 2001, in 2004 Ivanov admitted that the ministry had no housing for 145,000 servicemen's families and, at the same speed of progress, it would take more than fifty years until it did.[125] A year later only 9 percent of junior officers had apartments, 64 percent lived in hostels, and 13 percent in utility rooms.[126] In 2006 Putin and Ivanov pledged to resolve the army's housing problem by 2011–12.[127]

In early 2006 Prosecutor-General Vladimir Ustinov labeled the military an "army of criminals."[128] Crime and corruption—from insubordination and selling weapons to large-scale theft and embezzlement—have become commonplace: in 2005 the number of officers who committed crimes was enough to form two regiments, thefts alone amounted to $60 million ("enough to buy three dozen modern tanks"), about 16,000 military personnel were charged with a variety of crimes, including 100 senior commanders and eight generals or admirals.[129] Despite the occasional triumphant announcements of Ivanov and other Defense Ministry officials about having brought crime under control, the trend points in the wrong direction: the office of the Chief Military Prosecutor registered fifteen thousand criminal cases in 2004, compared with twelve thousand in 2002.[130]

Although drug trafficking and the sale of arms was a well-documented problem during the Afghan war, extensive criminal activity began during the army's withdrawal from Eastern Europe in 1990–93. Officers and soldiers openly sold uniforms and memorabilia in the region's markets, along with, a bit more surreptitiously, a wide range of arms from Kalashnikov submachine guns to tanks and heavy artillery pieces. It was around this time that President Yeltsin declared that the "embezzlement of weapons and military hardware . . . has acquired menacing proportions" and that the "corruption in the organs of power and administration is literally eating away the body of the Russian state from top to bottom."[131] In 1994 Deputy Defense Minister Burlakov was forced to resign owing to persistent allegations that he had accumulated a fortune from the sale of army property. In the same year, according to Vadim Poegli, a journalist who published an article with the title "Pasha-Mercedes: A Thief Should Be Put in Jail and Not Become Defense Minister," Defense Minister Pavel Grachev found himself in the middle of a scandal for diverting for his private use two Mercedes-Benz automobiles from funds earmarked for officer housing. Though Poegli was convicted of slander (and immediately amnestied by the Duma), Grachev has not been able to shake off the "Pasha-Mercedes" moniker.[132] The seemingly endemic corruption among the top brass is often difficult to prove although prosecutors have managed to hold some generals accountable. For example, Admiral Igor Khmelnov, commander of the Pacific Fleet from 1992 to 1995, received a comparatively light sentence in 1997 because prosecutors could not conclusively prove that he had sold sixty-four ships from his fleet to India and South Korea.[133]

The extensive corruption of the army leadership has scarcely abated in the new millennium. In 2003 a rear admiral was convicted of accepting a $2 million bribe in exchange for lobbying and a colonel general of selling $54 million of the Defense Ministry's domestic bonds.[134] In the same year the ministry spent 118 billion rubles (about $3.84 billion) on procurement yet few new weapons were actually acquired; experts seem to agree that a sizable portion of the money was misappropriated or just "disap-peared." In a November 2005 speech at the Ministry of Defense, Putin strongly criticized the chronic corruption and "unbridled thievishness" in the armed forces. He claimed that the military's resources were shame-lessly exploited by high-ranking officers who take foreign tourists on paid flights, operate illegal gas stations, and arrange treatment for crime bosses at military hospitals on a commercial basis. Speaking immediately after the president—and directly contradicting his own earlier statements about having gained the upper hand over corruption—Ivanov conceded that "misappropriations and waste" were increasing steadily in the army.[135]

There are several shortcomings in this regard that underscore the insti-tutional decay in civil-military relations. Defense officials can get away with offering unsatisfying explanations about how their funds are spent because the ministry publishes no financial reports of any kind, its ac-counts remain a state secret, and those in the know are prosecuted for disclosing how much the Ministry of Defense has spent on this or that project.[136] At the regional level only military prosecutors—many of whom are paid off by the officers they are supposed to watch over—have any form of control over the military's financial activities. The most funda-mental problem, of course, is that political and military leaders prefer to maintain a shroud of secrecy over the armed forces and, given the restric-tions on the media, not many journalists are courageous enough to pry into the ministry's business. To be sure, in many states under systemic transition the army becomes an organization characterized by fraud and mendacity. It is fairly isolated from society, it controls substantial re-sources, and civilians are usually all too content not to scrutinize its inter-nal affairs extensively provided that it does not interfere in political pro-cesses. As the Soviet Union was collapsing around the army, it became—emboldened by the simultaneous opportunities created by the hasty troop withdrawals as well as the reduction of manpower and equipment—per-haps the most fraudulent organization in the land. Fifteen years on, it remains mired in corruption.

IN COMBAT: AFGHANISTAN AND THE CHECHEN WARS

Given the enormous and growing literature on the Soviet Union's involve-ment in Afghanistan (1979–89) and Russia's two "Chechen Wars" (1994–96, 1999–), I do not offer detailed chronologies nor discuss issues such as the human rights violations of Soviet/Russian forces during these conflicts or the negotiations and political processes that concluded them. Rather, my objective is to briefly assess the performance of Soviet/Russian forces on the battlefield. The invasion of Afghanistan was a watershed event in Soviet history because it marked the first time that (1) the USSR invaded a Third World country; (2) a large number of Soviet ground troops were engaged in direct combat since World War II; and (3) Moscow's forces sustained many battlefield casualties.[137]

The Soviet Army's effectiveness in Afghanistan was impeded by several factors.[138] First, even in the face of much contradictory historical evidence, the Kremlin leadership seemed to expect that a mere show of force and a brief occupation would be sufficient to suppress Afghan opposition. Second, both the Soviet top brass and field commanders had underestimated the *mujaheddin's* staying power and competence in guerrilla warfare. Third, in terms of force structure, tactics, training, and logistics, the Soviets were totally unsuited for fighting a counterinsurgency war, especially so in Afghanistan's challenging geographic and sociocultural environment. Although the effectiveness of Soviet forces had improved with the passage of time, their adaptability to the kind of war they were forced to fight remained unimpressive throughout the conflict. Until the very end, their tactics were based on pressing their technological advantage—balancing heavy ground forces with massive artillery support and light infantry forces that could be airlifted with relative ease—but their counterinsurgency fighting skills were slow to develop as they consistently eschewed the sort of man-to-man combat and nimble small-unit operations their enemies excelled at.[139]

The most important advance in Soviet efficacy was achieved in the protection of their logistical and communication lines. This was chiefly the accomplishment of the air force that had gradually become a reliable supporter of ground troops. The quality of officers and soldiers brought into the theater had likewise increased somewhat as time went on, but even the *spetsnaz* (special forces) and other elite units—that performed comparatively well— at the final stages of the decade-long hostilities failed to match the *mujaheddin* in tactical flexibility and the ability to exploit the terrain for their purposes. Similarly, Soviet commanders were unable to forget the lessons they had learned from very different kinds of past conflicts. According to leading Soviet generals, the Afghan War demonstrated the profound gap between the theory of war officers were expected to master and the actual practice of counterinsurgency warfare they were forced to fight.[140]

Nonetheless, some analysts are confident that, had it not been for the massive U.S. assistance to the *mujaheddin*, the USSR would have easily won the war.[141] Even so, the price would have been high and holding on to Afghanistan would have been anything but easy. Soviet forces killed or maimed approximately 2.5 million Afghans, while one out of about every eight of their own soldiers (525,000 in all served in Afghanistan) died (13,833) or was wounded (49,985).[142] The Russian General Staff has put the blame squarely on Kremlin leaders for their "impetuous decision" to send their soldiers to Afghanistan, particularly because "they did not consider the historic, religious, and national particularities" of the country.[143] One of the key reasons for the war's outcome was the overwhelming popular resistance Soviet forces had encountered from the beginning, a resistance that had only become more resolute given the invaders' brutal tactics. They remained entirely oblivious to the common objective of most counterinsurgency wars, that of winning the "hearts and minds" of the local population.

A little more than five years after the withdrawal of the last Soviet soldiers from Afghanistan, Boris Yeltsin decided to send troops against Russian citizens in Chechnya. The Kremlin was worried that separatism in the northern Caucasus might inspire popular independence movements elsewhere in the country and, as Security Council secretary Oleg Lobov noted before the attack, "It's not only a question of the integrity of Russia. We need a small victorious war to raise the President's ratings."[144] The war was launched without adequate prior consultation with military commanders, many of whom—including three deputy defense ministers (Boris Gromov, Valerii Mironov, and Georgi Kondratiev)—spoke out strongly against the war. The First Chechen War demonstrated the true extent of the armed forces' decline. In virtually every respect, the Russian military failed the challenge it was supposed to easily master.

To begin with, planning for the war was hasty and careless. Defense Minister Grachev, famously boasted in late 1994 that he could take the Chechen capital, Grozny, with an airborne regiment in a couple of hours, even though only a few weeks before, in a testimony to the Duma, he declared that no army in the world was in as wretched a state as Russia's.[145] When in December 1994 Russian forces did enter Grozny, they possessed no proper equipment or even up-to-date city maps. The conscripts who comprised the bulk of Russia's forces were inexperienced, barely trained, and unprepared for the brutalities of urban fighting. The failed storming of Grozny in December 1994–January 1995 was a humiliating defeat for Moscow's troops at the hands of Chechen insurgents from which they never completely recovered.[146] The war also revealed to ordinary Russians for the first time how poorly prepared their armed forces, writ large, were for national security challenges. In contrast with the Afghan war, the First Chechen War was fought by an impoverished army whose soldiers occasionally sold their weapons to the enemy to raise cash for food.

The military proved itself to be "grossly deficient at all levels, from the commander-in-chief to the drafted private."[147] If the conflict in Afghanistan exposed the tactical rigidity of Soviet forces, the First Chechen War showed that few lessons had been learned. Russian officers were still expecting to fight the next large-scale war against NATO and entirely lacked training in modern urban warfare, mountain operations, and anti-guerrilla tactics.[148] Just like in Afghanistan, their massive advantage in firepower was of little help in a localized, low-intensity conflict—other than senselessly destroying entire cities and thereby deepening civilian resistance. Coordination and distribution of tasks between the armed forces proper and units under the command of the other power ministries (especially the Ministry of Internal Affairs) was especially unsatisfactory and led to many casualties because of friendly fire. Ground commanders devoted little effort to reconnaissance or planning and had to call off their ill-conceived attacks every time the Kremlin decided to start negotiations. Because of the lack of time to mold conscripts into combat teams, small-unit cohesion, crucially important in counterinsurgency maneuvers, was seldom realized. The First Chechen War was a disaster for the Russian military: it suffered more than six thousand casualties but failed to restore central government control over the breakaway republic before being withdrawn in 1996.

The armed forces' renewed attack on Chechen rebels three years later has been less controversial, in part owing to popular support (especially after terrorists allegedly—though it has never been conclusively proven—detonated bombs in Moscow). This second war is closely related to the rise of Putin's political fortunes. Indeed some commentators have called it an "electoral war" and human rights activist Elena Bonner even claimed that the "genocidal" war was "staged to bring Putin to power."[149] While the official justification of the first war was to "restore constitutional order" to a region wrecked by civil war and political turmoil, the second war was rationalized as a defense of Russia's population from the attacks of "international terrorist gangs" and irredentist attacks aiming to separate the North Caucasian republics from the Russian Federation.[150] From the perspective of the high command, it was an opportunity to overcome the humiliating 1996 defeat. Reliable information regarding the Second Chechen War is difficult to obtain, given that the Kremlin had devoted enormous resources in a largely successful effort to control reporting on the conflict and shut out the independent media.[151]

The Russian Army has performed better in the Second Chechen War. Under Kvashnin's leadership the General Staff took a critical look at the First Chechen War to identify lessons to be learned such as emphasizing preventive measures and setting clear goals when using force and—though only after 2002–3—employing heavy weapons selectively and minimizing collateral damage to the population and civilian infrastructure.[152] One of the key differences is the military's appreciation of the need to amass sufficient forces and supplies prior to beginning operations. Fewer tactical restrictions imposed by the Kremlin and the Defense Ministry combined with the absence of called-off operations due to political negotiations allowed battalion and regimental commanders more leeway to make decisions and increased their effectiveness. The power ministries stepped up training in antiguerrilla warfare and counterterrorism techniques. Moreover, Russian forces have been more willing to share the burden of fighting with Chechen loyalists—in all-Chechen units such as the Vostok and Zapad battalions—who proved invaluable in search-and-destroy activities.[153]

This time around the military—and the forces deployed by other power ministries—has also been better supplied and equipped. For instance, the Ministry of Defense managed to improve inter- and intraunit communication, one of the major deficiencies in the first war. Then troops used obsolete radio sets on which communication was easily compromised by their enemies who could not only eavesdrop on conversations but could also cut in and spread disinformation. Early on in the second war the army did get some "Akveduk" closed communications systems but only one set per unit and seldom the training required for its optimal usage. Morale and discipline improved as well, in large part as the result of deploying contract soldiers and the diminishing number (none, in fact, after 2005) of conscripts sent to Chechnya. Especially after 2004 *kontraktniki* serving in the war zone have been reasonably well paid: privates earn 15,000 rubles per month while a battalion commander can make as much as 22,100. Most volunteers come from the provincial towns of the North Caucasus and from the Siberian and Far Eastern Military Districts; hardly any of them are from Moscow or other major cities.[154]

Although some efforts were made to apply the lessons of the First Chechen War into practice, gains in performance and effectiveness should not be overestimated. Many troops entering the conflict are still inadequately trained, there is a lingering shortage of modern weapons, and the heavy and often indiscriminate use of artillery and air strikes has been the source of unnecessarily high (especially civilian) casualties. Consequently, counterproductive overkill—the gratuitous destruction of Chechen towns and villages and excessive cruelties against the local population—has characterized the armed forces' actions. The chief example is Grozny, which was so thoroughly destroyed in 1999–2000 that it could not function even nominally as Chechnya's administrative center until mid 2001.[155] Many disciplinary problems have been reported as well. For instance, in 2002 after an incognito inspection of vital checkpoints manned by armed forces personnel, Kvashnin complained that these groups were "bogged down in bribery and complete lawlessness."[156]

In the last several years Putin, Ivanov, and various military spokesmen have declared repeatedly that federal control was firmly established over Chechnya, that the war was over, and that drastic reductions in the number of troops stationed there were imminent. As Golts has put it, ordinary Russians have endured "endless lies from their leaders about the latest 'phase' of the 'operation' in Chechnya," but according to polls, the war did nothing to dent Putin's popularity.[157] In January 2005, Ivanov sought to convince his audience at the Council on Foreign Relations in New York that "the war in Chechnya is gone. There is no war, I can assure you . . . we're very much concentrated on human rights issues" there.[158] Nonetheless, only two months later he announced increases to the federal armed presence in the North Caucasus from 75,000 to 80,000 because the insurgency spread to Daghestan, Ingushetia, and North Ossetia.[159] Owing to the aforementioned problem of obtaining reliable data in Putin's Russia, the death toll of the Second Chechen War is not easy to estimate. For instance, according to the 2002 Russian national census Chechnya's 1-million-strong population had remained practically unchanged between 1989 and 2002, despite the deaths caused by the war and the departure of hundreds of thousands of refugees, who had fled the fighting and economic collapse. In August 2006 the Defense Ministry announced that 3,588 servicemen had been killed in Chechnya from the beginning of hostilities in September 1999. This figure is not only disputed by NGOs like the Soldier's Mothers Union but, in fact, is contradicted by the ministry's December 2004 announcement, according to which as of August 2004

5,362 soldiers had died in the Second Chechen War.[160] In August 2005, the pro-Moscow head of Chechnya's interim parliament, Taus Dzhabrailov, said that up to 160,000 civilians and soldiers have died or gone missing in the two wars.[161]

CONCLUSION

My main purpose in this chapter was to demonstrate, through a comparison of some key aspects of Soviet/Russian military affairs two decades apart, the extent of the army's protracted decline. Although the theoretical argument I outlined in the introduction is most germane to the following chapters, a couple of points inform the foregoing empirical analysis. The argument was chiefly concerned with explaining the changes in Russian civil-military relations with the help of the institutionalist approach. One of the manifestations of institutional decay is the acutely resource-poor environment, which has exacerbated the social ills that have plagued the armed forces. A major component of institutional decay is the erosion of long-held institutional norms revealed in our case study by high-level disagreements on strategy and doctrine, deteriorating professionalism and discipline, and the spread of large-scale corruption and unlawful behavior. In this instance the second formative moment I identified earlier, Yeltsin acquiescing to a new political environment, is significant. What is most relevant here though is not so much that Russia's first president consented to a certain kind of polity in which the military would play a political role but, far more so, that he permitted the evolution of a new organizational culture in the military establishment that condoned the kind of damaging phenomena I discussed.

As a result of numerous and mostly interconnected factors, contemporary Russia's army is merely a shadow of the USSR's once-proud fighting force. In virtually every aspect I examined, the army has been subject to a two-decade-long process of decay and deterioration. Russia wants to reclaim its status as a world power but its strategic and doctrinal documents are fraught with confusion and contradiction. Although military elites may say otherwise, their actions demonstrate that they believe the future security contingencies Russia needs to prepare for are not those produced by terrorism, separatism, and local wars but another all-out battle against the West, more specifically the United States and NATO. A major troubling legacy of the Communist era is the rigid and inflexible thinking of the military leadership which, in large part, is where these strategic-doctrinal incongruities originate.

The military's prolonged decay is most evident in its reduced budget and manpower and the deterioration of training programs and equipment. There is a noteworthy two-prong contradiction that emerges here. Quite simply, the armed forces' budget, manpower, training, and equipment are unsuited to fight both the large-scale conventional war the General Staff seems to want to plan for *and* the kind of low-intensity conflict that it, in all likelihood, should prepare for. Its budget, even after several years of double-digit increases, is still vastly inadequate to maintain a first-class, "global" army. Its equipment is similarly insufficient for that purpose—future acquisitions outlined by the Defense Ministry are unlikely to change this—and whatever is in Russia's arsenal tends to be poorly maintained. If, on the other hand, Moscow were to change its doctrine to accommodate current and likely future challenges—such as terrorist attacks and separatist rebellions—then its budget might be more or less adequate but it would have to drastically revise its training, rethink its weapons acquisition program, and reduce the size of its forces.

In the past twenty years the armed forces have been subject to a remarkable process of social and economic degradation and impoverishment. The drop in the military occupation's social prestige is as extraordinary as the plunge in the living standards of professional soldiers. Twenty years ago officers were considered the elite of Soviet society; today many live in poverty. The general morale in the armed forces is extremely low: the majority of officers are still in uniform because they could not find better berths for themselves outside of the military. Among the top echelons of the officer corps, in the meantime, corruption and embezzlement have reached levels alarming even by Russian standards. The situation of ordinary draftees has also significantly changed not so much regarding the conditions of their service—although in the USSR few soldiers went hungry or without proper uniforms—but because they are now virtually unprotected from the basest instincts of other young men of their cohort.

Not surprisingly, the army's battlefield performance has left much to be desired. The generals' resistance to change, even in the face of their units' dismal performance, is a symptom of their long-standing intellectual obstinacy. In fact, the ineffectiveness of Russia's troops in Chechnya is an apt demonstration of the many problems discussed in this chapter, from deficient training to low morale and discipline. Just as important, the Chechen conflict has also illuminated "the extremely unsatisfactory level of control the Russian public has of its military organization."[162] The continued degradation of the military establishment before and during the First Chechen War had provoked considerable resentment in the officer corps. It was one of the catalysts of the military's active and autonomous political involvement, the phenomenon that I will explore in the next chapter.

CHAPTER 3

Explaining the Military's Political Presence

> When the general is morally weak and his discipline not
> strict, when his instructions and guidance are not
> enlightened, where there are no consistent rules to guide
> the officers and men, and when the formations are
> slovenly, the army is in disorder.
>   —Sun Tzu, *The Art of War*

The widely recognized political role of Russian military elites is a puzzle that ought to intrigue political scientists, especially democratization theorists, civil-military relations scholars, and those studying Communist and post-Communist systems. Since the collapse of the USSR, active-duty officers have run for elected office with their commanders' support; politicians have met the unabashed insubordination of prominent generals with appeasement rather than retribution; and military leaders have successfully opposed and foiled state policy, to say nothing of intentionally deceiving their civilian superiors. In the meantime, the proportion of personnel with security and military backgrounds—although many more of the former than the latter—in the state administration has increased to the extent that Russian sociologists have developed a new concept, "militocracy," to describe the ruling elites in Putin's Russia.

The Russian Army's success in carving out an independent political role for itself is puzzling. The armed forces, to begin with, have not played an autonomous political role for more than two centuries. The military, to be sure, was an important political factor during the Soviet period, but then, unlike today, it would have been unthinkable for high-ranking officers to publicly voice their independent political opinions or refuse to carry out the party-state's directives and remain in office for long. An additional facet of this conundrum is that, notwithstanding their expanded political clout, post-Soviet generals are not interested in issues of sovereign power, let alone seizing control of the government. Indeed, a coup is widely regarded as highly unlikely, even though the armed forces have endured abuses—especially in the 1990s—typically seen as textbook motivations for revolt: drastically reduced budgets, occasionally humiliating treatment by political leaders and the media, and deployments unpopular within the military itself.

Though they may not be in favor of overthrowing the regime, Russia's generals have nevertheless proven themselves quite skillful at probing the limits of their political masters' tolerance and promoting the armed forces' corporate interests as well as their own. In so doing, they have stretched the boundaries of the army's political autonomy. This poses a range of normative, theoretical, and practical dilemmas. A politicized military goes directly against the fundamental principles of democratic civil-military relations. In the case of Russia, it also goes against the thrust of precedent. Understanding this departure from the Soviet pattern becomes all the more urgent given that the restoration of Russia's great-power status is a key objective of President Putin and his regime. The armed forces, after all, remain everywhere the classic means for the projection of state power; and for this reason alone, Russian generals can be expected to remain involved in issues in which they traditionally have had a direct interest: matters of doctrine and finance (particularly the size and distribution of defense budgets), foreign affairs (from NATO expansion to peace-keeping operations), defense reform, and combat-readiness.

Parallel to the unfolding empirical story I will show how useful are the theoretical tools I outlined in the introduction. The concepts of institutional decay and path dependence help explain the particular course Russian civil-military relations have taken since the Soviet Union's demise. In addition, some of the insights of the civil-military relations field add perspective to the picture drawn by the empirical analysis. While we do not need to rehearse the theoretical argument sketched earlier, I do want to reiterate that institutional decay illuminates the erosion of previously held norms and rules while path dependence outlines the course of historical change as it directs our attention to the formative moments critical to that change. Combining the strengths of the institutionalist approach and the civil-military relations literature results in a more penetrating understanding of Russian particularities while expanding our theoretical reach.

In this chapter I offer a detailed analysis of the depth and breadth of the Russian military elites' political activities and clout. First, I briefly summarize the first formative moment, Gorbachev's invitation of active duty army officers to participate in politics. In doing so, he put civil-military relations at the end of the Soviet period on a course that fostered the decay of long-held institutional norms. Second, I discuss the autonomous electoral participation of professional military personnel under Yeltsin. His consent to this development, which highlighted the evolution of a new institutional environment in which the military's independent political presence became not only acceptable but endorsed by the president, the legislature, political parties, and the judiciary, was the second formative moment. Because of the diminishing success of military candidates at the polls and, more generally, the decreasing importance of elections in an increasingly authoritarian polity, this electoral role declined during the 1990s.[1] For this reason, during the Putin era, the most important locus of the military's political presence shifted from the legislature to governorships and appointed political offices. This development—the presidential affirmation of military elites' political import—along with Putin's decision no to force the top brass to quickly implement a comprehensive defense reform, signify the third formative moment. The decay of institutional norms in Russia's army can be seen in several ways, such as threats of resignation by leading generals to elicit policy modification, the willingness of generals to mislead politicians, and the spread of large-scale corruption and criminal behavior, including the mistreatment and neglect of subordinates and materiel. In the last section I discuss what I consider the most illustrative manifestation of institutional decay in Russian military politics: the military elites' public criticism of and opposition to state officials and policy.

THE GORBACHEVIAN MOMENT

This is not the occasion to review the immense literature on Soviet civil-military relations. Nevertheless, in order to appreciate the massive changes triggered by Gorbachev's policies we need to take a brief look at some of the fundamentals. The notion of path dependence is valuable in pinpointing the formative moments and help us understand the institutional arrangements and the sociopolitical setting in which they are embedded.[2]

The Communist Party of the Soviet Union (CPSU) had co-opted top military officers into the party and state hierarchy long before the Gorbachev era. In fact, the "critical juncture" regarding one of the important phenomena of Russian civil-military relations, the practice of military officers serving in the legislature, may be traced back to the Bolsheviks who rewarded loyal generals with seats in Soviet-Russia's party and legislative bodies soon after they took power.[3] This important gesture of appreciation was, however, just that: it most certainly did not confer an *independent* political role on its recipients. High-ranking officers with watertight Marxist-Leninist credentials received seats in the CPSU Central Committee—where military representation fluctuated between 6–11 percent from 1934 to 1986[4]—and in the Supreme Soviet, even if their participation in these bodies was significant only to the extent that it was supposed to reflect the regime's inclusionary façade and its esteem for the armed forces.

Soviet military leaders were expected to unfailingly and unquestioningly implement even the most hare-brained schemes of the Kremlin. Although there were a few cases when high-ranking generals had gone beyond merely assisting in the formulation of state policy, when they exceeded the boundaries of the fundamental norms of civil-military relations, they drew swift censure from the party-state. For instance, Chief of the General Staff Nikolai Ogarkov was demoted in 1984 after repeatedly questioning the official line of the party-state.[5] Prior to Gorbachev's presidency, for military officers to *publicly* dispute party decisions, criticize state policy, or defy the orders of civilian superiors went directly against the widely accepted norms of civil-military relations. It would have been well-nigh unthinkable.

All this changed under Gorbachev, whose tenure was synonymous with the erosion of the behavioral norms that had theretofore governed Soviet military politics. In Douglass North's conception, the embedded norms of civil-military relations did suffer a "revolution" in the Gorbachev era. The changes his policies set into motion in the late 1980s had shaken up the bureaucratic culture in which Soviet officialdom was firmly anchored and spurred a remarkable transformation in the conduct of the Russian officer corps. Initially, that is, as long as they did not directly affect them, the generals grudgingly went along with *glasnost'* and *perestroika*. Nevertheless, once it came to issues that threatened the military's corporate interests—such as defense budget cuts and unilateral force reductions—they began to openly and publicly oppose them. Gorbachev had little understanding of military affairs, and his policies directly undermined the institution. He made matters worse by deploying the army in three blood-soaked political confrontations—Tbilisi, April 1989; Baku, January 1990; and Vilnius, January 1991—that resulted altogether in nearly three hundred civilians killed. These clashes were extremely unpopular with officers who were enraged by Gorbachev's modus operandi of ordering them onto the streets and then distancing himself from the consequences in order to maintain the fiction of his own liberalism by means of a convenient illness or absence.[6] The spirited opposition of the majority of officer corps to him and his reforms was entirely logical, albeit just as entirely unacceptable from the perspective of traditional Soviet civil-military relations.

By this point, however, Gorbachev's policies have resulted in a rapidly evolving political framework that not only allowed but actually *invited* the army's rank and file to participate in politics by publicly airing their grievances, voicing their political views, and running for office. This is the first formative moment in the evolving path of post-Soviet military politics, which quickly induced the decay of the age-old rules and norms of civil-military relations. After military personnel received what amounted to an open invitation to get involved in politics in 1987–88, the army "had begun to learn to walk on its own."[7] Soon, independent officers' assemblies sprang to life that began by criticizing the media's disparaging treatment of the military and then proceeded to openly denounce the government and even Gorbachev himself. The top brass' open opposition to state policy clearly demonstrated the decline in their long-held behavioral norms and standards, heralding the onset of institutional decay.

In the end, Gorbachev's defense and security policies had profoundly damaged the Soviet Army's social standing, cohesion, effectiveness, and ultimately, hastened its collapse.[8] For their part, military elites exploited the weaknesses of the CPSU leadership and acquired a great deal of autonomy, and actively opposed, obstructed, and/or publicly criticized state officials and policy, for the most part without any serious consequences. Invoking Roman generals whose political intervention Edward Gibbon regarded a key cause of the empire's decline might be far-fetched here.[9] Nevertheless, the August 1991 coup attempt—which clearly accelerated the Soviet Union's fall—was a direct consequence of these developments. The "Gorbachevian invitation" urging the armed forces' independent political participation was the revolutionary event, the formative moment, which set off the gradual breakdown of the behavioral norms and standards that had theretofore governed Soviet civil-military relations. He

filled the officers' earlier merely symbolic participation in the USSR's legislative bodies with substance. By the time the Soviet Union collapsed, military men had participated in the Supreme Soviet long enough and the
political system had changed drastically enough that it would have been
difficult to reverse the path his decisions initiated and ban the army from
the legislature. Gorbachev's challenge to the armed forces constituted an
about-face, aptly illustrated by Chief of the General Staff Sergei Akhro-
meev (an erstwhile Gorbachev advisor) who in his 1991 suicide note
wrote that everything in which he had believed was now destroyed.[10]

DEMOCRATIZATION, THE MILITARY, AND OCTOBER 1993

In the early 1990s the Russian officer corps became a political force to be
reckoned with, both as candidates for political office and as voters. Five
factors fomented the newly found electoral role of the armed forces. First,
Gorbachev's reforms gave armed forces personnel a legitimate outlet for
publicly venting their political views. Second, in August 1991 and in September–October 1993 the military was thrown into the political power
struggle, events that promoted their political maturation and activism.[11]
Third, the law does not ban active-duty personnel from running for or
holding political office (as incumbents they are on a suspended active-
duty status but continue to draw their salaries and may even be promoted).[12] Fourth, political parties—particularly in the early and mid
1990s—actively courted the military vote and recruited popular officers
as candidates for their electoral lists. And finally, the rapid breakdown of
the armed forces and all its attendant socioeconomic privations in the
wake of the Soviet Union's disintegration spurred on the officers to become politically active.

The task ahead of the new Russian state was to create the formal rules
of democratic civil-military relations and bring the army under institutionally balanced, constitutionally regulated, and nonpartisan civilian
control. As Marybeth Ulrich pointed out, "The prevalence of non-demo-
cratic patterns of political control and military professionalism in a state's
history" does not preclude "the expectation that democratic norms
should ultimately prevail as the process of democratization continues."[13]
Moreover, the existence of "democratic" states with undemocratic civil-
military relations (South Korea, Taiwan) only shows that these states
have not progressed far enough in their democratization processes.[14] In

democracies civilian supervision of the military has several indispensable components:

1. the armed forces must be subordinated to institutionalized control balanced between the executive and legislative branches;
2. the military's chains of command and the political institutions' areas of responsibility over the armed forces must be codified for all potential scenarios (peacetime, emergencies, war);
3. the conditions that warrant the use of the military in peacetime must be constitutionally regulated;
4. the executive and legislative branches must share exclusive fiscal responsibility over defense expenditures;
5. the armed forces must be depoliticized and their members must not be permitted to play any political role other than exercising their civic right to vote; and
6. civilian experts must be trained to provide objective advice to politicians and the public on defense-related issues and to staff pertinent state institutions (including the Ministry of Defense) and nongovernmental organizations.

In the past fifteen years Russia has made little headway in implementing these conditions. In fact, its democratization experiment held out realistic promise of eventual consolidation only for about two years during which the armed forces were forced to take sides twice between political contenders. This period began after the August 1991 coup attempt, which may be viewed as a last-ditch effort by forces in the CPSU and the power ministries to end Gorbachev's experiments.[15] Afterward, the military was first drawn into high politics in late 1991 when Russian president Yeltsin and Soviet president Gorbachev courted them for their support as they were about to decide the fate of the Soviet Union. Not surprisingly, the army failed to intervene on Gorbachev's behalf.

The turning point in Russia's democratization process was Yeltsin's face-off with the legislature in the fall of 1993. In late September of that year, to put an end to the prolonged conflict between the Kremlin and the Supreme Soviet, Yeltsin issued Presidential Edict 1400 that disbanded the legislature, called for new elections, and scheduled a constitutional referendum.[16] The hard-line members of parliament responded by deposing and impeaching Yeltsin and installing an acting president—Yeltsin's vice president Aleksandr Rutskoi—and a new "government" (complete with a "defense minister," the outright Stalinist general Vladislav Achalov).

The September–October 1993 crisis was also a turning point in Russian civil-military relations. Both sides demanded the army's support. Rutskoi, a bona fide hero of the Afghan war, urged his fellow officers to take a stand against the president—in essence, inviting a mutiny—while Ruslan Khasbulatov, the Supreme Soviet's chairman declared that "we must have military units here today . . . not just men in military greatcoats, but military units."[17] Finally army units came to Yeltsin's rescue but only after he agreed to give in writing his unconstitutional order instructing Defense Minister Pavel Grachev to storm the White House where renegade lawmakers took refuge.[18]

The casualties included 149 killed, many more wounded, and Russia's democratization process. At this point the period of democratization ended and, with the December 1993 Constitution, a new "superpresidential" polity began to take shape in which the legislature's influence has gradually decreased. To be sure, I am not suggesting that all remnants of democratization dating from the mid 1980s had ceased to exist in one fell swoop following the 1993 crisis. Rather, I contend that since then the arrow signaling the direction of Russia's political trajectory has pointed not toward further democratization but toward an increasingly authoritarian model.[19] This trend only accelerated with the beginning of Putin's presidency.

How does the military fit into this system? After the USSR's fall the armed forces were not depoliticized but "departified." The abolition of the CPSU's domination of the military created a vacuum that has not been filled by balanced and stable civilian control. Instead, the process of establishing and institutionalizing civilian oversight authority turned into a protracted power struggle between the executive and legislative branches—a struggle that culminated in the triumph of the president in 1993. The resultant system of civilian control, far from balanced or effective, is a personalistic and unregulated arrangement based on the president's overwhelming political power and his ability to play off institutions and individuals against each other.

The opportunity to put civil-military relations on a democratic footing fell onto Yeltsin's shoulders but he was not equal to this task. It was Yeltsin who was not just passively present at the creation of a new political system in 1992 but who, as Russia's first president, could have and should have persevered to reverse the institutional decay in civil-military relations that began under Gorbachev. He and other political leaders should have barred active-duty military personnel from the legislature

and other elected political positions, should have insisted on training objective civilian defense experts to eliminate the virtual monopoly of uniformed Defense Ministry personnel of military-security knowledge, and
more generally, should have demanded the establishment of institutional
norms and rules compatible with democratic civil-military relations. In
all likelihood, doing so would not have been easy given the difficulty of
path-reversal and overturning decisions that many benefited from. But it
certainly would have been easier at this point to derail Russian civil-military relations from its antidemocratic course than it would have been
later. Yeltsin's acquiescence to the formation of a political and legal system in which the military could continue to enjoy an increasingly legitimate and growing political presence is the second formative moment mentioned earlier.

THE ARMED FORCES IN ELECTORAL POLITICS

Although military officers had served in the legislature throughout the
Soviet period, in terms of acquiring real political influence, the first meaningful election took place in 1990—the last one of the Soviet era—when
forty-four of them won seats in the Congress of People's Deputies of the
Russian Republic. They ran as a result of the mounting political activism
in the armed forces fostered by Gorbachev's policies. Once the Soviet
Union collapsed and the new rules of the political game were being ham-
mered out, to push military officers out of legislative bodies would have
been far too difficult. First, by this time there was a history of military
cadres holding elected political office going back several decades; a
"path" that was not easy to break. Second, a large number of them were
already *active* members of these institutions and would have, in all likelihood, vehemently opposed any proposal aimed at excluding them. In
fact, by October 1992, three of them had chaired parliamentary commissions. In the June 1991 election for the Russian presidency, generals fig-
ured prominently again, with Albert Makashov placing fourth, Boris
Gromov placing second (as Nikolai Ryzhkov's vice-presidential running-
mate), and, most important, Aleksandr Rutskoi running on Yeltsin's side.
The military's growing electoral participation became a pattern that per-
sisted until the late 1990s, which is to say, it continued for as long as

elections remained a more or less meaningful exhibition of Russian popular will.

After the August 1991 coup attempt, Defense Minister Grachev publicly argued for the military's subordination to civilian authority. His contention to be sure, meant no departure from the past because civilian oversight had been the iron-clad theory *and* practice during the Soviet period. The fact that Grachev had thought necessary to declare the continuation of the age-old dictum suggests, however, that the political role of officers in the new Russia needed to be clarified. This was so because by the time Grachev took office in May 1992—as a reward for his support of Yeltsin during the heady days of the August 1991 political crisis—the officer corps was heavily politicized. Initially, Grachvev intended to deal with this situation by insisting that political and military careers were incompatible and pressuring reformist officers to decide between the two. This was a prudent stance because a number of officers by this time had emerged as vocal advocates of policies and views that ran counter to those of the high command. Forcing them to choose supported the cause of ridding the Defense Ministry of reformist officers, an objective that had been more or less achieved by late 1993. An instructive example is that of Major Vladimir Lopatin, a former Supreme Soviet deputy, who worked closely with civilian reformers, tried hard to put radical defense reform on the political agenda in the late 1980s, and less successfully, to keep it there after the fall of the USSR.[20]

Grachev had tried to keep the military out of politics also by actually discouraging officers from running in the December 1993 parliamentary elections. Despite his efforts, this turned out to be the first post-Soviet election in which the armed forces had played an important role. At the time the Ministry of Defense employed 2.3 million uniformed personnel, most of them facing grim professional prospects. By this time the army had been devastated by years of unparalleled governmental neglect, vastly inadequate funding, and massive corruption. Not surprisingly, all but four of the sixteen contending parties succeeded in enticing military officers onto their electoral lists with promises of more resources for the armed forces. Vladimir Zhirinovsky's misnamed Liberal Democratic Party of Russia (LDPR) alone ran nine officers aspiring to a seat in the Duma. Most of the officers, however, were allied with parties that could not pass the 5 percent electoral threshold. As a result, only eleven of them were elected to the 450-seat Duma and only one, Dmitri Volkogonov, was nationally known.

President Yeltsin conceded that the LDPR attracted one-third of the military ballots, though it may have taken an even larger share. It is important to note that there is no way to ascertain precisely the voting behavior of the armed forces. Having said that, some experts have estimated that the LDPR garnered 72 percent of the vote in the strategic rocket forces, and in the important Taman and Kantemir divisions, based near Moscow, 87.4 percent and 74.3 percent respectively.[21] According to military sociologists, "more than 60 percent" of what they call "military electorate" voted for Zhirinovsky's radical nationalist party.[22] A potent mixture of nostalgia, resentment, and solidarity explains the military's support for the LDPR. For example, Zhirinovsky's plans of imperial revival, though absurd, stuck a chord with officers who longed for the glory days of the USSR. In addition, military personnel deeply resented Yeltsin's tendency to embroil the armed forces in his political battles. Finally, to the extent that esprit de corps can translate into political identification, it mattered significantly that a relatively large number of officers ran under the LDPR's colors. All in all, in the 1993 elections military candidates did less well than many had anticipated along with progovernment and proreform parties. Moreover, the new military members of the legislature failed to arrest let alone reverse the accelerating deterioration of the armed forces' conditions. After the crisis Yeltsin continued to neglect the military all the more so because its support of him during the crisis was most reluctant.[23] Therefore, as we shall see in chapter 5, he began to utilize the paramilitary organizations maintained by the power ministries to build an effective institutional counterbalance to the regular army.

Not surprisingly, the Defense Ministry's initial disapproval of its personnel's electoral forays was nowhere to be found by the next parliamentary elections. Indeed, the December 1995 Duma elections turned out to be the high point of the Russian military's electoral participation, in good measure because this time around Grachev and the ministry leadership had actually encouraged officers to stand for election. He even granted aspiring deputies temporary leave with pay for the duration of their campaign. By this time the previously cozy relationship the ministry had enjoyed with the legislature had deteriorated, and Grachev wanted to fill the Duma Defense Committee with military men of his liking.[24] The Ministry of Defense had hoped to place a large number of soldier-deputies in the legislature assuming, wrongly, that they would act as a "khaki-colored voting bloc" that would hasten the adoption of more defense-friendly policies.

The top brass urged officers to run as independents in order to maintain a nonpartisan façade. In the end, taking advantage of incentives such as extra salary and fringe benefits, 123 officers ran as independent candidates and more than 40 others ran on party lists.[25] Only 22 military men were elected, however, and of these only 2 were the ministry's own (i.e., independent) candidates. Their poor showing resulted from a combination of factors, of which three stand out. First, the officers' uniform had lost some of its luster after army units stormed the White House in October 1993 on Yeltsin's orders. Second, the military's performance in the ongoing war in Chechnya was widely viewed as a major embarrassment. And last, the Defense Ministry was legally banned from using state resources to support its candidates who, running as independents, could not receive campaign funding from parties and coalitions either.[26]

Presidential politics attracted individuals closely associated in the public mind with the military. The 1996 election featured a leading retired general as an important candidate. General Aleksandr Lebed, who came in third in the first round of the elections with 15 percent of the vote, posed a credible challenge to Yeltsin's reelection bid. Had Lebed enjoyed the support of a major political party and more robust financial backing, it is likely that he would have been even more successful at the polls. Known for his integrity and willingness to take on politicians and Defense Ministry bureaucrats alike, Lebed was popular both in the army and the general public. As a result of a political compromise, he agreed to terminate his campaign in Yeltsin's favor in return for being named the administration's point man on national security. Lebed's leadership style—marked by abrasive statements, provocative meddling in bureaucratic politics, and the capricious sacking of top generals—quickly used up Yeltsin's patience, however. No longer having a compelling reason to appease him, the president fired him in October 1996. After 1996 no military man—on active duty or retired—played an important role in presidential elections.

The number of military officers competing for seats has declined sharply in post-1995 Duma elections. There are several reasons for this. First, although Yeltsin was not prepared to bar military personnel from electoral politics, a May 1997 presidential decree denied salary and benefits to officers seeking elective office from the time of registering their candidacy until the elections. The reasons for this change were that the government refused to pay its employees when engaged in something other than their jobs and did not want to, in effect, subsidize the campaigns of its likely opponents. Second, fearing negative state response, the Ministry of Defense no longer promoted the campaigns of aspiring officers. Third, given the lackluster electoral performance of military candidates, parties interested in bolstering the presence of individuals with defense-security backgrounds on their rosters preferred to turn to other power-ministry (such as interior and emergency situations) personnel.

In the 1999 parliamentary elections only about twenty-nine members of the armed forces—one-fourth as many as four years before—stood as candidates, nearly all of them generals, although the number of those representing other power ministries had significantly increased. The number of the Defense Ministry's putative supporters in the legislature actually grew because those considered in the "military bloc" (including veterans and active-duty personnel nominated by the Defense Ministry) won thirty-four to thirty-six seats and comprised roughly 8 percent of Duma deputies.[27] These individuals—even if they might not have actively promoted the ministry's interests—at the very least represented a considerable presence of viewpoints and mindsets approved by the military establishment. The trend of declining military participation continued during the 2003 legislative elections and was paralleled by the decreasing success of officers at the polls. Only a handful of them were elected and none of them officially represented the armed forces.

It is important to reiterate that, while there is no foolproof way to measure the precise voting patterns in the military, it is possible to make educated guesses. During the Yeltsin era, the 1993 elections were the last one in which the military voted in a more or less predictable manner, that is, against the incumbent and for nationalist and/or Communist candidates. For the rest of the 1990s the armed forces did not constitute a coherent electoral constituency because military personnel were divided by several cleavages such as rank (strongly correlated with age and education); service in Afghanistan, Chechnya, and other armed conflicts; location (Moscow or other metropolitan area versus the provinces); socioeconomic background; and family status. In subsequent elections a large proportion of military voters favored Yeltsin's rivals at the polls—owing to the president's mistreatment of the army—in contrast with those employed by the other power ministries. So much so, that throughout the rest of the 1990s the opposition not only considered the military an ally against the president but even believed that it might overthrow him.[28] Nonetheless, Yeltsin still had a support base in the armed forces, especially in the higher echelons where many officers were beneficiaries of the presidential inattention toward the army that made the virtually unchecked corruption possible.

Following Putin's ascent, the armed forces' vote has become more predictable as individuals affiliated with the security-military sector have come to overwhelmingly support him. As a presidential candidate in March 2000, Putin was widely popular in the army owing to his backing of the Chechen campaign and his efforts to increase defense funding. Just as important, Putin did not tell the military how to fight the Chechen War and left, more or less, internal matters to the armed forces to sort out. Unlike his predecessor, Putin was perceived by soldiers as someone who "makes manly decisions and sticks to them."[29] Most reports agree that he received a large majority of the defense-security vote, then again, he received the large majority of all votes. Still, his backing in the armed forces proper has been estimated to be 30–50 percent higher than in the country as a whole. Defense Ministry spokesmen announced that more than 80 percent of servicemen voted for Putin and more than 85 percent in the peacekeeping units stationed in Bosnia and Herzegovina and in the Black Sea Fleet based in Sevastopol.[30] According to Irina Isakova, active and retired defense- and other power-ministry employees along with their dependents—that is, those who are defined by Russian election experts as possessing "a military frame of mind"—may comprise as many as one-third of the total of the approximately 60 million eligible voters.[31] This figure is likely to be inflated but it underscores Putin's extraordinarily high-level of support in the armed forces.

Although the military appear to be, by and large, in Putin's corner, they do not necessarily form a docile voting bloc. The implementation of policies that harm the armed forces' corporate interests and the well-being of its members are likely to be met with diminished electoral support. In early 2005, for instance, numerous veterans' associations—whose votes Putin could ordinarily count on—organized major demonstrations protesting the deteriorating social status of servicemen, in part due to the Kremlin's social-benefits reform. The respected military expert, Aleksandr Golts, noted that officers were "infuriated" by the authorities' failure to improve their social standing while a poll found that 80 percent of Russian officers were dissatisfied with the government.[32]

When considering the armed forces' voting behavior it is important to keep in mind that the vast majority of the conscripts do not want to be in the military, and their political preferences approximate those of their nonserving cohort rather than those of their superiors. At the same time, things appear to have changed little since 1989 when Aleksandr Lebed, as commander of the Tula garrison, was instructed to ensure the election of a Kremlin-friendly candidate.[33] The law forbids political campaigning in military installations and thus personnel have more limited access than other voters to electoral campaign information from candidates and parties. In reality, commanders have been quite capable of influencing electoral outcomes in the barracks.

Grachev, for instance, pressured the armed forces to vote for the pro-government Russia's Choice Party in 1993. In early 2000 the decorated general, Gennadii Troshev, openly urged his soldiers at a polling station in Grozny, Chechnya, to remember "who supports us" and that "the most important thing is not to make a mistake, but to choose the most worthy," referring to then-acting president Putin.[34] Commanders usually are able to manipulate the information flow available to draftees by controlling the television programs they can watch and permitting only certain newspapers and magazines on base. "Managing" the voting process in army garrisons, where the ballot is notoriously easy to falsify and difficult to monitor, continues to be a time-honored tradition. Allegations of electoral falsification in the barracks arise virtually every time elections are held.

In the main, military officers have had only a modest impact on the legislature. The partial exception, of course, is the role some of them have played regarding defense- and security-related issues.[35] Even in this policy domain, however, one could argue that the most influential voices have belonged to politicians with nominal or no military service (Alexei Arbatov or Boris Nemtsov, for example). What accounts for this? First, military officers often lack the skills to make substantive contributions to policy debates on nonmilitary issues. Second, this weakness and their poor electoral performance after 1995 have eroded the appeal of army officers as potential candidates in the political marketplace. Third, the fact that few political parties have evidenced a sustained interest in defense issues underscores the diminished attractiveness of military men to them. Parties have also have been aware that most Russian voters do not seem overly concerned with military matters other than the thorny issue of conscription. Finally, military MPs were spread across numerous political parties whose platforms they were obligated to support. In any event, they showed no inclination to unite around a common set of military-related objectives.

In sum, at the beginning of the post-Soviet era President Yeltsin had the opportunity to reverse the trend of growing military activism by insisting on the depoliticization of armed forces personnel—as other postsocialist states had done. Instead, he and the Russian polity agreed to new institutional rules (i.e., the 1992 Defense Law) that legitimized the norms dating from the Gorbachev period. To make matters worse, the law also permitted military personnel to hold positions in government while serving in the armed forces, a regulation that further weakened the prospects of accountability and created a conflict of interest. In other words, the type of constitutional control over the armed forces that was emerging in Russia did not require the exclusion of the military from politics and was a source of the officer corps' further politicization.

By the late 1990s the importance of military officers' parliamentary service largely declined, but the legislature was only one of the arenas of the army's political activity. Some of its new political clout has been generated not by its legislative role but by the service of many high-ranking officers in the state administration. That is where the army's real political weight is best gauged.

FROM COMMUNIST OFFICERS TO OFFICER POLITICIANS

After a virtual absence of more than seventy years from national politics, high-ranking military officers emerged as independent political figures of consequence since 1991. To be sure, Marshal Georgi Zhukov was rewarded for coming to Nikita Khrushchev's aid with full Presidium membership—at that point the highest party post ever held by a professional military figure—in 1957. Still, "Khrushchev regarded his political debt to the Marshal of sufficient magnitude to pose a genuine threat to his rule, making a preventative purge imperative" a few months later.[36] Defense ministers and marshals Dmitri Ustinov and Andrei Grechko were also full members of the Politburo in 1973–76 and 1976–84, respectively, and thus might be considered other exceptions. Nonetheless, neither of them ever really emerge from the shadow of their mentor, Leonid Brezhnev.[37]

In contrast, many military men who had grown disillusioned with their civilian leaders became influential politicians in their own right in post-Soviet Russia. In addition to those who served as Duma members, dozens have been elected as governors, appointed as powerful presidential envoys

to Russia's federal regions, or established their own political organizations. They fall into two broad categories: "independents," who carved
out their own political niches; and "appointees," who received their positions from a powerful patron (usually the president). Another typology
that captures most of the noteworthy generals-turned-politicians distin-
guishes between them on the basis of service in the Afghan War (e.g.,
Gromov, Grachev, Rutskoi, Lebed) as opposed to in the Chechen campaigns (e.g., Rokhlin, Kvashnin, Troshev).[38]

The careers of leading post-Soviet generals are not only interesting from
the perspective of Russian military history. They are also illustrative of
the extent and kind of political influence they had gradually acquired.
More important for our purposes, their behavior at crucial junctures in
their professional lives clearly exhibits the negative changes in behavioral
norms that underscore the institutional decay in Russian civil-military
relations. A few brief portraits of Russian generals who have been the
pivotal actors of post-Soviet military politics expose the differences and
similarities in their political impulses and motivations, and reveal their
varying connections to fellow officers and politicians.

During the Yeltsin era, a number of factors combined to favor the political ambitions of renegade generals, most notably, the less structured political environment of the first post-Soviet years, the still ambiguous rules
of the political game, and the often enthusiastic support of the military
rank and file. These generals recognized the magnitude of the Russian
army's decline, at times openly defied their civilian and military superiors,
and partly as a result, gained significant support both from ordinary soldiers and officers and from the general public. The military and political
career trajectories of the numerous "independent" generals have been
quite different.

Aleksandr Rutskoi

The son and grandson of professional soldiers, Rutskoi commanded a
regiment in the Afghan War. He was a prisoner of war held by the *mujaheddin*, and on his release returned to the Soviet Union a war hero.
In 1988 he became deputy commander of the Army Air Force and was
recognized as a Hero of the Soviet Union. Rutskoi was Yeltsin's vice presidential running mate in the 1991 elections. As a widely respected officer,
in the early 1990s he was in demand by political parties trying to boost

their popularity. In 1992 he was approached by the Civic Union, a centrist formation that failed to take root in the political system. Rutskoi's relationship with Yeltsin soon soured after their triumph at the polls. He was one of the key players in the 1993 crisis, having cast his lot with the legislature and declared himself Russia's lawful president. Following the showdown Rutskoi was incarcerated but was pardoned in February 1994. In that year he established his Derzhava (Power) Party, ran in the 1995 Duma elections but failed to pass the 5 percent barrier. In 1996, however, he was elected as the governor of his native Kursk Oblast (region).

In the 1999 Duma elections Rutskoi and his party were loosely affiliated with the opposition Fatherland-All Russia ticket (known in Russia by its acronym, OVR—Otechestvo-Vsia Rossiia), although later they broke relations and he threw his support to Unity, the political formation backing the government. Rutskoi proved to be a relatively effective governor, yet in November 2000 he was removed from the ballot by a Kremlin-inspired judge for, among other things, offending Putin. (He criticized the president's mismanagement of the *Kursk* tragedy.)[39] Although he famously lamented after the accident that "a trolleybus driver in [the city of] Kursk gets more [salary] than a submarine commander,"[40] as a politician he was not a forceful advocate of the armed forces.

Aleksandr Lebed

Notwithstanding Rutskoi's high profile, he was by no means the most prominent soldier-politician to emerge after the fall of the USSR. That distinction belongs to the aforementioned General Aleksandr Lebed, the kingmaker of the 1996 presidential elections.[41] Lebed was a battalion commander in Afghanistan, and in 1988 he was appointed to head the Tula Paratroop Division, one of the most elite units of the Soviet Army. He participated in operations in numerous "hot spots" in the USSR: in the conflict between Armenians and Azeris in Baku, Azerbaijan (1988–89), in the clashes in Tbilisi, Georgia (1989), and in the unrest in Baku and other Azeri towns (1990). Lebed was elected a member of the Communist Party of Russia's Central Committee in 1990. During the failed coup attempt in the following year his unmistakable presence bolstered the spirits of the defenders of the Russian Federation Supreme Soviet building (the "White House") in Moscow.[42] In 1992 Lebed was sent to Tiraspol to end the armed unrest in the Transdniestr region and was soon appointed the commander of the Fourteenth Army stationed there. After numerous run-ins with his civilian and military superiors, he was retired by Presidential Order in June 1995 and was elected to the Duma to represent Tula later that year.

While in Transdniestria, Lebed repeatedly refused to carry out the orders of President Yeltsin and Defense Minister Grachev, individuals whose incompetence and crookedness he thoroughly despised. His insubordination was tolerated, however, because he got things done and he enjoyed broad popular and military support. Lebed's strong opinions and uncompromising views suggested a proclivity to put his foot in his mouth on occasion. During the 1996 presidential campaign he extolled the virtues of general-turned-politicians such as Charles de Gaulle and Augusto Pinochet. He was fond of pointing out that Pinochet compiled a superior record of economic development while killing "no more than three thousand people!"[43] In his short tenure as the secretary of the Security Council, Lebed's main achievement was to secure an uneasy truce concluding the disastrous first Chechen War. His success in Chechnya cemented his reputation both as a no-nonsense, can-do politician and a serious rival to Yeltsin who now had yet another reason to fire him. Two years after Yeltsin finally sacked him, Lebed successfully ran for the governorship of the enormous and resource-rich Krasnoyarsk Krai (region), which he ruled competently until his death in a helicopter accident in April 2002. (Incidentally, Lebed's brother Aleksei, a former colonel, has been the governor of Khakassiia, a neighboring region in Siberia.)

Igor Rodionov

One of Lebed's first and boldest maneuvers as national security tsar was to replace his old nemesis, Grachev, with another maverick general, Igor Rodionov, in July 1996, only thirteen days after the second round of the presidential elections. Prior to his appointment, Rodionov, a brilliant writer on military and strategic issues, was the widely respected head of the General Staff Academy (GSA). In 1985–86, Rodionov commanded the Fortieth Army during the most intense combat period in Afghanistan. Ten years later Rodionov drew criticism for the extraordinarily high casualties under his command but those who criticized him—particularly retired general and Duma member Konstantin Kobets—were his potential

rivals in senior-level postings in the Defense Ministry.[44] Even more controversial was Rodionov's role in the April 1989 suppression of the riots in
Tbilisi during which his troops reportedly killed twenty civilians. In fact,
in August of that year Rodionov was removed from his command, although later he was appointed to lead the GSA. His detractors called
Rodionov "the Butcher of Tbilisi," while others maintained that he prevented an explosive situation from getting worse.

As defense minister, Rodionov repeatedly and publicly criticized the
Yeltsin administration's national security policy—after Lebed's dismissal—and condemned its slew of broken promises made to the army.
Rodionov seemed intent on introducing genuine defense reform but he
had neither the time nor the necessary support inside or outside the Defense Ministry to succeed.[45] He was one of the few generals who recognized the importance of providing noncommissioned officers with better
training so they could take on additional responsibilities and lighten the
load of the already overextended junior officer corps. Nonetheless, Rodionov, like so many of his colleagues, had seemed not to have made the
transition to post–Cold War geostrategic realities. In a December 1996
statement he enumerated NATO countries, Iran, China, Pakistan, and
Japan—in essence, the full Soviet-era list—as Russia's potential enemies.[46]
Not surprisingly, Rodionov only lasted eleven months as defense minister.
The main reasons for his dismissal were his often publicly vented disregard for his civilian superiors, his ongoing fights with bureaucrats—such
as Defense Council secretary Yuri Baturin—concerning the inadequacy of
the defense budget to support meaningful reform, and his close links with
the anti-Yeltsin Russian Communist Party (KPRF). And, because Rodionov was essentially forced on the president by Lebed as a condition for
terminating the latter's presidential bid, his loyalty to Yeltsin always remained doubtful.

Since his dismissal from the ministry, Rodionov has remained active in
politics. He has seldom missed an opportunity to decry the mistreatment
of the armed forces and has organized and participated in numerous anti-
government demonstrations and has been the signatory of many public
letters condemning the policies of presidents Yeltsin and Putin. Rodionov
has represented several parties in his political career. In the 1999 Duma
elections he received a prominent position on the KPRF's electoral list.[47]
In February 2002 Rodionov was elected as the leader of the new People's
Patriotic Party whose program was more radical than that of the KPRF

but, as he insisted, it would respect parliamentary rules.[48] In early 2005 Rodionov, now representing the Rodina Party in the Duma, signed a petition—along with nineteen other deputies, including the ultranationalist and virulently anti-Semitic retired general Albert Makashov—calling for the suppression of all Jewish organizations in Russia.

Lev Rokhlin

Rodionov was one of the key supporters of General Lev Rokhlin and his All-Russia Movement to Support the Army. Unlike the preceding three individuals, Rokhlin made his military career not in Afghanistan but in Chechnya. Nonetheless, because he was an "independent" politician who made his own political career and because it coincided with Yeltsin's presidency, it seems appropriate to discuss him here. Rokhlin's distinguished service in Chechnya earned him a Hero of Russia decoration, which he refused to accept from the president owing to his utter disappointment in the Kremlin's conduct of the war.[49] Within one year, Rokhlin moved from the battlefields of Grozny to the chairmanship of the Duma Defense Committee (DDC) as a member of the Our Home is Russia Party. He used his position to harangue Yeltsin and his government for their criminal neglect of, and "rash and ill-considered decisions" regarding, the army.[50]

Rokhlin established his All-Russia Movement to Support the Army in the summer of 1997, while still chairing the DDC. The movement's founding statement called not only for improvements in the living standards of military personnel but also for the removal of President Yeltsin.[51] Rokhlin appealed to officers and servicemen to unite, organize assemblies, disobey Yeltsin, and to convey their "legitimate demands" to the Kremlin in order to "preserve" the army.[52] His successor, Viktor Iliukhin, urged the military to commit acts of insubordination because "the legal means to decide the question of power in Russia had been exhausted."[53] The organization's size and its antagonism to civilian authorities continued to increase until Rokhlin's death, at the hands of his wife, in July 1998.[54] Afterward, the movement—staffed primarily by retired officers and veterans—gradually lost its momentum and its influence within the armed forces because it did not represent the army as a whole let alone the voters considered the "military bloc." By the 1999 Duma elections it had become a fringe group and received only 0.59 percent of the popular vote.[55] Although Rokhlin seemed to have the chance to make a national impact, in essence he—unlike Lebed, Rutskoi, and most other generals-turned-politicians—continued to focus his political activities on a single-issue: the armed forces. His impassioned advocacy of the army drew public attention on its plight but his uncompromising stance against the political establishment did not aid his cause.

These "independent," self-made general-politicians put a strong mark on the civil-military relations of the Yeltsin-era. Their actions vis-à-vis their civilian masters—especially with respect to the commander-in-chief—clearly show the decay in the institutional norms of civil-military relations.

Putin's Moment

When in 2000 Vladimir Putin became acting and then elected president, he did have the opportunity—just like Yeltsin before him—to reverse the increasingly antidemocratic path of Russian military politics emblematized by the army's growing political influence and institutional decay as marked by laws, regulations, and behavioral norms incompatible with democratic civil-military relations. Russia's new president was not up to this challenge. To be sure, he restored the strength of the central state and brought the military under his control, but he actually *reinforced* the course of military politics by (a) appointing military personnel to important political positions; (b) allowing the top brass to successfully resist radical defense reform—reform that Putin himself was initially a strong advocate of; and (c) co-opting generals he rightly dismissed for their inappropriate behavior by giving them responsibilities in the state bureaucracy. This was the third formative moment in the evolving path of civil-military relations.

Since Putin's ascent to the presidency, the military has maintained a prominent position in Russian politics, though its power now pales in comparison to that of the internal security (former KGB, now FSB) apparatus. There are important differences in the generals' political role in the 1990s and since then. In the increasingly authoritarian environment created by Putin, the political clout of influential generals is invariably dependent on the president's good graces. In other words, they are no longer "independents"; they are "appointees." If under Yeltsin only the generals' own ambitions limited their political prospects, in the Putin era their roles, though significant, have been confined to their appointed positions and limited by the loyalty they owe their patron. Moreover, while Yeltsin's Kremlin aimed to foil the political ambitions of generals after

1995, Putin has filled important posts in his administration with military and especially security officers and encouraged others to run for elected office. Indeed, the Putin era has been a boon for the *siloviki*, individuals whose professional background is rooted in the power ministries. How to account for all this?

In the past, Soviet-Russian leaders had gradually built up their personal support bases as they ascended in the party-state hierarchy. But Putin's meteoric rise simply left him no time to cultivate a cadre of supporters. This meant that he could only rely on the backing of his former colleagues in the security establishment and in the St. Petersburg city administration. Not surprisingly, former KGB (and, to a far lesser extent, armed forces) personnel and St. Petersburg politicos have been the primary beneficiaries of his staffing decisions—hence the term *militocracy* mentioned at the outset. In this polity FSB (internal security service), Interior Ministry and Ministry of Defense bureaucrats have come to make up an unusually high percentage of the governing elite (e.g., 33 percent of federal government, 35 percent of all deputy ministers, 58 percent of the Security Council, 70 percent of presidential envoys).[56] There are now thousands of former military and especially security service men at all levels of government.

Putin has also lent his support to trusted generals who run for elected office and has urged them to enter politics, especially on the regional level where his control is somewhat less pervasive. Many of them have succeeded, and a handful have become governors. In the 2000 regional elections, for instance, three of the four generals who ran for governorships won (Kaliningrad, Ul'yanovsk, and Voronezh regions); many were elected to head city administrations or gained other posts. The newly elected governor of Ryazan Oblast (and former commander of the Airborne Forces), Georgi Shpak, claimed in 2004 that all of the regions with *silovik* governors (which also include Moscow Oblast) "have made considerable economic progress" and he could not see "why the idea of a man in epaulets in a position of authority should be seen as something weird."[57] Nonetheless, particularly owing to the president's success in reducing the regions' autonomy, they must do their best to stay on the Kremlin's good side. Putin has also shown a proclivity to select security-military cadres to head the country's federal districts as presidential envoys (also known in Russia as "governors-general" and "viceroys").

Moreover, Putin has repeatedly extended important appointments to members of the military elite he had previously dismissed, thereby presumably not only preempting their opposition to him but, in fact, turning them into loyalists. To be sure, this practice already began under Yeltsin who, in 1998, rehired former defense ministers Grachev and Dimitri Yazov, former chief of the General Staff Mikhail Kolesnikov, and a number of other high-ranking army officers as well-paid "advisors" to the Defense Ministry or to the state-owned arms exporter Rosvooruzhenie, an organization described at the time as resembling "a system of 'common racketeering.' "[58] Putin, however, has expanded this custom starting with, as I noted in chapter 1, the rehiring of the admirals he fired for their role in the *Kursk* accident. In September 2004 Putin named former General Staff chief Anatolii Kvashnin, whom he had sacked for fomenting the long-standing conflict between the General Staff and the Defense Ministry only two months earlier, as his representative in the Siberian Federal District. Let us briefly look at Kvashnin and Gennadii Troshev, two generals who have played notable, albeit rather different, political roles in the Putin era.

Anatolii Kvashnin

As chief of the General Staff, Kvashnin received the Legion of Honor, France's highest decoration (for his role in developing Franco-Russian security cooperation) only six months before he was dismissed by his commander-in-chief. A "Chechen general" like Rokhlin, Kvashnin was the commander of the North Caucasus Military District prior to his appointment to head the General Staff. He was not a fast-track officer but his consistently superior performance in a number of different capacities—including a stint at the General Staff from 1992 to 1995—and a personal resumé untainted by corruption charges or scandals soon focused the attention of the newly appointed defense minister, Igor Sergeev, on him in 1997.[59] Putin (and Yeltsin) apparently had great faith in Kvashnin's effectiveness, and in 1999 they gave him what amounted to a blank check to take any steps necessary for the total defeat of the enemy in Chechnya. Although Kvashnin could not deliver—in fact, command over the operations was transferred first to the FSB in early 2001 and then to the Ministry of Internal Affairs in mid 2003, an act that symbolized the military's relative loss of status in the new president's regime *and* that Chechnya was an *internal* matter—Putin did not find it necessary to dismiss him until July 2004. Moreover, during the Second Chechen War (in 2000) he appointed Kvashnin to the Security Council, an event that signified the first time since the creation of that body that the chief of the General Staff held a seat there on the same level as the defense minister.[60]

Kvashnin's tenure heading the General Staff was perhaps most remarkable for the unprecedented public conflict between himself and Sergeev. Things got so far out of hand that, in March 2001, Sergeev lost his temper in public and accused Kvashnin of "criminal stupidity" and of attempting to "harm Russia's national interest."[61] The fact that this sort of controversy could have occurred at all is in itself strong argument in favor of the armed forces' civilian management. According to his detractors, Kvashnin—who, in contrast to Sergeev, urged less reliance on nuclear weapons and a build-up of conventional forces—jeopardized Russia's future status as a great power and undermined its ability to maintain a nuclear balance with the United States.[62] In the next chapter we will hear more about these two generals, because their conflict centered on contradictory conceptions of defense reform.

Kvashnin seemed to have recognized the magnitude of the military's problems but throughout his seven-year tenure as the head of the General Staff he improved matters little if, indeed, at all. Rather, he invested most of his energies fighting Sergeev and later Sergei Ivanov during a period that had seen unprecedented politicization and infighting within the Ministry of Defense. Kvashnin shared the top brass' outdated views on defense reform partly out of conviction and, one would presume, partly to further the political ends of the General Staff vis-à-vis the Defense Ministry. Although a frequent critic of Putin's military polices who was rumored to have political aspirations of his own, Kvashnin's appointment as presidential envoy in Siberia is likely to have taken the wind out of his ambitions for higher political office.[63]

Gennadii Troshev

Kvashnin's successor as commander of the North Caucasus Military District was Gennadii Troshev, another prominent general who distinguished himself in Chechnya. In fact, Troshev was an old "Chechnya hand," having commanded the Fifty-eighth Army there, and had risen to his district command in April 2000 after he had already served there as deputy commander.[64] He did not last long in his new capacity, however. In December 2002 Putin sacked the outspoken Troshev from his post, most likely because he had publicly rejected Defense Minister Ivanov's proposal that he be transferred to command the Siberian Military District. Troshev, who

many believed was jockeying to start a bid for the Chechen pr(
said that accepting the transfer would be "a betrayal of the Checl
ple." By refusing to take the assignment, Troshev managed to le,
army and embark on a political career while at the same time creat.ug the
perception of being in opposition to the government—just as other generals like Lebed and Rokhlin did before him. Troshev's dismissal was one
of the few high points of Russian civil-military relations. Presidential aide
Sergei Yastrzhembskii called Troshev's statements "unacceptable," noting
that "generals should not publicly discuss suggestions and orders from
the defense minister."[65] A talented general with a penchant for threatening
his civilian and military superiors with resigning his command at the most
inopportune times if he did not get his way, Troshev was out of line one
time too many.

Actually, Troshev had not developed a soft spot for Chechens. In 2001
he called for the public hanging of captured Chechen rebels: "Gather them
all in a town square, hang them up and let them dangle for all to see," he
said.[66] He was among those politicians and military leaders—including
Defense Minister Ivanov and General Vladimir Shamanov—who expressed their compassion for and voiced their disapproval of holding Colonel Yuri Budanov responsible for raping and killing a girl in Chechnya.[67]

In the 2003 Duma elections Troshev ran on the list of the People's Party
of the Russian Federation—a left-of-center propresidential formation established along the lines of the People's Deputy faction in the legislature.
This was the third-largest group—after the Communist and the Unity-
Unified Russia factions—in the Duma, with sixty-two single-mandate
deputies at its peak. Since 2003 Troshev has been one of President Putin's
military-security advisers "on Cossack affairs." The most important function of presidential advisers is to prepare documents for the president on
relevant issues. Significantly, they have the right to request information
from federal ministries and agencies regarding their field of competence.

What tentative generalizations emerge from these brief portraits of
Kvashnin and Troshev? Both served in Chechnya in top command positions, both locked horns with Putin and with their political and military
superiors, both—particularly Troshev—cultivated political ambitions,
and in the end, both received presidential appointments to important
posts. This last point sets them sharply apart from the group of generals
we met earlier. Rutskoi, Rodionov, and Rokhlin acquired their positions
independently and, one could argue, even *against* the wishes of President
Yeltsin. Lebed is only a partial exception: he was a maker of his own

political fortunes and the one presidential appointment he briefly held was his payoff in a clear-cut political deal. Nonetheless, he was in the position to reach that deal because of his own accomplishments—being a creditable presidential candidate—and, of course, he was elected as governor on his own merits. The point is that the first group of general-politicians was not indebted to the president. The second group certainly is and this notion is the result of clever politicking by the Kremlin.

In contrast with the armed forces' uneasy relationship to Yeltsin, the military and Putin have forged links advantageous to both sides. It helps that they seem to share similar views, and that many in the armed forces consider the president one of their own. For Putin, who is best viewed as a pragmatic bureaucrat, security-military cadres are the type of people he best knows and understands. With the Kremlin's success in turning governorships into appointed positions—in yet another step away from democratic pretensions—and if the president's past personnel choices are indicative of future ones, it is likely that the military's (and, to a far larger extent, the security forces') political presence in Russia will further expand. Growing presence does not necessarily mean rising *influence* in the case of military cadres, however, as there is no evidence that the generals who receive lofty political appointments from the president act to further the armed forces' interests. Clearly, however, the large number of high-ranking bureaucrats with military (and security) backgrounds denotes a particular mindset and way of thinking.

Opposition to State Policy

What are some of the actual manifestations of the Russian officer corps' political activism resulting from the two-decade-long institutional decay of civil-military relations? Perhaps the most glaring outcome in the last fifteen years has been the frequent contestation of state policy by the armed forces as an organization and the individual commanders' acts of direct insubordination to their civilian and military superiors. These deeds—along with the armed forces' electoral role and political status—complete a triad of behavioral incongruity should one take the Soviet period as a point of departure. The military's active political involvement and its tolerated opposition of policies it considers injurious to its interests go against fundamental democratic standards and constitute the kind of revolutionary change in informal institutional norms North and others have identified.

In this section I want to mention only a few of the many examples of institutional and individual acts of misconduct that run counter to governmental programs and initiatives and, at times, hurt Russia's interests. The fact that prominent generals like Lebed, Rodionov, and Kvashnin were seldom held responsible for their actions is just as important as the instances of insubordination they committed. There are several reasons for this, some of them contextually determined. Russian presidents would hate to alienate the armed forces whose backing they need. Moreover, those officers who publicly misbehave—refuse to carry out orders or publicly criticize the government and/or its policies—often enjoy some popularity among voters so disciplining them could entail political costs. In some circumstances tolerating the military's opposition to certain policies might also be politically convenient: politicians can shift the blame to the top brass for stonewalling the implementation of policies in which progress has been lacking.

The habit of insubordination was born in the late 1980s: by 1990, military officers would openly criticize Gorbavhev's policies and incompetence. Under Yeltsin's presidency military leaders were often able to get away with open insubordination more or less with impunity. Although John Lloyd probably overstated his case when he wrote, in 1998, that the military "became a consensual organization in which major orders could no longer be given but were replaced by a bargaining or on occasion a voting process,"[68] the trend of diminishing professional discipline is beyond doubt. A renowned example that became a prime lesson in the rewards for disobeying orders occurred in Chechnya in 1994 when Defense Minister Grachev had to haggle with his regional commanders for troops and air support.

General Lebed provided numerous illustrations of individual misbehavior. Grachev sent him to Moldova's Transdniestr region to grasp control of the situation there. Although he did succeed in his mission, Lebed committed several acts of gross insubordination while serving in Transdniestria. He held press conferences even though Grachev categorically forbade him to do so. When in 1994 Grachev dispatched Deputy Defense Minister Matvei Burlakov to assess Lebed's command, Lebed not only did not allow Burlakov to review his troops but publicly called him a "thief." His actions earned him the admiration of his subordinates, cemented his broad political support base, and made him the most popular general in the land.[69] Incidentally, in 1993 Burlakov himself publicly warned that the army's support of the president was conditional and suggested that the military deserved a restoration of the special treatment it had been accorded during the Cold War.[70]

In June 1999 Anatolii Kvashnin masterminded the surprise action of Russian paratroopers who left their bases in Bosnia and raced to the Kosovar capital of Prishtina to seize control of its airport without any coordination with NATO forces. This move was Moscow's in-your-face reminder of its displeasure with the secondary role it was allowed to play in the region and that it was capable of bold independent action. From the perspective of civil-military relations, however, this incident was important because President Yeltsin not only approved the action but also permitted Kvashnin to leave the government—including Defense Minister Igor Sergeev—in the dark about it.[71] The "Prishtina Dash" signified Yeltsin consent to Kvashnin's disregard of the chain of command within the Defense Ministry and the government. Incidentally, this case also compounded the ambiguities created by the 1996 Defense Law that signaled the elevation of the General Staff to or above the level of the ministry. This, in turn created a troubling and confusing situation that was only resolved five years later when modifications in the law clearly subordinated the General Staff to the Ministry of Defense.

In view of this event it was not quite surprising that a year later, in the summer of 2000, Kvashnin once again bypassed Sergeev, and sent his own defense reform proposal to President Putin. This was another flagrant violation of the chain of command—in essence, Kvashnin acted as if he had only one direct superior, the president—and, to make matters worse, the incident quickly became public knowledge. Instead of immediately firing Kvashnin for his gross breach of conduct, Putin and his advisors treated the incident as an intellectual discussion between military specialists and pretended that nothing was amiss.[72]

Resigning one's command to express one's dissent over policy is a perfectly legitimate alternative to insubordination if all other legal avenues of registering one's disagreement have been exhausted. In Chechnya, however, leading generals have been occasionally allowed to overrule or blackmail their putative civilian masters with impunity. For instance, in November 1999, when the government was undecided about a strategic move at the Terek River, General Shamanov threatened to quit if the operations were halted. (As I noted above, General Troshev had also used the same tactic.) At this point Putin—who was still prime minister but already in charge of the Chechnya operation because Yeltsin, conveniently, divested himself of this responsibility—declared that "Russia doesn't have many generals like Troshev and Shamanov" to explain why he did not accept their resignation and appoint a replacement.[73]

To be sure, hundreds of thousands of Russian officers have resigned their commissions since 1991, and it is impossible to know how many of them left the armed forces in order to protest policies or for better career opportunities outside of military service. Nevertheless, there have been numerous cases when generals and high-ranking officers chose to retire rather than to become accessories to what they considered the Kremlin's and the Defense Ministry's misguided course of action. For example, prior to the beginning of the First Chechen War in 1994, several prominent generals who were pegged for major command positions—among them General Eduard Vorobyev, deputy head of Russia's ground forces, who was to lead the entire Chechen military operation—and more than five hundred officers quit the army as a form of protest.[74]

In terms of democratic development, instances of the generals' resistance to state policies are, of course, far more worrisome than individual misconduct. The Russian military, as an institution, has passively resisted and/or actively opposed state policies in areas that pertain to their interests. Russia has long emphasized the armed forces as the most important instrument of its foreign policy and has designated supporting roles to diplomatic, economic, and other means.[75] Accordingly, Soviet-Russian military elites have traditionally regarded voicing their views and concerns in the policy domain of foreign affairs as their prerogative. Since 1991, however, generals have at times actively contested and publicly countered a wide array of the state's expected and actual foreign policies. The Defense Ministry has aggressively promoted its interests in the Commonwealth of Independent States by delaying, for example, the division of the Black Sea Fleet with Ukraine and the withdrawal of its troops from elsewhere, such as Georgia and Tajikistan (the exception was its rapid departure from Azerbaijan).[76] Military elites resisted the Kremlin's anticipated readiness to abandon Soviet bases in Cuba and Vietnam and to reach a compromise with Japan on the issue of the Kurile Islands and with NATO on the 1998–99 Yugoslav crisis. The top brass have consistently opposed the strengthening of strategic relations with the United States and NATO, because it directly threatened their corporate interests. Following the rapid improvement of Russian-American relations in the aftermath of 11 September 2001, the generals expressed serious concerns with what they saw was Moscow's overly permissive attitude toward NATO expansion, Western attempts to gain a military foothold in the CIS, and in ABM Treaty negotiations.[77]

The Foreign Ministry has not been the Defense Ministry's only nemesis in the government. The high command has also repeatedly clashed with the Ministry of Finance over the latter's calls for decreased military expenditures and occasional refusal to disburse approved funds to the Ministry of Defense. Moreover, the military leadership's steadfast refusal to provide proper accounting of the state funds entrusted to them has also occasioned repeated clashes with the legislature. Entire books could be written about these and other government initiatives and how the top brass have tried—occasionally with considerable success—to foil their introduction or realization. The military elites' active obstruction of policy is a quintessential part of contemporary Russian civil-military relations. They have been most successful in blocking the implementation of a substantive defense reform, the policy that most directly affects the lives and career prospects of officers. The bottom line is that "the military's upper echelon," as Golts has recently written, "is the only segment of the federal government that can afford to ignore or even undermine presidential orders."[78]

CONCLUSION

Russian generals are not praetorian officers who become leading political actors by virtue of their use or threatened use of force. There has been no hint of any segment of the officer corps contemplating a political takeover, even if throughout the Yeltsin era "the possibility of a military coup was a hot topic."[79] Demonstrations by military personnel have been relatively small in size and frequency—the largest protests in favor of defense reform were organized by political parties and involved few participants from the armed forces—even though Russian officers and soldiers have had plenty of legitimate grievances in the last fifteen years. As one expert noted, owing to the armed forces' institutional history and the survival of strong threads of professionalism, third world models of military politicization fail to explain Russian and Soviet behavior.[80] In other words, as Brian Taylor persuasively argued, the Russian army's organizational culture is not hospitable to the idea of overthrowing the government. But, the military's political involvement can and—as I showed above—does take forms other than coups d'état or threats of military takeovers.

The unique window of opportunity for establishing democratic civil-military relations was the first few months of 1992, the very beginning of the new Russia.[81] At this point the erosion of civilian control over the armed forces could have been halted and reversed using the appropriate political and legal instruments. The Kremlin, the government, and the legislature should have established the conditions for a balanced civilian oversight of the military (as well as of the armed formations of the other power ministries). President Yeltsin, who had little interest in the armed forces—and, to be sure, who was handicapped by numerous and arguably more pressing issues on his agenda along with a dearth of financial resources—preferred to avoid this responsibility and let the military enlarge its institutional autonomy and solidify and increase the political role it had gained during the 1980s.

Yeltsin consented to new formal institutions, such as the 1992 Law on Defense that permitted officers to serve as people's deputies in the legislature *and* to hold leading positions in the government simultaneously while also serving in the armed forces, a regulation that weakened the prospects of effective institutional accountability and created a conflict of interest. For instance, in the early 1990s, when Sergei Stepashin was Yeltsin's deputy minister of security, he was also a member of the Duma and chaired its Defense Committee.[82] In other words, the type of constitutional control over the armed forces that was emerging in Russia did not require the exclusion of the military from politics, a mistake that, as I tried to show, was a source of the officer corps' further politicization. I disagree with Robert Barylski who contended that the presence of military professionals in the Duma had improved the flow of accurate information between the armed forces and the political elite.[83] Rather, most of the military members in the legislature—aside from a few prominent exceptions such as Rokhlin and Rodionov—failed to become advocates for the armed forces. In the meantime, the top brass' reluctance to release information useful to the Duma had changed little.

The institutional decay that began in the late 1980s has been at work now for two decades and is evident, among other things, in the Russian officers' electoral participation and their occasional resistance to state policy. The breakdown of Russian civil-military relations and the trend of increasing military influence in politics originate in the late-Soviet period. Under Communism the army behaved as the subservient executor of the

Communist Party's will. The political status that leading generals might have enjoyed was entirely dependent on the party's magnanimity and control. Gorbachev's ill-conceived and inconsistently implemented policies had a devastating effect on the armed forces. As a result, the long cultivated iconic image of the obedient, self-sacrificing, and heroic "Soviet Warrior" has been replaced in reality and in the public mind with the image of the corrupt, incompetent, irresponsible, and impoverished Russian soldier. Fifteen years after the end of the Soviet Union the party-state's oversight of the armed forces has now become synonymous with presidential control. At the same time, the absence of institutionally balanced, consistent, and firm civilian supervision combined with the decline of military professionalism has resulted in the generals' political participation and obstruction of state policy. The clearest example of this behavior is their steadfast resistance to meaningful defense reform, the subject of the next chapter.

((((

CHAPTER 4

The Elusive Defense Reform

Not since June 1941 has the Russian military stood as
perilously close to ruin as it does now.
   —Alexei Arbatov, "Military Reform in Russia," 1998

The period of radical reform is finished.
   —Vladimir Putin, speech at the Ministry of
      Defense, October 2, 2003

Taking the quotes above at face value, one might assume that during the five years that elapsed between them the Russian military
establishment had been comprehensively rebuilt. In contrast to
President Putin's proclamation—often repeated in campaign speeches
prior to the 2003 parliamentary elections—his country's armed forces
have yet to weather the sort of transformative reform necessary to bring
them in line with post–Cold War economic, geopolitical, and security realities. Three months after the Putin's announcement, Defense Minister
Sergei Ivanov publicly conceded that though the military's "reform" had
been completed, a period of "regimentation" was just beginning. He depicted the coming era as one in which a "more radical reforming of the
army" would occur, which would include improving command structures, modernizing weapons and equipment, and preparing new regulations.[1] Putin himself admitted at a July 2005 Security Council session that
those responsible have "not yet managed to implement the agreed military
reform programs."[2]

In fact, the armed forces require massive changes if they are to fit into
Putin's vision of a Russia restored to great-power status. They remain

impoverished, demoralized, and largely ineffective in spite of substantially boosted budgetary allocations since 2000. Nevertheless, the chances of radical change in the military establishment in the near term (say, in the next five to ten years) are slim because several formidable obstacles— from still inadequate budgets to a number of social problems—continue to impede substantive reform.

The greatest barrier to meaningful defense reform, however, has been political, not economic or social. Despite constant rhetoric about military reform in the past fifteen years, the Kremlin has been unwilling to force generals to transform the defense establishment in line with the profound changes in Russia's domestic and international circumstances. Therein lies an intriguing puzzle: even though the Russian executive's power has increased sharply since 1991 and even though the Kremlin has ostensibly wanted comprehensive defense reform, little has been done. This outcome is primarily explained by the opposition of the army leadership—whose cooperation, of course, is indispensable for the implementation of the president's reform agenda—to the reform and, in the final analysis, the president's willingness to tolerate this opposition.

This chapter is divided into four sections. I begin by taking stock of the progress Russia *has* made in transforming its armed forces since 1992. I continue with a summary of what *needs* to be done to prepare Russia's armed forces for the challenges of the present and the foreseeable future. Then I briefly outline and evaluate the reform proposals generated by political parties and the Ministry of Defense. Finally, I explain the absence of substantive reform, focusing on the role of the president and the opposition of the armed forces leadership.

WHAT *HAS* BEEN DONE AND WHAT HAS NOT?

The modern Russian Army was established in May 1992 following Moscow's failed attempts to maintain unified ground and air forces with Ukraine and other states within the framework of the Commonwealth of Independent States. Since its creation, the military has been the target of numerous reform proposals. Reforming the post-Soviet armed forces is a gigantic task that cannot be accomplished quickly or easily. Still, I contend that the *radical, comprehensive, transformative* changes that Russia's armed forces so clearly need have not been implemented and some of the changes that have been put into place have been ill-conceived or poorly executed. This is certainly not to say that nothing has been done or that the armed forces have remained unaffected by the epochal changes around them. In a few areas, in fact, important changes *have* taken place.

Force Reduction

The most readily apparent difference between the armed forces of 1992 and 2005 is that they have become considerably smaller. The downsizing process—implemented in several stages and including the repatriation of more than 1 million troops and dependents from Eastern Europe and the Baltic States—has progressed relatively smoothly and has resulted in force reductions of more than 50 percent. Though much of the armed forces leadership has bitterly resented state demands to decrease the military's size, the generals have completed this massive operation on time and without incident. This is a tremendous accomplishment.

Since January 1999 no major troop reductions have taken place despite Defense Minister Igor Sergeev's 2001 promise—itself a reiteration of Putin's pledge of the previous year—of further decreasing the army's size by 365,000 officers and soldiers and 120,000 Defense Ministry employees.[3] According to its own data, in May 2003 the ministry employed 1,162,000 uniformed personnel and 840,000 civilians.[4] Nevertheless, the Ministry of Defense announced in late December 2004 that as of January 2005 the total strength of the Russian armed forces, after cutting 100,000 troops from its rosters, would be 1,207,000 servicemen and 876,000 civilian personnel.[5] As this discussion suggests, accurate statistics about the armed forces are notoriously hard to come by. The military's manpower *may* be significantly lower than published figures indicate because base commanders routinely inflate the staffing levels of their units for two reasons. First, if the ministry orders additional cuts in personnel those can be easily "implemented" by scrapping vacant slots. Second, overstating the number of troops enables commanders to collect food and equipment rations as well as salaries and benefits allocated to nonexistent personnel, which can then be used to alleviate the unit's financial difficulties or to line one's own pockets.

Most important, *reduction does not equal reform*. The army's quantitative diminution by no means signifies its simultaneous qualitative improvement. Force reduction does not necessarily enhance either the effectiveness or the combat-readiness of the armed forces; it just makes them smaller.

Reorganization and Restructuring

The restructuring of the armed forces has been a contentious process mainly because military leaders have often subordinated the national interest to the interests of their own services. For instance, former defense ministers Grachev and Sergeev insisted on enlarged responsibilities to and preferential treatment of the airborne troops and the strategic nuclear forces, respectively, despite the imperatives of substantive reform. Some structural changes have taken place in the past twelve years, most during Sergeev's tenure (May 1997–March 2001), but even the high command has since recognized that a number of them have not been sufficiently thought through. The reforms included the abolition of the Ground Forces Headquarters, the merging of the air defense branch into the air force, and the reduction of the number of military districts to six with the amalgamation of the Siberian and Trans-Baikal districts and the Volga and Ural districts. (Actually, the headquarters of the former Volga Military District were re-designated as the headquarters of the Second Army and thus no units were disbanded.)

Two of Sergeev's reforms were quickly reversed under his successor, Sergei Ivanov: both the ground forces headquarters—their importance is underscored by the several armed conflicts on Russia's borders—and the space forces were reestablished as independent entities, and the latter was integrated into the air force. As a result of the recent consolidation of various branches—for instance, the air defense forces have been folded into the air force—the Russian armed forces now maintain four separate services: army, navy, air force, and the strategic missile forces. The seemingly logical innovation of transferring army aviation to the Ground Forces did not take root and was reversed; these units have been reintegrated into the air force where they are "clearly regarded as a burden."[6] The result of all these reforms and reversals is that the structure of the current armed forces is not very different from what it was in the Soviet-era.

More recently, building on the lessons of the wars in Chechnya, the army began to form a new force in the Caucasus: brigades of mountain troops. According to Chief of the General Staff Yuri Baluyevskii, the hostilities in Chechnya have finally taught the Russian Army the wisdom of using self-sufficient battalions rather than the less flexible division-regiment configuration with its more strict organizational structure.[7] Moreover, a total of 209 units were to be assigned to "permanent combat-readiness" category, which requires that their staffing levels be raised to at least 80 percent (all volunteer contractors), that they should be fully equipped, and that they are capable of fulfilling combat missions in peacetime and wartime without additional mobilization.[8] By April 2003, 72 such units existed and, although aggregate figures have not become available since then, it is clear that increasing their number (by 29 units in 2005, 20 units in 2006, and 11 units in 2007) remains a priority for the Defense Ministry.[9] In a May 2006 speech President Putin said that the government's objective was to secure two-thirds of the army manned by contract personnel forming 600 units on constant combat-readiness by 2011.[10]

The public debate between political parties, the government, and the defense establishment regarding the professionalization of the armed forces is now more than a decade old. The main dilemma has been the ratio of volunteers versus draftees in the armed forces. Again, from the conflicting numbers actual facts are often difficult to sort out. Ivanov said in March 2006 that there were 60,000 professional soldiers and sergeants on active duty at the time. But, in a May 2003 report Chief of the General Staff Kvashnin stated that contractors "now account for 21 percent of the Russian army's privates and non-commissioned officers, which means that every fifth man [232,400] is a professional soldier."[11] Ivanov's figure probably deserves more credence—the Russian media often features stories about the difficulty of recruiting and retaining *kontraktniki*—but the questionable credibility of numbers with respect to defense matters cautions against making unqualified assertions.

The ministry has not been fully satisfied with the quality and discipline of the recruits, many of whom, in turn, have not found the terms of service attractive enough to renew their contracts. Nonetheless, it anticipates that further inducements will raise the proportion of contracted volunteers to 70 percent in the armed forces by the end of 2008.[12] Recent reports indicate that these expectations will not be fulfilled, and moreover, the "idea of creating a contract-based army is failing."[13] In late August 2006, the army was said to be in a "feverish state over the mass early cancellations" of service contracts by soldiers and sergeants. A Defense Ministry document noted that no more than 19 percent of contract soldiers reenlisted, owing to low wages and poor living conditions.[14] According to data collected by the General Staff, every third *kontraktnik* in combat situations deployed in Chechnya abandoned military service ahead of schedule.[15] The manpower situation is likely to further deteriorate in 2008 when the term of service for conscripts will be reduced to one year.

Depoliticization and Patriotic Education

The demands of (re-)establishing civilian control after the fall of the USSR required the military establishment's comprehensive depoliticization. This has not happened. Instead, the military was "departified" in 1991 when President Yeltsin issued a decree that abolished Communist Party organizations in the KGB, the Ministry of Internal Affairs (MVD), and the armed forces. A large proportion of the military elite endorsed the party's banishment from the army and the abolition of the Main Political Administration (MPA), which was responsible for political-ideological in-doctrination. Political officers, the MPA's foot-soldiers, were replaced with division-level "educational officers," though in practice the identity of the individuals often did not change. At the same time, while the political officers of old were present with the troops and played an important role in motivation and indoctrination, the educational officers are far more removed from the soldiers and enjoy considerably less influence over them. In 2002 Anatolii Kvashnin reinstated political officers at army- and corps-command levels.

President Putin has described himself as "a pure and utterly successful product of Soviet patriotic education," which in part explains the increased emphasis on this kind of instruction since his rise to top governmental positions.[16] Not surprisingly, the well-documented decline of patriotic fervor among young Russians—in 1987, 93 percent of respondents had regarded themselves "patriots of the fatherland," but by 2003 their proportion had fallen to 23 percent[17]—has not failed to make an impression on him and his advisors. In March 2001 the government unveiled a five-year plan for patriotic education to "awaken patriotic consciousness" and feelings of loyalty to the country. The governmental "Decree on the State Program 'Patriotic Education of the Citizens of the Russian Federation for 2001–2005'"—which earmarked 170 million rubles ($6.4 million) was published in its entirety in *Rossiiskaia Gazeta*.[18] Furthermore, in July 2005 an amendment to the law "On Education" brought back basic military training as a mandatory school subject—it was cancelled in 1991.

Military leaders had long been concerned with what they occasionally describe as the post-Soviet "moronization" of Russia's airwaves. To counteract this undesirable trend, in February 2005 *Zvezda* (Star), a new government-owned military-patriotic television channel, began broadcasting in Moscow. The station is said to be the brainchild of Defense Minister

Ivanov who wants it to provide "effective informational and ideological influences," especially among those who now go to great lengths to avoid military service. According to its general manager, it is a civilian, commercial, and market-oriented channel with a state-patriotic concept. *Zvezda*—whose satellite broadcasts cover virtually the entire country—shuns "Western film products" with their violence and pornography.[19] Instead, its programming is tilted toward patriotic Russian films and documentaries as well as materials from the Defense Ministry's archives. Early notices suggest that *Zvezda* needs to become much more professional and engaging if it is to fulfill the ministry's expectations.[20]

Conscription and Alternative Service

Most experts agree that the mandatory and unpopular conscription system is at the heart of Russian defense reform. One of the main problems surrounding the draft is that, in fact, only a small proportion of young men serve (according to recent ministry figures only about 9 percent).[21] There are many ways to legally avoid military service and those who cannot, often bribe the appropriate officials or simply dodge the draft.

For tens of thousands of youths every year the way to get out of conscription is to enroll at a civilian college or university where military training (in so-called "cadet departments") is available that allows students to qualify as reserve officers without actually serving in the armed forces. In recent years these departments have produced approximately a 170,000 reserve officers annually, over ten times more than needed.[22]

Incidentally, Putin, Ivanov, and both of Ivanov's sons, along with the vast majority of Russia's elite have managed to avoid military service this way. In the summer of 2005 Education Minister Andrei Fursenko decided that of the 229 civilian institutions of higher education where this option was available only 35 would retain their cadet departments. The remaining institutions are going to be upgraded to orient them toward students who genuinely want to serve in the armed forces, and they will have to serve as contract officers for a period of five or six years, depending on their specialization.

This change was in line with a key provision of the Defense Ministry's 2003 reform proposal that decided to expand conscription and simultaneously shorten the draft period. Reducing the number of deferrals for conscripts, another important step in this direction, was accomplished in 2006 when nine of the twenty-five draft deferment categories were abolished by the State Duma.[23] (Rural doctors and teachers, athletes, artists and cultural workers, young men with pregnant wives or very young children, and those caring for elderly parents are no longer exempt.) The new restrictions will come into effect in 2008 together with the halving of the length of military service. The latter is actually going to be a two-step process. Under the terms of the new June 2006 bill the period of military service will be reduced to 18 months starting in January 2007 and to 12 months from 2008 for men between the ages of eighteen and twenty-seven.[24] The Defense Ministry's hope, obviously, is that the outcome of these reforms will significantly improve the size *and* quality of its conscript pool.

The right of draft-age young men to opt for civilian service instead of conventional military duty was already enshrined in the 1993 Russian Constitution. This right, however, was not only not guaranteed by proper legislation for nearly a decade but, in fact, individuals who intended to choose alternative service were hauled off to jail as recently as 2000. The legislative work on this bill was influenced by the Defense Ministry's lobbying efforts to make civilian service as unappealing and burdensome as possible in order to deter prospective conscripts from claiming their right to avoid armed service. The resulting law that Putin finally signed in July 2002 obligates those who use this option to serve for three-and-a-half years, almost twice as long as the term of regular conscription. Furthermore, the law—which came into force in January 2004—says that alternative service must be performed away from the individual's normal residence. This stipulation creates new opportunities for corruption (i.e., influencing the decision of where civilian service might be performed) and makes it an expensive option to regular armed duty because those choosing alternative service must pay for their accommodation. The new reductions in the conscription period might affect the length of alternative service as well, although, as of the summer of 2006 no decision has been taken in this regard.

Not surprisingly, the number of those who sign up for alternative service is minuscule: 186 out of about 155,000 draftees in the spring 2005 conscription cycle, down from 314 in the previous fall 2004 round.[25] According to the reports of the Committee of Soldiers' Mothers, military commissioners in Moscow were usually demanding bribes (up to $800) even to accept applications for alternative service.[26]

Budgetary Oversight

One of the critical issues of civil-military relations is civilian control over the defense budget. In the past fifteen years the Russian legislature has not gained sufficient authority over the federal budget, one-third of which is taken up by the power ministries. The government, and especially the Ministry of Defense, routinely refuses to share pertinent information with the legislature or supply opaque data. Few details of the defense budget are accessible even to Duma deputies whose budgetary oversight is limited, owing to their lacking capacity for the independent analysis of the budget or of defense policy. At the same time, the government appears to view the legislature's attempts at scrutinizing the armed forces' finances as hostile acts. This lack of transparency actually violates the 1998 Law on Budget Classification.[27]

President Putin has been displeased with the Duma's budgetary process and particularly with the deputies' "bargaining." In 2001 he suggested that the federal budget should be put together by the government and the Duma would simply approve it or reject it without discussion. In 2002, nonetheless, deputies of the liberal Union of Rightist Forces (SPS) successfully negotiated for the partial declassification of the 2003 draft defense budget by threatening the entire SPS faction's vote against it if transparency did not improve. Transparency was only marginally improved in 2003 when the government agreed to make public some additional elements of the 2004 military budget. But the difference for members of the legislature was getting fifty-nine lines instead of the previous five lines of text from the Ministry of Defense, much of it containing little useful information or traceable figures.[28] The December 2003 parliamentary elections, in which whatever robust opposition existed to Putin (and the quasi-party United Russia) was rendered irrelevant, seemed to obviate the need for increased transparency. Much of the defense budget is still shrouded in secrecy. For instance, not even Duma members—to say nothing of the press and the general population—could determine what proportion of the substantially increased 2005 defense budget would be spent on research and development.[29] Moreover, even Duma Defense Committee members are furnished with virtually no details about how the Defense Ministry actually spends the funds once they are allocated. Members of the Russian legislature do not have information about the price of a particular weapon model. In the best-case scenario, they do know the aggregate number of weapons the ministry procured and their total value. In the 2006 state budget 44 percent of the military's outlays were entirely classified.[30] As Pavel Zolotarev, president of the Foundation for the Promotion of Military Reform and a general in the reserves, recently wrote, the budget is structured in a way that it

> does not allow either parliamentary or civilian oversight of the military sphere. . . . The impression is created that somebody has, as it were, deliberately set the goal of not allowing anyone else to understand all the nuances of appropriations for defense and security needs. Meanwhile one budget exists, as it were, for the government and so that it can be shown to people. But the Defense Ministry has its own—internal— budget and its own structure of items of expenditure. These two budgets do not intersect, and therefore there is nothing to oversee.[31]

Increasing Civilian Presence in the Military

As a symbol of civilian oversight and a practical issue of the civilian management of the military establishment, the appointment of a civilian defense minister is an important ingredient of democratic civil-military relations.[32] For most of the 1990s Russia's military leaders publicly opposed the idea of a civilian defense minister. They argued that there were no civilians with the military expertise necessary—a clear snub to the eminently qualified First Deputy Defense Minister Andrei Kokoshin—and, as Grachev contended, that "people in the military would not understand it" and "when the Army is flooded by so many problems, for goodness' sake let someone who has breathed its air all his life deal with them."[33] Technically, Igor Rodionov became Russia's first civilian defense minister in December 1996—five months after being appointed by Yeltsin—when the president transferred him to the reserves in order to "reflect the progress of Russian democracy." Actually, the emptiness of this gesture was demonstrated by the fact that the Ministry of Defense had continued to be staffed entirely by military men and by the active-duty status of Rodionov's successor, Igor Sergeev.

Russians finally did get a civilian defense minister of sorts in March 2001 when Putin appointed his close associate, Sergei Ivanov, to the post.

A former SVR (Foreign Intelligence Service) general, Ivanov became the most politically powerful defense minister in Moscow since Dmitri Ustinov in the Brezhnev era. The president made another important civilian appointment naming a woman, Lyubov Kudelina, as deputy defense minister in charge of financial affairs. Kudelina, who previously served as deputy finance minister responsible for the defense sector, has been an advocate of keeping the Defense Ministry's finances secret and limiting the legislature's oversight authority.

Russian political elites have discouraged the rise of civilian specialists on military-security issues because they have nothing to gain and much to lose from the independent scrutiny of the defense establishment. The rising significance of a small but influential cadre of civilian defense experts or *institutchiki*—mostly concentrated in the Institute of the USA and Canada and the Institute of World Economics and International Relations—in the Gorbachev era has been reversed; these people have been excluded from the policy mainstream under Yeltsin and, especially, Putin. There are few autonomous organizations that focus on military matters, and they tend to be supportive of state policy. Another factor thwarting the emergence of civilian defense specialists is the continued obsessive secrecy in Russia—virtually everything having to do with security and defense is considered a "state secret"—which has deterred individuals from trying to acquire expertise on these matters.

The Kremlin has also applied growing pressure on the few newspapers that publish articles critical of the military reform's progress. In October 2003, for instance, it compelled the editors of *Moskovskii Komsomolets* (and pressured managers of others newspapers) to stop publishing the columns of Pavel Felgenhauer, one of the country's few independent security experts. Even more troubling has been the prosecution of researchers working on defense-related issues (e.g., Igor Sutiagin) and military journalists (e.g., Aleksandr Nikitin, Grigorii Pasko) who ask inconvenient questions. They can be—and have been—jailed for years without proper trial, the eventual outcome of which is rarely in doubt. "When the authorities decide that they are going to convict you of something," as one scholar comments, "there is absolutely no way to win."[34]

In sum, "defense reform"—to the extent that what has taken place since 1991 may be called that—has fallen far short of radically transforming Russia's armed forces. A decade after the fall of the Soviet Union Colonel-General Leonid Ivashov, the former head of the Defense Ministry's Main

Directorate for International Military Cooperation, lamented that "we have been doing nothing but talking about the reform of the armed forces and making some incomprehensible attempts in this direction."[35]

The various aspects of defense reform draw attention to the usefulness of Alfred Stepan's work because it points out the dramatic increase in the military's political influence in post-Soviet Russia. His typology of the military institutional prerogatives reveals that the Russian armed forces' political role is troublesome (i.e., "high") in two important respects.[36] First, at present the military does not provide the legislature with the type of detailed information that would allow actual oversight of the defense budget. Second, contemporary Russia is a textbook case of Stepan's sixth military prerogative: "active duty military officials fill almost all top defense sector staff roles" and civilians are essentially shut out from this occupational field. In several other areas, one would place the military's institutional prerogatives somewhere between the "high" and "low" grades. For instance, although there are no uniformed military personnel in ministerial position in the Russian cabinet, there are plenty of officers in prominent political posts. Also, the armed forces enjoy a "major role in setting the boundaries" of promotions even if the Russian executive does have considerable latitude in this regard. In contrast, the Soviet Army, of course, was under a strict system of multifaceted civilian control, its budget was entirely dependent on the CPSU's decisions—though the high command naturally lobbied for growing defense outlays—and its generals did not hold independent political positions.

THE REFORMS RUSSIA'S MILITARY NEEDS

Although the primary focus here is *why* transformative defense reform has proven elusive in Russia, it seems worthwhile to outline what changes ought to be put in place. In order to ascertain the kind of armed forces Russia needs one must look at the stated objectives of its foreign policy. The problem immediately facing us, however, is the many-faceted incongruity, contradiction, and confusion between strategy and doctrine, reforms and implementation. Leading politicians frequently change their views of fundamental foreign policy objectives (for instance, cooperation or discord with NATO and the West) based on the political developments of the day. Underscoring these disparities are the significant and troubling discrepancies between Moscow's stated goals (e.g., preventing nuclear proliferation) and actions (i.e., selling sensitive materials to countries like Iran whose nuclear development program has been a source of profound concern for the United States, Britain, and other Western democracies). This state of affairs has led a prominent Russian military expert to publicly contend that "Russian foreign and security policies do not meet the criteria of 'policy.' We have some kind of uncoordinated actions, we seem to dart about like firemen to one situation or another—I mean the Kremlin, the Kremlin administration."[37] Though these may be strong words, another prominent defense specialist, Dmitri Trenin, deputy director of the Carnegie Foundation's Moscow Center, seems in perfect agreement. He argues that it is imperative that Russia give very serious thought to both its threat perceptions and security needs. In essence, Moscow has yet to find its place in the post–Cold War international system and has yet to bring its foreign policy ambitions in line with its military capabilities. Although Russia is certainly not the only state that has found it difficult to transform its military according to new realities, its record of defense reform—fraught with false starts, reversals, and sloppy implementation—is perhaps the most unimpressive, even though it has changed by far the most in terms of territory, population, and capacity to raise funds for defense spending.[38]

It is hard to disagree with Trenin who maintains that a careful reassessment of Russia's current challenges and the constraints within which it has to operate is highly unlikely to take place, chiefly because there is a severe communication problem between the country's political and military leaders.[39] This problem is exacerbated by the continuing absence of transparency in defense-security affairs. Fundamentally, the executive and the legislative branches only find out about the armed forces what military elites are willing to reveal, and politicians—including President Putin—have displayed little enthusiasm for prodding the generals. Furthermore, given the growing restrictions on media freedoms and the success of the Kremlin's ongoing intimidation campaign targeting those inquiring about "sensitive" subjects, the public has scant understanding of Russia's security challenges. Then again, one might argue that in an increasingly authoritarian state like Putin's Russia even an informed public would be powerless to influence political decisions.

Russian political and defense elites must come to terms with the reality that the greatest threat to their security comes not from traditional Cold War adversaries but from the nationalist and separatist forces along their southern borders. The chances of an all-out land-sea-air war with the

United States and its NATO allies are virtually nil, no matter how much the old guard in the Defense Ministry and the General Staff would like to believe (and convince whoever they can of) the contrary.[40] Instead, as the events of the past decade and a half have suggested, Moscow's attention should be focused on nuclear proliferation, international terrorism, and radical Islamic upheavals. These are, of course, the same threats Western democracies also face, hence the opportunity and need for closer cooperation with them. The first step, therefore, would be to bring the country's military doctrine and strategic concepts in line with these realities.

What kind of defense reform *does* Russia really need? The three-stage program outlined by Alexei Arbatov and others some years ago still looks both reasonable and feasible.[41] Start with the reduction of the armed forces to 800,000, then continue with the establishment of an all-volunteer force emphasizing quality rather than quantity and significantly increase the wages of personnel to attract the kind of individuals the military needs. As several experts, including Arbatov and Aleksandr Golts, have pointed out, the costs of such a transformation are not beyond Russia's means especially when the size, wastefulness, and corruption of the contemporary armed force are considered. For instance, maintaining some units in all branches of the military on high alert is unnecessary, expensive, and a testimony to the surviving Cold War paranoia of the military leadership. Eventually, the army should be reduced to 550,000–600,000 troops that—if fully professional as well as appropriately trained and equipped—"could ensure the highest quality for Russia's armed forces for the next ten to fifteen years."[42]

The key issue of the practical aspect of military reform has been the conscript versus volunteer dichotomy. Military leaders and politicians supporting the draft have argued that it needs to be maintained in order to continue the age-old tradition of the army making boys into men and the patriotism, camaraderie, and shared experiences that obligatory military service have—at least in the eyes of its supporters—signified in many places. Their main objection to an all-volunteer force, however, has little to do with sentiments and everything with money and self-interest, as detractors claim that the country simply cannot afford an all-professional army. Military experts and politicians who have pushed for substantive defense reform have demonstrated that not only is Russia perfectly capable of bearing the economic burden posed by a volunteer force but, in fact, it would be far better off with such a force. Nevertheless, their calculations are predicated on unrealistic assumptions: a changed Russian mindset, a different politico-military establishment, and more specifically, a defense budget opened to genuine public scrutiny. Arbatov's outline of an ideal Russian military reform has virtually no chance of being taken seriously by the high command. In the end, one ought to be skeptical regarding the probability of a major doctrinal-strategic reassessment and the subsequent implementation of a defense reform consistent with it.

In practice and deeds—if not necessarily in theory or words—Russia is still preparing to fight the next war against the West. The large size of the armed forces, the continuing emphasis on the conscription system, the deployment patterns of the forces (nearly 80 percent are concentrated close to Russia's western and eastern borders), the objectives of training, and the weapons acquisition program (pressing nuclear submarines and heavy bombers) all indicate a defense establishment readying for a large-scale conventional war instead of present and probable future conflicts. In October 2003 Defense Minister Ivanov explained to NATO generals that the principal obligation of the Russian Army was to protect the country against an attack from the air or from space.[43] Clearly, only one potential adversary, the United States, is currently capable of executing such an attack. Recent evidence shows that fundamental change in Russian strategic thinking is some time away. In July 2005 Ivanov announced that the Pacific Fleet was to acquire at least two new nuclear submarines in the following two years.[44] Two months later the newly appointed commander of the navy, Admiral Vladimir Masorin, declared that his focus would be on developing strategic nuclear forces in his service.[45] Needless to say, these weapons can only be directed against the United States and NATO and are hardly useful against fighting the low-intensity conflicts Russian politicians are ostensibly worried about.

When in his 2006 State of the Nation address Putin declared that Russia "must be able to fight in global, regional, and local conflicts simultaneously", he was, in effect, lending further support to the agenda of military elites.[46] As a perceptive Russian journalist recently opined, "Money available for defense is not the problem. . . . However, Russia is spending it just like 20 years ago. All we need to change is the mentality of Russia's top brass. Otherwise, the Russian Army will remain the Red Army."[47]

THE OPTIONS: QUALITY VERSUS QUANTITY

In chapter 2 I reported on the shape Russia's armed forces are in. Let us now see what options Russian politicians have advocated and the contours of the reform that is ostensibly being pursued.

Reform Proposals under Yeltsin

Although the dire need for defense reform was obvious even at the time of the creation of the new Russian Army in 1992, few coherent reform programs had emerged. President Yeltsin appointed numerous commissions to study military reform, most of which faded into oblivion a short time after their formation. The policy of Russian governments until the mid 1990s was to cut budgets, postpone substantive reform until the economy's eventual turnaround, and reduce manpower. In terms of changing the military, downsizing was the most important achievement of the Yeltsin era.

After the 1995 Duma elections three distinctive approaches emerged in the legislature regarding defense policy in general and military reform in particular.[48] The first view was emblematized by retired generals who argued that Russia's economic, social, and foreign policies should be adjusted to accommodate the needs of the military establishment. The second group was represented by the ruling elites (the Our Home is Russia [OHR] party as well as supporters of the Yeltsin administration) who perceived military reform as reconciling the army to meager defense budgets and tended to underestimate the armed forces' crisis. The third group was comprised of members of the parliamentary opposition who advocated a balanced and consistent defense policy, including higher defense outlays to support military reform. Given the post-1995 dynamics of Russian politics it was hardly surprising that the second approach dominated. Prior to the 1995 Duma elections, the OHR enticed the popular general, Lev Rokhlin, to join its ranks, assigning him the third place on its electoral list. After the election the OHR nominated him to the chairmanship of the Duma's Defense Committee, its most important organ on military affairs. In that post, Rokhlin turned out to be an uncompromising critic of the administration's defense policy, however, and was pushed out of his chairmanship in May 1998.

Aleksandr Lebed was the leading advocate of military reform in the armed forces. He believed that Yeltsin's election promise to end the draft and create a fully professional army by 2000 was absurd. Lebed called for force reduction by a third and the creation of a smaller number of fully manned, combat-ready divisions (he referred to them as "small mobile fists to solve all problems").[49] After his dismissal from his national posts, however, he ceased to be a factor in the defense reform debate.

There is a fundamental reason why no substantive defense reform took place during Yeltsin's presidency. In essence, Yeltsin made only two reform-related demands of the military leadership: speedy withdrawal from Central and Eastern Europe and substantial force reduction. Beyond that, the president pretty much gave his implicit promise to the top brass of not interfering with the way they ran the armed forces, and in return, he did gain their support, however qualified and grudging it might have been at times. (I want to underscore that I have in mind military elites here, not the officer corps in general let alone the NCOs or conscripts.) This arrangement gave a green light to the unprecedented corruption in the armed forces *and* virtually guaranteed that no military reform was going to take place.

Reform Proposals under Putin

Between 2000 and 2003 the discussions of military reform intensified, particularly because conditions in the armed forces in many respects had continued to deteriorate and because during this period there was still a relatively robust opposition to Vladimir Putin's supporters in the Russian legislature. Moreover, Putin's interest in bringing about military reform had become keener after the August 2000 tragedy of the *Kursk* submarine and its aftermath. In a speech delivered shortly after the accident, he remarked that "discussions of military reform have been going on in our country for quite a while—for at least eight years and maybe even a decade—but, unfortunately, there has been little headway in this respect. I hope very much that we will be able to secure positive changes."[50] For a short time, the U.S. military victory over the Iraqi army in the spring of 2003 lent further momentum to reform discussions. The crushing defeat of the Iraqi armed forces, which, in many ways (inflexible tactics, low-tech arsenal, low morale, bloated officer corps) were a smaller replica of Russia's own forces, exposed the large and growing gap between American and Russian capabilities and made an indelible impression on Russian military and political elites. It also proved wrong the numerous Russian politicians and generals who publicly predicted a major American defeat prior to the war.[51]

The wide-ranging debate spawned numerous reform concepts. The most vocal supporters of defense reform were political parties, particularly the Union of Rightist Forces (SPS). It is important to emphasize that in the December 2003 Duma elections the parties that were willing and able to criticize Kremlin policies—particularly the pro-Western SPS and Yabloko—did not succeed in passing the 5 percent threshold necessary for representation. Moreover, only a total of six of their delegates gained seats in single-mandate races. The future importance of potentially troublesome independent deputies was counterchecked in the fall of 2004 when, in a further step to assure a thoroughly compliant legislature and, more generally, noncompetitive politics, Putin's regime eliminated the single-member district system for the Duma. In the summer of 2003, however, it seemed that the SPS and other parties still had some chance of substantively contributing to the policy debate.

THE UNION OF RIGHTIST FORCES

From the mid 1990s until the fateful 2003 parliamentary elections Boris Nemtsov, the cochairman of the liberal SPS was the most ardent and consistent proponent of radical defense reform in Russia. The fundamental premise of the SPS's proposal was that conscription was unfair, unpopular, and inefficient, and it had to be abolished as soon as possible. The SPS, together with the Institute of Transitional Economy, developed an ambitious and comprehensive reform plan the key proposal of which was to end conscription and transform the entire armed forces into contract-based professionals in no more than four-to-five years (some versions deemed as little as eighteen to twenty-four months sufficient).[52] The plan, which was estimated to cost 90 billion rubles (about $2.9 billion) and required only a 2 percent increase in defense outlays according to its backers, allowed for the introduction of a voluntary six-month military training course at the end of which participants would have had the option to sign a contract with the military or return to civilian life. It also called for doubling the contract soldiers' salaries to about 15 percent above the average wage and to supplement it with various bonuses (e.g., for combat duty) in order to attract qualified and motivated candidates. At the same time, Nemtsov and his colleagues argued, manpower needed to be further reduced to around 800,000–850,000, in line with the Defense Ministry's own long-forgotten plans unveiled in 2000. In addition, the SPS promoted retraining programs and covering the costs of higher education for veterans.

Nemtsov and his party were scathing critics of the Pskov experiment in which the top brass had sunk a great deal of financial and political capital. They argued that the General Staff used the conversion of the Seventy-sixth Airborne Division in Pskov—a town eight hundred miles northwest of Moscow—to volunteers as a ploy to prove the staggering cost of professionalization. Military leaders estimated the cost of converting every conscript position to contract status at 1 million rubles (about $32,250) and, accordingly, requested and received 3 billion rubles (around $96 million) from the Ministry of Finance to hire the three thousand soldiers necessary to staff the division. In line with their financial request for the Pskov experiment, the General Staff claimed that for the professionalization of the entire army (as the SPS proposed) the Ministry of Defense would need to convert 400,000 conscript positions to contract-soldiers with the overall price-tag of 400 billion rubles ($13 billion). As Nemtsov said, "We [the legislature] will never find R400 billion and therefore there will never be any reform."[53]

The SPS was quick to point out that the generals spent the bulk of the 3 billion rubles in Pskov on unnecessary capital investments, such as building apartment blocks for contract soldiers. SPS politicians contended that the army would be much better off renting apartments to volunteers with families, raising salaries, and improving its arsenal rather than spending scarce funds on apartment construction. Certainly, the Defense Ministry's ploy to run up the cost estimates of the military's conversion could not have been more transparent. After all, why were the generals all of a sudden so intent on building apartments for privates when, according to their own data, in late 2002 168,000 officers and their families had no apartments to live in? In any event, by 2006 even the military recognized the experiment with the Seventy-sixth Airborne Division as a dismal failure.[54]

OTHER PARTIES

Many politicians and parties, however, have been opposed to the end of conscription. Their view of defense reform largely corresponds to their ideological hues. For example, the left-wing opposition, led by the Communist Party of the Russian Federation (KPRF), supports the restoration of Russia's great-power position and insists that the United States remains the country's primary enemy. Together with the Working Russia movement, the KPRF agrees with the General Staff that maintaining a large conscript-based army is a top priority.[55] The Unity Duma faction—a strong supporter of the president—has proposed that Russian youth be allowed to avoid military service by taking a six hundred dollar, six-month course of military training.

In contrast, the liberal democratic Yabloko—along with the SPS one of the few sources of democratic opposition to Putin until the December 2003 parliamentary election—was sharply critical of the shortcomings of defense reform.[56] Its leaders advocated increased defense spending to allow the rapid abrogation of conscription and conversion to a contract-based army, force-reduction to a total of 800,000 uniformed personnel, doubling the salary of all servicemen and officers, and changing the ratio of the current budgetary spending to 50 percent on maintenance and 50 percent on technical upgrading. Yabloko repeatedly pointed out the inconsistencies between the Kremlin's and the Defense Ministry's doctrinal and reform conceptions, such as the former's recognition of the absence of traditional security threats to Russia while the General Staff was predicting and was intent on preparing for a large-scale conventional war. Yabloko's effectiveness, however, was limited by the fact that after the 1999 elections it captured only 17 seats of the 450-seat Duma. Following the 2003 parliamentary elections, both Yabloko and the SPS have become severely weakened and largely irrelevant. Their influence has correspondingly declined, leaving little opposition in the legislature for the Defense Ministry to contend with. Several NGOs also proposed more or less comprehensive programs for military reform. Among them the most important was the Moscow think-tank, the Council for Foreign and Defense Policy, which put forth a military reform plan in 2003.[57]

THE MINISTRY OF DEFENSE

Sergei Ivanov—who dismissed the SPS's plan as "slapdash populism"—and the Ministry of Defense also privileged manpower issues in their reform proposal. Their plan was to fill most of Russia's 209 combat-ready units (in eleven divisions, seven brigades, and ten regiments) with contract servicemen by 2007. Nonetheless, conscription would continue and draftees would serve in all branches with the exception of combat and rapid-deployment units. The plan also included cutting compulsory military service from two years to one and the cancellation of many draft exemptions, changes that were made into law in 2006. Conscripts would receive a six-month basic training and serve out the rest of their military service in noncombat units. A task force of government experts estimated a 35-billion-ruble ($4.34 billion) price tag for this plan—based on the aggregate cost analysis of individual units—most of which would go to wages and rebuilding barracks. Moreover, the ministry apparently realized that the dearth of professional training of NCOs was a serious shortcoming, as Ivanov promised to remedy the situation.[58]

To alleviate the anticipated shortage of qualified contractors, Ivanov announced a plan—endorsed by Putin and quickly approved by the government—to lure CIS citizens into the Russian Army with the promise of Russian citizenship to be conferred following three years of service.[59] Given that this proposal is in direct conflict with legislation in several CIS states (e.g., Georgia, Ukraine), its legal implications are unclear. The ministry's plan to allow women (who are not subject to the draft) to volunteer for combat units also requires new legislation. Ivanov noted that contract soldiers would be primarily recruited to staff units in the "Northern Caucasus" (i.e., Chechnya), which is likely to make professional service less appealing.

THE DECISION AND SUBSEQUENT MOD PLANS

In July 2003 the government decided to back the Defense Ministry's proposal of incremental expansion of volunteer service over the fast-track and less expensive reform suggested by the SPS. According to the government-approved reform, by 2007 nearly half of the military will comprise contract personnel, salaries will be increased, and conscripted service will be cut to one year. The Kremlin announced that the reform would cost 79.1 billion rubles ($2.6 billion), which is considerably less than the military leadership's estimates. The General Staff had to be disappointed because it did not want the reform launched until 2010, hoping—one assumes—to outlast Putin and that under his successor there would be even less talk of a radical transformation of the military.

In February 2006 Ivanov predicted that by 2008 "frontline units will be manned by 140,000 soldiers and sergeants serving under contract," the army as a whole will become 70 percent contract based, and the number of conscripts—serving for one-year—will be increased. He failed to explain how, even with the reduction of deferments, this would be possible, given Russia's profound demographic problems and the army's difficulty to attract qualified volunteers.[60] The ministry's Military Development Plan for 2006–10 prioritizes three areas: maintenance and development of a strategic deterrent sufficient for repulsion of contemporary and future military threats; development of conventional forces; and development of combat training.[61]

In a January 2006 interview with the army's daily newspaper, Chief of the General Staff Baluyevskii indicated that the top brass were contemplating further restructuring the army to transform the current military districts into "operational and strategic directions" and the reorganizing of divisions and armies into more flexible units with enhanced maneuverability.[62] More specifically, this reform proposal would replace the current six military districts and four fleets with three regional command centers (Far Eastern, Central Asian, and West European; that is "East," "South," and "West") and "cut the armed forces by 100,000 men—down to 1 million servicemen—with a view to saving budget funds."[63]

If recent history is any guide, many of these proposals will not be implemented and will amount to little more than momentary news items. They merely confirm, once again, that there is no firm blueprint for defense reform and that statistics propagated by the military leadership remain unreliable. Skeptics suggest that the Defense Ministry's original reform proposals—like others preceding it—would be long forgotten by 2007, their supposed completion date and even if not, Ivanov could always blame the inadequacy of defense spending or some other factor for lackluster outcomes. They charge that "there is no reason to expect changes for the better"; after all, in five years Ivanov has failed to transform the military or improve Russia's defense capacity and resorted to blaming others for his failures: in essence, the Russian Army still very much looks like a smaller, poorer, and demoralized version of the Red Army.[64] By opting for the Defense Ministry's reform framework, the government, once again, favored the generals over a population that, according to a slew of opinion polls, overwhelmingly supports comprehensive defense reform.[65] The question is, why?

Explaining the Absence of Genuine Reform

How can we explain the long-delayed radical defense reform in Russia where there is a strong president who is apparently eager to implement reforms and a military establishment that has traditionally been a reliable executor of state policy? Although there is no simple answer to this question, some of the insights of civil-military relations theory combined with an understanding of the profound changes in the nexus between Russian political and military elites since the mid 1980s go far toward providing a satisfactory explanation.

The President and Military Reform

His oft-repeated rhetoric aside, it would seem logical to expect the Russian president to want to drastically reform the armed forces, given their abominable state. Putin is certainly aware of popular opinion that has become increasingly interested in military reform. Moreover, one of the recurring themes of his speeches has been the return of Russia as a great power, which would be difficult without the wholesale reform of the armed forces. But how potent are these reasons to expect robust reform activity from the state? Public opinion is often disregarded even in consolidated democracies; it is hardly a reliable predictor of political action in contemporary Russia. And, the Kremlin may well be interested in attaining the trappings of great-power distinction—securing permanent membership in elite international forums such as the G8, gaining respect for the country and its representatives—rather than in its substantive dimension of expensive, messy, and thankless responsibilities.

Still, all things being equal, Putin appears genuinely to want substantive military reform. When he came into power in 2000 he appeared quite intent on pushing defense reform, announcing, for instance, that troop strength would be decreased from 1.2 million to 800,000. Soon, however, force reduction was forgotten about and lip-service replaced the preparations for restructuring. It has been argued that during his first presidential term it was the military-security area where Putin compiled "the worst record of success while encountering the most damaging challenges to his leadership. The conclusion that four more years were lost for rehabilitating the military structures appears now self evident."[66] All things are, thus, not equal: the incentives to embark on substantive reform are far outweighed by the virtually insurmountable difficulties.

After the culmination of the political struggle between the executive and the legislature in 1993, the Russian head of state acquired "superpresidential" powers.[67] The president's prerogatives vis-à-vis the defense establishment further increased after Putin expanded his control over the power ministries (ministries of defense, interior, emergency situations, and others) at the expense of the government. As noted in chapter 3, given Putin's swift rise in the state bureaucracy and therefore, his inability to generate a support base, he was forced to rely on the backing of his former colleagues in the security sphere and, to a lesser extent, in the St. Petersburg city government. Putin has been exceedingly popular among the power-ministry personnel, and he knew that he could alienate this large support base by forcing the military through an unpopular reform. Furthermore, without the generals' backing who could Putin have entrusted with the implementation of whatever military reform he might eventually have wanted to introduce? To be sure, as Taylor convincingly explained, the military's organizational culture makes its violent political interference in defense of its institutional prerogatives extremely unlikely. At the same time, the armed forces have resorted to what Colton described as political bargaining—offering continued support to Putin and his regime in return for implicit assurances that no reform would be forced on them—to uphold their interests.

A similarly salient issue is the war in Chechnya, with which Putin's ascendance was intimately connected. The army's performance in the Second Chechen War—even if superior to its abysmal record in the First—might in itself be an argument for military reform. Nonetheless, it is hard to see that Putin would force the very generals who supported his decision to reinvade Chechnya and managed the first stages of the war to implement a reform they oppose. In fact, it has been argued that the Second Chechen War became the reason for and the instrument of burying military reform with enthusiastic backing from the top brass.[68]

All of this is not to suggest that Russian presidents have been impotent pawns in the hands of generals. Yeltsin was willing to impose his will on the military on numerous occasions (e.g., the army's withdrawal from Eastern Europe, the inception and conclusion of the First Chechen War, let alone the drastic annual budget cuts). Putin has been more careful in antagonizing the armed forces, but he, too, has made decisions that did not please the army elite. For instance, he ordered reluctant generals to cooperate with the United States over Afghanistan, stifled their opposition to the U.S.'s use of Central Asian military bases on Russia's periphery, and postponed promised defense-sector salary increases when budgetary restrictions so required.

Russian presidents also know that there is no consensus on defense reform even among the elites supportive of the state's agenda. Therefore, a resolute executive campaign for a drastic makeover of the military establishment might not make for good politics. There are three additional points connected to the presidency that go a long way toward explaining the absence of serious defense reform. First, an underlying reason for the military's successful opposition of defense reform is that Russian presidents have not been able to curb the armed forces' organizational independence, the magnitude of which is unparalleled in democracies.[69] Primarily owing to the fact that in Russian and Soviet society only military officers were able to acquire specialized expertise relating to defense and security issues, members of the officer corps have been able to portray themselves as the monopolists of such know-how for ages. This tradition has changed little in the post-Soviet era, what with the limitations on the media, the intimidation and persecution of those researching "sensitive issues," and the continued aversion to opening up the institution itself to civilians and to public inspection. As a result, throughout the last three centuries the military has attained a high level of administrative and operational autonomy that makes it difficult for the state to impose on it unpopular policies, such as defense reform. Given the Russian polity's authoritarian direction and "superpresidential" executive, only the head of state could significantly weaken the military's institutional independence, but neither Yeltsin nor Putin have done so.

Second, there is a long-standing deference to the military in Russian culture that dates from before the Soviet period, at least as far back as the reign of Peter the Great (1705–25).[70] For much of Russia's history since then, the armed forces have been a highly respected institution that successfully protected the state and the nation repeatedly, most recently in World War II. Even if the army's prestige has been considerably tarnished in the last decade and a half, the traditional reverence to the institution, if not necessarily to its current leaders, is still evident and to some extent it prevents outsiders from interfering with it. In general, both Russian presidents have behaved deferentially toward the military. This is especially true for Putin. Recall, for example, his reluctance to punish those responsible for the *Kursk* disaster (he took a year to fire them). In that case he began what turned into a long-standing pattern: disinclination to hold high-ranking military officers accountable followed by cushioning the blow, as it were, by giving them plum jobs in the federal bureaucracy to ensure their soft landing. Putin frequently pays homage to the armed forces, their history, their role in the country's successes, and wants to enhance the age-old societal reverence toward them.[71] Although part of the explanation for the presidents' publicly demonstrated admiration for the armed services might be to counteract young Russians' increasingly lackadaisical view of things military, the result is that in a deep sense the army remains the "sacred cow" of state institutions in the mind of many, especially older, citizens.

Third, an obvious though often overlooked point, is that there are many pressing matters confronting Putin and the Russian government; reforming the armed forces is just one of them. Considering the magnitude of the numerous other challenges Russia faces—a multitude of social ills, economic problems, to say nothing of domestic and international political issues—the delays in the transformation of the military establishment are easier to understand.

In sum, the argument is not that the president and political elites in general could not succeed in getting the army to execute state policy abhorrent to them: this has been done many times before. Rather, the point is that *combined with* other priorities—the dearth of sufficient resources, the imperatives of the Second Chechnya War, the military support base for the president, and traditional deference toward the armed forces—defense reform faces a daunting set of obstacles and loses its urgency and privileged spot among the other items on the state's to-do list. The single most important source hindering military reform, however, is the army's own opposition to it.

The Military Opposition to Defense Reform

The 1996 Defense Law (Article 13, Section 2) granted the Ministry of Defense and the General Staff fundamentally equal status that virtually ensured that they would compete for decision-making authority. In June 2004, however, in response to the protracted conflict between the two institutions, the Duma modified the Defense Law and formally established the defense minister and the ministry's superiority over the General Staff and its chief. The amended version of the Defense Law entrusts the Ministry of Defense with the administrative and operational command and control of the armed forces. Although the law omits all references to the role of the General Staff, it may become a research institute or think tank, the "brains of the army," charged with preparing threat-assessments and doctrinal documents for the ministry to review. This was potentially the most important defense-related legislation in the past several years, and it codified the General Staff's worst-case scenario. "Potentially," because laws passed by a mostly rubber-stamp legislature can mean very little in Russia, they can be open for varying interpretations or rewritten as changing circumstances demand. In any case, it is difficult to envision the General Staff's loss of command and control functions at the stroke of a pen before an alternative structure is put in place.[72] The fact that until this point the General Staff and its chief were not formally subordinated to the minister and his ministry was a major shortcoming in the legislation that allowed a decade-long destructive feud between the two institutions and their leaders.

The protracted conflict between the two bodies has been one of the main reasons for the poor prospects of substantive military reform. The armed forces are far from homogeneous: the most important chasm is between the Defense Ministry bureaucracy and the General Staff. This intrainstitutional dichotomy is best explained by the traditional notion that ministry personnel primarily serve political interests whereas those in the General Staff are the guardians of the military's own prerogatives. But there are other notable cleavages within the officer corps, based on assignment, location, branch/service, age, and rank. Conservative officers have managed to dominate both entities largely because they have succeeded in purging the military leadership of independent thinkers. Since the mid 1980s they have developed the skills necessary to successfully probe the Kremlin's limits of tolerance and oppose or foil state policy with impunity. On the other hand, the government has been often willing to cut the generals some slack in order to retain their support, especially if the issue at hand was not weighty enough to warrant an all-out conflict with them.

One of the fundamental differences between the ministry and the General Staff has to do with Russia's military doctrine. This discord was muted under the ministerships of Grachev (May 1992–July 1996) and Rodionov (July 1996–May 1997), because they saw eye to eye with the General Staff. Also, Yeltsin allowed generals to adopt a military doctrine in November 1993 largely of their own design partly as a reward for rescuing him a month earlier, even though it sharply contradicted his personal blueprint.[73] (This document, in effect, gave a retroactive approval for military intervention in domestic political disputes.)[74] A serious rift developed, however, between Defense Minister Sergeev (May 1997–March 2001) and Chief of the General Staff Kvashnin (May 1997–July 2004), which was rooted in their disagreement over spending priorities and, more broadly, over Russia's defense doctrine and future military stature. Sergeev, a loyal Yeltsin appointee, wanted to concentrate defense outlays on the strategic nuclear forces (not incidentally, his own branch of service). Kvashnin, on the other hand, had long advocated boosting investment in conventional weapons and maintained that, in order to protect its interests, Russia needed a large army capable of waging war anywhere in the world. Eventually, Putin came down on Kvashnin's side in this often public feud. He strengthened Kvashnin's position in August 2000 when he fired six senior commanders, all ardent Sergeev supporters, and—a few months later—replaced their patron himself.[75]

By naming Sergei Ivanov as the new defense minister in March 2001, Putin signaled the elevation of the ministry over the General Staff. Ivanov distinguished himself in his previous job as secretary of the Security Council: he acquired a great deal more authority than Andrei Kokoshin, his most prominent predecessor in the job, and he raised the profile of his position by giving frequent interviews.[76] Nonetheless, his new appointment did not suggest a move toward more robust civilian control of the armed forces nor did it portend a radical transformation of the military. The main reason is that Ivanov initially did not receive a mandate from the president beyond overseeing the implementation of the defense budget and increasing the ministry's foreign contacts and international exposure (e.g., via the planning of joint exercises with important partners like China).[77] Moreover, Ivanov has been unable to gain the generals' confidence even though, as has been widely noted, in most critical situations he tackled he took the generals' side rather than Putin's.[78] In 2003, for example, he announced that changing Russia's defense priorities was premature and no radical military reform was necessary presumably because, as he also noted, it has "largely been completed."[79] Although he arguably has one of the most thankless jobs in Russian government and has had some successes in managing the ministry's finances, Ivanov has failed to alleviate, much less solve, a number of major problems such as the pervasive hazing of recruits, the widespread corruption in the officer corps, and the need for a coherent doctrine and development program.

Even after Ivanov's appointment, some disputes between the ministry and the General Staff had remained, although they became more polite. First, Kvashnin and the generals recognized the close relationship between Putin and Ivanov and were mindful of the risks of antagonizing Ivanov. Second, the new defense minister had come around to support many of the General Staff's views regarding doctrine and military reform. For instance, as Security Council secretary, Ivanov approved a cut of 480,000 in the armed forces' manpower in 2000 but three years later, as defense minister, he stated that force reduction was completed even though virtually no personnel cuts had been implemented.[80] Third, unlike Sergeev, Ivanov has not played favorites among the branches, perhaps because he does not have special professional ties to them, having never served in the military.

Nonetheless, Ivanov did not fully succeed in either consolidating his power over the armed forces or lessening Kvashnin's influence prior to his dismissal. The differences between the two mostly centered on resource allocation, restructuring, and especially on the tempo of defense reform (the defense minister wanted to expedite action, which was against the interests of the top brass).[81] Putin had remained on the sidelines of these quarrels but, by the summer of 2004, he apparently had had enough of Kvashnin's persistent defiance that not only impeded the reforms but also fueled the tension between the Ministry of Defense and the General Staff. The June 21–22, 2004, insurgent attack in Ingushetia which resulted in 97 dead and 105 wounded soldiers and civilians, along with Kvashnin's sharp public criticisms of the 2005 preliminary defense budgets, served as convenient reasons for Putin to fire him in mid July.[82] Kvashnin's departure could not but improve relations between the General Staff and the Defense Ministry. His successor, his former first deputy, Yuri Baluyevskii, is a pragmatic general who is expected to follow presidential and ministerial directives.

As we have seen, since 1991 army leaders have often actively contested state policy. The generals have traditionally viewed foreign affairs as a policy area in which voicing the military's institutional interests was their prerogative—as Stepan and Colton suggested—and, emboldened by the changes in civil-military relations that started under Gorbachev, have publicly countered a wide array of expected and actual government policies. The institutional decay that then began allowed these negative trends to develop between the armed forces and their putative civilian masters. More specifically, Russian generals have been able to get away with consistently opposing the strengthening strategic relations with the United States and NATO and, in general, abandoning the bridgeheads developed or acquired during the Cold War. No issue has raised their ire more than military reform because it goes against their vital material and political interests.

Quite simply, in contemporary Russia defense reform means, almost by definition, the conversion of the conscript-based military to a contract-based force of volunteer soldiers. Retaining the draft, however, is in the direct interest of the top brass for several reasons. First, generals maintain that only a large standing army is capable of effectively countering Russia's strategic challenges and only a draft-based army will allow them to call up millions of reservists if need be. The old Soviet-type strategic thinking is so deeply ingrained in current military elites that they seem incapable of developing new tactical and operational concepts demanded by the new security environment or to appreciate the changed realities underscoring the perceptions of the civilian leadership. As a recent meeting of the top brass made clear, the generals oppose further size reductions because they still maintain that Russia needs an army to defend the motherland in a potential war against the United States or NATO.[83] Since, they insist, Russia cannot afford a large *professional* army, it follows that conscription must not only be continued but ought to be expanded (especially in view of dire demographic prospects) by eliminating many of the current deferral options.

Second, high- and middle-ranking officers materially benefit from using the conscripts as a cheap workforce to build their homes or to barter their labor for cash, food, coal, or supplies with local politicians and businessmen. Third, there is little accountability over the treatment of draftees who have few avenues to protect their interests. Volunteers are harder to bully around, they feel less at the mercy of their commanders, and are more willing to pursue their rights to seek redress to their injuries. For these reasons, the General Staff has consistently supported keeping the two-year conscription term, the expansion of the draft-base by the cancellation of most deferrals, and efforts to make alternative service as difficult as possible. Finally, the generals well realize that a volunteer army would necessarily be smaller and would ultimately lead to the trimming of the bloated officer corps.

The military leadership has publicly opposed even the limited reforms recently approved by Putin. In July 2003 First Deputy Chief of the General Staff Baluyevskii, who succeeded Kvashnin a year later, revealed the General Staff's official recommendation that defense reform be halted. Not unexpectedly, Baluyevskii and his generals applauded the presidential announcement marking the "conclusion of radical military reform."[84] They must have been equally pleased with repeated declarations by Putin and Ivanov that "it would be impossible for Russia to switch to an all-volunteer military force," that the draft would be expanded, and that "we are destined to have a strong army . . . in the range of 1.134 million."[85] As Golts noted, senior military officers will not accept defense reform unless it is forced on them.[86] But Russia's presidents have been unwilling to do that and are unlikely to change in this regard in the foreseeable future.

CONCLUSION

In this chapter I depicted one of the key consequences of the institutional decay of Russian civil-military relations. The protracted negative changes in formal and informal institutions helped create an environment in which the armed forces leadership could successfully resist adopting and implementing a comprehensive reform program. Yeltsin's consent to the type of polity that was taking shape after 1991 and Putin's confirmation of the military's political role practically encouraged and legitimized the top brass' opposition to defense reform. If we use Colton's work to gauge the Russian military's political role, it is easy to see that the generals forcefully present their official prerogatives, provide expert advice, and do not shy away from political bargaining when their interests so require.[87] Nonetheless, they certainly do not exert influence in issue areas not involving the army's primary concerns. In other words, if we rate Russia's army by the criteria proposed by Colton (and Stepan), we get a picture that accurately reflects reality. Russia is an authoritarian state and its armed forces enjoy political influence commensurate with that designation. Their political clout is a good deal less than militaries hold in dictatorships but a lot more than they possess in democracies. The strengths of these two studies are that they help us place the military's political influence on a hypothetical scale of political interference.

In order to successfully engage the security challenges of the twenty-first century, Russia needs compact, mobile, highly trained, and well-equipped units that can quickly react to the small-scale "soft" security threats it should anticipate in the foreseeable future. The armed forces need to be professionalized and their manpower reduced to no more than 800,000 and, according to some experts, once their equipment and training permit, even further. Military education on all levels should be revised to take account of the recent revolution in the technology of warfare and the massive changes in the strategic environment; this restructured education should encourage individual initiative, independent thinking, and personal accountability, and develop a rigorously prepared corps of professional NCOs. The majority of Russians—if opinion polls can be trusted—would support this kind of military reform.

Although some reforms *have* been put into place, the sweeping changes needed have not been implemented and the decline of Russia's armed forces has not been reversed, the Kremlin's proclamations notwithstanding. To be sure, one partial explanation might be that—unlike in Central and Eastern Europe where the prospect of NATO membership was a powerful incentive for the governments to undertake meaningful defense reform—no such external pressure has really been applied to Russia. For a number of entirely logical reasons, moreover, it is highly likely that radical defense reform will not take place in the foreseeable future either. The top brass has fought meaningful reforms tooth and nail because such reforms are synonymous with their further loss of prestige and privileges. Not surprisingly, Russian generals have used their political clout to protect and further their corporate interests.

"Successful reform," Larry Diamond writes, "requires a long-term policy vision, driven by political leadership."[88] In contemporary Russia there is no such long-term vision let alone the kind of leadership that would see through a difficult reform process. The state is unwilling to accept the financial sacrifice real military reform entails, is confronted with many other more pressing issues, and is reluctant to antagonize a military leadership that is loath to lose its large army. If public dissatisfaction with the Kremlin's unpopular policies—such as the ill-prepared pension reform in winter 2004–5—does gain expression in widespread demonstrations and the like, it is likely that Putin and his regime would be even more dependent on the support of the military-security establishment in the future. Defense reform will also not succeed until military and political elites clearly and publicly recognize that the main threat to Russia's security does not come from the United States or NATO. This, too, is unlikely to happen in the near future because the generals have a basic interest in maintaining the myth of that threat.

In sum, the prospects of real military reform in contemporary Russia discourage hope that the country will soon field a modern and effective army. Likewise, there are no signs that would indicate that civil-military relations will soon be put on a democratic footing in the country. More generally, this analysis is in line with the disappointing record of Russia's democratization experience. The institution most responsible for this outcome is the presidency, the focus of the next chapter.

((((

CHAPTER 5

Civil-Military Relations and Superpresidentialism

The word "democratization" is a slogan behind which
either there is nothing or there are dangerous
consequences. The attempt to democratize according to
Western values is utterly naive or a conscious provocation.
—Sergei Ivanov, interview, July 2005

The September–October 1993 crisis between the legislature and
President Boris Yeltsin profoundly affected Russia's political development. From this point on Moscow's political trajectory has been
characterized by increasing centralization, the growth of executive power
with the corresponding decline in the legislature's influence, and the
steady erosion of rights and freedoms. Although experts at times refer to
contemporary Russia as a "managed," "façade," or "quasi" democracy,
these labels only serve to avoid calling it what it has become: an authoritarian state.

In chapters 3 and 4 the focus was on the armed forces' side of the civil-
military relations equation as I explained the generals' political presence
and opposition to radical defense reform. In this chapter the analysis of
military politics continues but the spotlight shifts to two crucial civilian
institutions, the presidency and the legislature. A short time after the collapse of the Soviet Union the presidency had emerged as the pivotal political institution in Russia with the incumbent acquiring "superpresidential"
powers. For the most part, Yeltsin obtained this power at the expense of
the legislature, the elected representatives of the Russian people. What
powers does the president currently enjoy vis-à-vis the legislature in terms

of the armed forces' civilian oversight? To what extent has the Duma been successful in asserting its prerogatives regarding the military and its budget? One of the tasks of this chapter is to find answers to queries such as these.

Another objective is to briefly examine a group of noncivilian or para-military institutions, or perhaps it would be better to define them as the militarized contingents of civilian bodies. I am referring to the "power ministries" (other than the Defense Ministry) and their hundreds of thou-sands of troops in uniform—sometimes inelegantly called the "multiple militaries"—that have played important political and security roles in the past decade and a half. These institutions had become politically signifi-cant under Yeltsin who used them as counterweights to the regular armed forces. Once Vladimir Putin took office, power ministry personnel, the *siloviki*, emerged as his most important support base. I will consider their political influence, especially in view of the regular armed forces' role.

This chapter is divided into four sections. First, I assess President Yelt-sin's policies toward the military. Then I explain the changing character of the Security Council and the power ministries in contemporary Russian politics. In the third part my emphasis shifts to the legislature and its declining influence in Russian politics, especially regarding its significance as an overseer of the armed forces. Finally, I will discuss President Putin's relationship to the generals.

YELTSIN AND THE ARMED FORCES

Although the coup attempt of August 1991 actually took place a few months prior to the collapse of the USSR, it seriously affected the develop-ment of Russian civil-military relations.[1] The coup was conceived and supported by a group of politicians opposed to democratization and com-mitted to the preservation of the Soviet Union. The plotters—whose ranks included a number of top politicians such as Soviet defense minister Dmi-tri Yazov—were unable to impose their will on the commanders of Mos-cow-area military detachments who carried the day by convincing their subordinates of the coup's folly. The army's decision not to support the overthrow of Russian President Boris Yeltsin effectively prevented a suc-cessful coup.

The military's part in the political upheaval underscored the dilution of civilian control over the armed forces that had begun under Mikhail

Gorbachev. Right after the coup attempt, Yeltsin issued a decree that abolished Communist Party organizations in the armed forces, the KGB, and the Ministry of Internal Affairs. A crucial defect of Russian civil-military relations is that the vacuum created by the elimination of party-based control has not been filled with an institutionally balanced system of civilian supervision. Instead, in the first couple of years after the USSR's collapse the president, the legislature, and a variety of political forces repeatedly attempted to recruit the military to do their bidding. For much of the first post-Soviet decade, Russian politics had been marked by an ongoing power struggle between the president and the legislature, and the outcome of this confrontation had been the gradual evolution of dramatically increased presidential powers, in effect, a form of "superpresidentialism."[2]

In a study published in 2000 Steven Fish wrote that the concept of superpresidentialism (or superexecutivism) denotes a form of democratic but, more frequently, a type of semidemocratic, regime.[3] It is different from autocracy to the extent that regular and reasonably free elections are held. Superpresidentialism suggests an anti-institutional bias given that an extremely powerful president has no incentive to promote the building of institutions that could potentially challenge him later. In polities where power is dispersed among political institutions, politicians are often guided by an institution-building imperative.[4] In contrast with moderate presidential and semipresidential systems, Fish goes on, superpresidentialism is characterized by

> a huge apparatus of executive power that overshadows other state agencies and the national legislature in terms of its size and the resources it uses; a president who controls most or all of the levers of public expenditure; a president who enjoys the power to make laws by decree; rules that make impeaching the president exceedingly difficult or impossible; a legislature that enjoys little real oversight authority over the executive branch; and a judiciary that is appointed and controlled largely by the president and that cannot in practice check presidential prerogatives or even abuse of power.[5]

Since these words were written, Russia's polity has become far more authoritarian, but viewing it as a superpresidential system remains useful still.

The concept of path dependence also helps to explain the particular evolution of the Russian political system. Timothy Colton and Cindy Skach showed that successive constitutional decisions political elites took in the late Soviet period and at the birth of the new Russia—such as the ambiguously differentiated roles between the legislative and executive branches and the vague power relations in the triangle of the government apparatus, the Supreme Soviet, and the president that, in effect, led to the 1993 crisis—put its political development on a path that was difficult to escape.[6]

Notwithstanding his extensive powers, Yeltsin repeatedly broke the law and trespassed on the legislature's prerogatives. For instance, the September 1992 Defense Law required the president to obtain parliamentary consent for top military appointments, but Yeltsin did not abide by this rule. Though amended hundreds of times between 1991 and 1993, the Constitution was nonetheless clear in denying the president the right to dissolve parliament, yet that is precisely what Yeltsin did on 21 September 1993. The new, December 1993, Constitution—one of the practical outcomes of the president's victory over the Supreme Soviet two months earlier—reflected the emerging power configuration. It shifted responsibilities over the armed forces once possessed by parliament to the executive and endowed him with near-dictatorial powers. A January 1994 presidential decree subordinated all "force organs" to the president. In spite of his enlarged authority, Yeltsin broke the law once again in December 1994 when he ordered Russian troops to invade Chechnya. He violated Articles 8 and 88 of the Constitution by informing neither the Duma nor the Federation Council (the legislature's lower and upper house, respectively) prior to taking action. To make matters worse, in August 1995, the Constitutional Court created a troubling precedent by refusing to rule against the president, concluding that the use of armed forces in Chechnya was legal.

Yeltsin equated civilian oversight of the armed forces with presidential control. He repeatedly courted the army leadership at times critical to his own political fortunes and failed to deliver on his promises once the military agreed to back him. Just before his final showdown with Gorbachev in December 1991, Yeltsin announced a 90 percent pay raise to all military personnel, proving once again that he was far more astute in enrolling the generals' backing than his rival. Until his October 1993 clash with the legislature, the president was relatively effective in gaining the armed forces' support with assurances of pay increases, the disbursement of overdue salaries and benefits, and increased military prerogatives in defense reform. In the meantime, as Pavel Baev argued, the army succeeded in "forging a new identity as a presidential institution, answerable only to the Commander-in-Chief and relying on his special attention."[7]

Just prior to the September–October 1993 events, the president transferred extensive bonuses to selected units and, after a reluctant military came to his rescue, rewarded loyal generals with medals, promotions, and a 40 percent salary increase to all armed forces personnel. On the eve of the 1996 presidential elections, Yeltsin once again found it expedient to placate the army leadership by ordering payment of overdue wages, increasing salaries, and promoting all five senior commanders to the rank of army general. In mid 1997—around the time Duma Defense Committee chairman Lev Rokhlin started to organize his All-Russia Movement to Support the Army, which openly called for the president's legal removal— Yeltsin once again began to entice military personnel with promises of quick financial relief and other perquisites.

A more important method Yeltsin employed to reward and appease the top brass was to permit them to make decisions directly affecting national security without extra-institutional interference. In other words, he bought whatever military support he did enjoy by promising not to interfere. Needless to say, such a pledge is a virtual death sentence to any future military reform. Perhaps the best example of this aspect of his rule was when he allowed the army leadership to draft Russia's military doctrine as a reward for coming to his rescue in the fall of 1993.[8] More generally, Yeltsin consented to the military elite's making numerous important decisions about the prospective defense reform and its implementation, insisting only on the expeditious withdrawal of forces from abroad and drastic cuts in the army's manpower. He was careful, however, not to press for the downsizing of the military's central administration that, as a result, had become even more bloated vis-à-vis the rest of the armed forces.

Yeltsin appears not to have fully recognized the magnitude of the army's problems—and thus the need for substantive defense reform— until its disastrous performance in the First Chechen War. According to former prime minister Yevgenii Primakov, in 1995 the president even contemplated resigning because of the fiasco in Chechnya.[9] His overall approach to defense reform, not unlike other policy areas, was disorganized and erratic, driven by momentary political expediencies rather than some thoughtful assessment of the country's long-term defense needs. For instance, without serious consultation with the top brass, he decided in 1992 to reduce the length of compulsory military service from twenty-four months to eighteen months. This decision had to be reversed in 1995 owing to manpower shortages. Another example was his promise—announced with much fanfare during the 1996 presidential campaign—to end conscription by 2000. It is hard to imagine another pledge that would have been more popular. Still, a decade later the end of the draft is a fanciful dream; in fact, it is being expanded.

Yeltsin's preferred way of dealing with defense reform was to establish, with much publicity, committee after committee to study a particular issue and then, apparently, forget about the problem. Ordinarily, these groups were comprised of top politicians to demonstrate the supposedly high priority of the matter on the presidential agenda to an electorate that had become increasingly cynical about the corruption-ridden armed forces. Prime ministers Sergei Kirienko and Viktor Chernomyrdin and First Deputy Prime Minister Anatolii Chubais all headed commissions on defense reform. In a short time, however, most of these governmental and presidential committees had faded away without accomplishing anything tangible. Events also seem to have conspired against Yeltsin. In 1997 he did approve a package of defense reform ideas one of the committees presented him with but the state's financial meltdown the following year prevented its implementation.[10] In this instance, at least, the economic collapse provided a convenient excuse for the protracted absence of serious reform. But another, equally significant factor that would have also precluded its completion was the military's opposition to it. Yeltsin failed to consult the very institution he intended to transform prior to issuing the decree in July 1997 on military reform. On hearing of the decree, Defense Minister Sergeev immediately warned him that the generals would be sure to sabotage his reform efforts.[11]

The political and economic turmoil in 1998 presented another major challenge to Russian democratization and economic transition processes. Yeltsin's attitude toward the army did not change, however. In August 1998 he announced that he would take direct control over military policy in order to ensure that officers and soldiers were paid.[12] Throughout the crisis the president met on several occasions with Sergeev who assured him of the armed forces' loyalty. By the end of his tenure political upheavals, sharp decline in popular and elite support, and poor health had weakened the president. Sergeev—one of Yeltsin's few superior choices in personnel—was duly rewarded for his allegiance with a promotion to the rank of marshal in November 1997. Incidentally, this action displayed the president's unpredictable decision-making yet again, given that he declared earlier that no one would receive that rank in peacetime.

Yeltsin's impulsive dismissal of several prime ministers, starting with the firing of Chernomyrdin in 1998, actually had a positive overall effect on the armed forces. The reason is that no Russian government had paid less attention to the military than Chernomyrdin's. Not surprisingly, the top brass endorsed all prime ministers who succeeded him. In turn, Kirienko, Primakov, Sergei Stepashin, and Vladimir Putin (prime minister, August–December 1999; acting president, January–May 2000; president, May 2000–) continued to confirm Sergeev in his post. During his short tenure Primakov took charge of financial levels and vowed that the army would not have to go for months without pay in the future. After a career spent entirely in the internal police and security apparatus, Stepashin elevated national security on his cabinet's list of priorities, especially owing to NATO's 1999 spring war against Yugoslavia, which reawakened the concerns of Russia's political elites about national defense and their interest in pan-Slavism.[13] In June 1999, Yeltsin was eager to share the political rewards of the surprise deployment of Russian troops in Kosovo, particularly after several weeks of humiliation at the hands of NATO leaders who had ignored his appeals to call off air strikes against Serbia, one of Russia's historic allies.

The myriad of organizational shifts during his reign betrayed not only Yeltsin's informal "checks and balances" scheme but also his confused and unpredictable approach to military-security affairs. In order to strengthen his own, highly personalistic control over the military, he relied on casual exchanges and networks and thwarted the evolution of structured, balanced, and stable mechanism of civilian oversight. Yeltsin concentrated decision-making on these issues in his personal staff and, more broadly, in the presidential administration. He subordinated to himself a number of security organizations to offset the influence of the armed forces and encouraged rivalry between the Ministry of Defense and the "power bloc." The key objective of civil-military relations under Yeltsin was the safeguarding of the president's personal power.[14] Ultimately, his permissive attitude toward the military—that is, the second formative moment—fostered its further institutional decay and impeded the chances of substantive defense reform.

PRESIDENTIAL COUNTERWEIGHTS: COUNCILS, COMMITTEES, AND THE POWER MINISTRIES

In the 1990s, civilian control over the Russian armed forces had developed as a loose arrangement of checks and balances created by Yeltsin, who—when his interests so required—played off individuals and institutions against each other. The president set up and/or leaned on several institutions to aid him in controlling the armed forces. Some of these, most importantly the Security Council, have endured and have become loci of power under Putin, while some have faded into irrelevance and others—such as the Defense Council and the Ministry for Defense Industries—were abolished as suddenly as Yeltsin launched them, highlighting his erratic leadership style and the specific political contingencies that justified their formation in the first place.

The Security Council and Other Organizations

The Security Council (SC) was originally established by Gorbachev. Its members—the relevant power ministers (defense, foreign affairs, and interior among others) and other high ranking defense/security officials—are appointed by the president who not only chairs the council but also selects its secretary. Under the Constitution the SC was supposed to resolve strategic tasks, devise military policy and doctrine, and consider outstanding issues with the former Soviet republics. A short time after coming to power, however, Yeltsin had decided to transform the SC into a sort of presidential consultative-advisory body. Consequently, a 1992 executive decree established it as an administrative organ that coordinated the work of power ministries and monitored the implementation of the executive branch's decisions on security issues.[15] Until the First Chechen War, as one staffer observed, the military's predicament was issue "number ten of ten" on the Security Council's agenda.[16] Since 1994 it has enjoyed a significant but shadowy role in deciding defense, foreign, and security policy, though bureaucratic infighting has often reduced its effectiveness. First and foremost, the council has been a loyal presidential institution supporting the executive's positions—no matter how ill-conceived they may have been—vis-à-vis the legislature over defense and security issues. For example, at its 27 November 1994, session the Security Council voted unanimously to invade Chechnya even before discussing the issue.[17]

The most influential Security Council secretary under Yeltsin was Andrei Kokoshin who in his six-month long tenure in 1998 turned it into a well-organized body capable of dealing with a large number of defense issues. Kokoshin had an eventful career in the military-security realm. His job titles included first deputy defense minister, secretary of the Defense Council, and head of the State Military Inspectorate. Nevertheless, he fell victim to political machinations, the generals' hostility, and to poor political choices—at least poor choices in Yeltsin's eyes—that derailed his career. The latter included working with the Duma on a number of issues and backing the president's archenemy, Moscow mayor Yuri Luzhkov, for the prime ministership in 1998. Yeltsin, who was not known to forgive acts of personal disloyalty, could not stomach either of these blunders.[18]

During the first fifteen months of Putin's presidency there were indications that the Security Council might become an important policy-initiating and policy-debating forum devising new approaches and concepts. In late summer 2000, just before the *Kursk* accident, the council prepared a report on defense reform that called for the reduction in the size of the regular armed forces (by 350,000) and in the various other power ministries (by 250,000) and, more generally, deep cuts in all branches of the armed forces.[19] Hopes that the Security Council might emerge as an engine of defense reform were soon dashed, however. The report had the unintended consequence of uniting defense and security chiefs on the Security Council and beyond—for the first time during Putin's presidency—in their unyielding resistance to real, substantive defense reform. At the 27 September 2000 council meeting major proposals about defense restructuring were shelved owing to the generals' opposition.[20]

At the beginning of Putin's tenure, the Security Council had quickly become the institutional bailiwick of the entrenched security-defense elite, Putin's primary support base. The eminent sociologist, Olga Kryshtanovskaya, likened the influence of the Security Council, where over half the members were uniformed officers, to that of the Communist-era Politburo.[21] The fact that in the first year of Putin's presidency it had gained unprecedented political clout was largely because in Sergei Ivanov—who was appointed as the council's secretary in November 1999—Putin found someone with apparent dynamism and unquestioned personal loyalty, a person "he felt a kinship with and trusted the most."[22]

Once Ivanov left the Security Council to head the Defense Ministry, the overall political influence of the former had diminished. It is not engaged in formulating the national security strategy despite the fact that this is supposed to be its main prerogative.[23] It appears that under its current secretary, Igor Ivanov, studying national security issues has been the Security Council's chief activity. In May 2006 Putin instructed Igor Ivanov to prepare hearings on the three key issues the government considers as the most important threats to the country: the "threat of possible technological breakdowns"; the threat posed by the "unfavorable demographic developments"; and the "threat in the sphere of national security, defense issues primarily."[24] In any event, the Security Council has become neither

the locus of civilian oversight nor an institutional sponsor of defense reform for the perfectly commonsensical reason that many of its members
are directly threatened by those very same prospects. Still, given the com-
position of its membership, the Security Council should have been a logical institutional choice to coordinate the diverse forces in both wars in
Chechnya but, in fact, it had failed to do so.

Yeltsin established the Defense Council (DC) in July 1996 to serve as a
counterweight to retired General Aleksandr Lebed whom he appointed
Security Council secretary the month before. Fundamentally, the DC was
a powerless intradepartmental consultative body. It was entirely up to the
president to adopt the DC's recommendations by issuing decrees that
were to be implemented by the relevant ministries.[25] Yeltsin had no further
use for the DC after Lebed's forced resignation (in October 1996), and
he unceremoniously abolished it in March 1998 and incorporated its personnel into the already burgeoning Security Council bureaucracy.

Although, strictly speaking, the Ministry for Defense Industries was
not a presidential institution, in practice Yeltsin created it for short-term
political reasons in 1996 and disbanded it a year later. As a result of the
relentless pressure and lobbying of the military-industrial complex, he
agreed to form a ministry that expanded the defense industries' access to
the state, eased the licensing of arms exports, and allowed more effective
lobbying for military contracts. Yeltsin's key response to the military's
unfolding crisis was the forming of "extra-legal and extra-constitutional
commissions to usurp existing state functions of the Defense Ministry."[26]
In May 1997 he organized two new commissions on military affairs, although in retrospect this seems to have been a mere public relations ploy
to satisfy certain constituencies rather than a substantive policy decision.
In February 1998, Prime Minister Chernomyrdin appointed Chubais to
chair a new commission to hasten the financial recovery of the defense
industry. There have been separate commissions for military construction,
finance, and reform, but in practice they have done little. They were created, usually with much publicity, only to be forgotten some months later.

The Power Ministries

The underlying reason for President Yeltsin's strong support of the power
ministries was his disappointment with the reluctant backing he got from
the Defense Ministry in October 1993 and, consequently, the need to cultivate more dedicated instruments of power. He succeeded in removing

the paramilitary units of the power ministries from parliamentary supervision and bringing them under presidential control. These uniformed bodies are made up of the dozen or so organizations spawned by the KGB, the Ministry of Internal Affairs (MVD), and other Soviet-era armed formations. Aside from MVD troops they include the units of the Border Guards, the Presidential Guards, the Federal Security Service (FSB), the Foreign Intelligence Service, the Prosecutor-General's Office, the Federal Agency for Government Communications and Information, and a few other organizations. In 1996, the combined manpower of these forces exceeded 2 million men.[27] Their numbers decreased little in the past decade: in 2005 the MVD alone employed 1.4 million uniformed personnel.

In order to build an effectual counterweight to the regular armed forces, Yeltsin selected the commanders of the paramilitary forces based on their personal fealty to him and rewarded them according to the Kremlin's perception of their usefulness. He had followed the political maxim, *divide et impera*, with remarkable skill as manifested by the growing enmity between the Russian Army and the paramilitary formations. The president created a system under which the various branches of the regular armed forces (army, air force, navy, strategic rocket forces) had to compete for resources and conscripts not only with each other but also with the "multiple militaries." During Yeltsin's tenure the power ministries had tended to dominate this rivalry: they were dramatically strengthened in terms of personnel and equipment.[28] For instance, in 1994 the army received five helicopters in contrast to the fifty obtained by the MVD troops.[29] Naval units fighting in the First Chechen War were outfitted with obsolete gear and weaponry, such as thirty-pound bulletproof vests and combat helmets manufactured during World War II, while MVD troops received the latest equipment.[30] The Border Guards—along with MVD units—were especially pampered with resources in large part because of the effective lobbying of their first post-Soviet chief, General Andrei Nikolaev.

Generally speaking, the *siloviki*, who comprised one of the most privileged social strata in the Soviet era, had the most to lose by democratization. It was not surprising, then, that they were eager to be enticed by Yeltsin and his successor. The numerous paramilitary forces pose a special threat to Russian democratization because the only real civilian control over them has been exercised by the president, not the government, and because their use in domestic scenarios has not been clearly regulated. Their leaders are easily dispensable as was shown by the example of the Ministry of Security chief Viktor Barannikov, a presidential appointee, who was promptly replaced by a more compliant colleague when he refused to break the law for Yeltsin in 1993.[31] The ease with which units of the power ministries may be deployed in domestic contingencies was shown in the fall of 1994 when Presidential Guards raided the offices of MOST Bank and when the head of the Federal Security Service extended his authority over arms exports and technology transfers.[32] During the 1998 crisis, Yeltsin once again turned to the power ministries by instructing Interior Minister Sergei Stepashin to put MVD (Ministry of Interior) units on alert around Moscow. In the end, the political resolution of the crisis did not require their deployment.

One of the public justifications of building up the power ministries' troops was to allow them to make substantial contributions to fighting in internal contingencies. This was especially important because, if nothing else, the embarrassing tragicomedy of errors that was the army's December 1994 assault on Grozny must have convinced even the most thick-headed politicians that the military was incapable of suppressing the insurgency in Chechnya. So, in a sense, the Kremlin was forced to take on other armed structures to do what the military could not. Many Ministry of Interior units have received specialized combat training and have served in the Northern Caucasus.[33] Armed units of the Federal Counterintelligence Service and various other power ministry formations have also been heavily involved in the fighting in Chechnya from the beginning.[34] Still, the coordination of these disparate units—as the First Chechen War had clearly exposed—had been remarkably unsuccessful, owing largely to the Security Council's incompetence. The political leadership must have recognized, given the many blunders committed by the generals, that incompetent commanders should not stay in place at all cost without being held accountable. Consequently, in the Second Chechen War operational responsibility was transferred to the FSB in 2001 and to the Ministry of Interior in 2003. Another purpose behind relieving the Defense Ministry of its command was to underscore that this was an internal matter of the Russian state.

The privileged situation of the security and paramilitary forces vis-à-vis the Russian Army is reminiscent of the preferential position of the *Securi-tate* in Nicolae Ceauşescu's Romania or of the Republican Guards in Saddam Hussein's Iraq. The various security services have proven themselves just as immune to the changes they need as the armed forces. This is hardly surprising given that they allied themselves with Yeltsin and then Putin against the legislature and in doing so effectively protected themselves from any genuine reform.[35] The corporate interest of the power ministries signifies a full-court return to authoritarianism. Their opposition to all political forces that manage to retain some autonomy is perfectly consistent with this concern. For instance, in May 2005 FSB director Nikolai Patrushev told the State Duma that NGOs—such as the Peace Corps of the United States or the British-based medical charity Merlin—were little more than front organizations for spying.[36] It may not be purely coincidental that six months later the government introduced legislation that drastically reduced the autonomy of NGOs operating in Russia.

The security services have seen a tremendous increase in their institutional stock since Putin's ascent to the presidency but for a very different reason. Yeltsin needed to cultivate them as an institutional counterweight to the regular armed forces. The rise of the *siloviki* under Putin, however, can be explained by his own background and the unusual rapidity of his rise in the political hierarchy, which precluded the possibility of methodically building up his support base. He appointed leading members of the power ministries to an astonishingly large number of important political positions. As the president has brought under his control a growing number of organizations—from media outlets to regional administrations—more and more of the *siloviki* have ended up with jobs of political consequence. Approximately 75 percent of Putin's appointees have a background in the internal security apparatus, intelligence, law enforcement, or to a lesser extent, the military, and they occupy more than one-third of the influential posts in the three top tiers of government.[37] In Mikhail Gorbachev's administration in 1988 power ministry personnel comprised 5.4 percent of government personnel and 4.8 percent of the top leadership. In Putin's Kremlin the corresponding numbers were 32.8 percent and 58.3 percent in 2002, and they have only increased since then.[38]

"Militocracy"—the term some sociologists use to depict the contemporary Russian polity—is a somewhat misleading concept, however, because there are many more bureaucrats with prior employment in the security services than in the army and the two groups differ in various ways.[39] There is no doubt that both security services personnel and members of the regular armed forces are vastly overrepresented in state administration. The most privileged institution is the FSB, the direct successor of the KGB, where the president had spent most of his career. In 2003 more than six thousand former KGB officers held senior positions in the state apparatus.[40] Many of the president's top advisors—Igor Sechin, Viktor Cherkesov, Vladislav Surkov, Viktor Ivanov, along with the Interior Minister Rashid Nurgaliev, to mention but a few—are former senior KGB officials.

On occasion, Putin has held up the high morale of the FSB—and other security services—as an example for the military to emulate.[41] As a result of administrative reforms in mid 2004 the FSB's status was made equal to that of a ministry. Putin has given access to political influence to many former security officers but not necessarily because of some diabolical scheme to transfer the state to them. Rather, he appointed a large number of *siloviki* owing to his personal conviction that these individuals were professionals, they had useful administrative and organizational skills, and they possessed the corporate values and integrity he was looking for. In sum, these people are "straight shooters" whose personal loyalty Putin could be confident of. At the same time, from the perspective of democratic development security officials are not the sort of individuals one could expect to promote transparency in politics, the accountability of public figures, or a robustly independent civil society.[42] Given Putin's authoritarian predisposition, this is hardly a reason to overlook them.

In a summer 2005 interview Defense Minister Sergei Ivanov—who, in November 2005, was named one of three deputy prime ministers and is considered a likely successor to Putin—made some revealing statements about the role of *siloviki* in the Russian state.[43] Ivanov said that he agreed with a fellow member of the State Security Committee, Viktor Cherkesov, who stated that the "Chekists" (veterans of the security forces) must take on fully the leadership in Russia. Further, Ivanov noted, he felt that he was a member of a group with a special responsibility, a group that "share[s] the analysis of the situation. In the security services one gets used to making realistic assessments and not seeing what one wants to see. There is less self-deception and one may also have a heightened sense of danger." It is not surprising, then, that Ivanov has given many of the top posts in the Ministry of Defense to former FSB comrades. In late 2004, for instance, the second most powerful person in the ministry, General Andrei Chobotov, the head of its central apparatus; General Nikolai Pankov, head of the Defense Ministry's personnel directorate; and Colonel Sergei Rybakov, the defense minister's assistant for special missions were all erstwhile colleagues in the internal security apparatus.[44]

The Legislature's Function in Civilian Control

Until 1993 Russia did have a relatively independent legislature that could have filled a significant role in the establishment of institutionally balanced civilian oversight of the military. The country's presidents, however, were interested neither in sharing their authority with parliament in general nor in jointly controlling the armed forces in particular. In the past fifteen years executive power has grown as the political influence of the legislature has diminished. The legislature's very limited role in overseeing defense-security affairs, then, is directly attributable to "superpresidentialism" and may be the greatest failure of Russian civil-military relations. In the current Duma, elected in 2003, the propresidential United Russia (UR) Party controls more than two-thirds of all seats. The rest of the deputies belong to a few smaller parties favored by the Kremlin and to some minuscule and routinely vilified opposition parties. All twenty-nine Duma committees are chaired by UR members. In short, whatever noteworthy parliamentary opposition existed was eliminated in the December 2003 elections.

The democratic institutions of the First Russian Republic (1990–93)—the Congress of People's Deputies (CPD), the presidency, and the Constitutional Court—were grafted onto the preexisting and undemocratic Soviet-era basic law through various amendments.[45] The 1,068-member CPD elected a much smaller working legislature, the Supreme Soviet that had discharged day-to-day legislative duties. Prior to the introduction of the presidency in 1991, the first chairman of the Supreme Soviet was none other than Boris Yeltsin who used his position to great effect in his battles with Gorbachev over the status of the Russian Federation. Once the presidency was established, it was superimposed onto the existing parliamentary system without the necessary constitutional changes to limit legislative power. This shortcoming, in turn, had become the source of institutional conflict between the legislature and the presidency. The problem, in a nutshell, was that Yeltsin felt that the Supreme Soviet—elected under the old communist rules—was not a democratic and representative body while the parliament suspected him of autocratic ambitions.[46] Not surprisingly, prior to the September–October 1993 crisis, the president and parliament had been locked in a political battle for authority over several major institutions, including the armed forces.

Since 1993, the power of the newly created Duma to oversee military affairs has been greatly reduced. The 1993 Constitution removed controls over the armed forces once possessed by parliament. For instance, the legislature lost its authority to appoint top military leaders. Duma members did have the opportunity to use whatever limited power they still enjoyed to control the budget, especially in 1993–96, the period between the new Constitution and the 1996 Law on Defense. Instead, legislators—most of whom have little knowledge of or interest in the details and technicalities of defense matters—chose not to engage concrete problems or priorities and appeared to agree with the military in their aim to avoid pushing even the most-needed defense reforms.[47] An important, though often overlooked, reason for this is that regulations require parliamentary deputies who serve on the Defense Committee to sign a Secrecy Act. Their signature essentially confirms that they recognize that they will view classified materials and understand that they can only travel abroad with special permission. This, in turn, virtually guarantees that the committee would be staffed with retired military officers because few Duma members want to serve under such restrictions, particularly when they are seldom keen on dealing with military affairs—and potentially intimidating generals—in any case. The Duma, as a whole, therefore, is neither "cleared" nor "competent" to seriously engage military-security issues.[48]

The 1996 Law on Defense was a further major step toward authoritarianism as it denied the legislature virtually all checks and balances over national defense policy. As a result of the law's ambiguities and loopholes, the president could now commit Russian forces even without consulting with the Duma. This bill entrusted only two important powers to parliament pertaining to the armed forces: to pass the defense budget and to write pertinent laws. Although the law required the president to report to the Federation Council, he was not, in fact, accountable to it. Legislative oversight is also thwarted by the fact that no law prohibits military officers from serving as Duma representatives *and* in government (i.e., in both the legislative and executive branches) simultaneously. Because Yeltsin succeeded in creating a highly personalized nexus with Duma leaders, poor personal relations between the Duma Defense Committee (DDC) chairman and the Kremlin—for example during Rokhlin's term in 1996–98—tended to be detrimental to the committee's work in particular and for civil-military relations in general.

The long-serving DDC chairman, Andrei Nikolaev—a former army general who was also the commander of the Federal Border Service and was elected to the Duma in 1998—had rarely been afraid to speak his mind, yet he succeeded in remaining on Putin's good side. In early 2002, for instance, he announced that the military was undergoing not a reform but rather "an absolutely thoughtless reduction of the armed forces that is dangerous to the country."[49] A few weeks later he said at a press conference that the army's reform had yet to begin and that neither the General Staff nor the Ministry of Defense had any logical concept of the sort of reform that was needed.[50] Nikolaev, and a few other Duma leaders—such as Boris Nemtsov—interested in defense reform, repeatedly pointed to the significance of the Iraqi army's inferior performance against U.S. forces in 2003. He noted the Russian military's many similarities to Saddam Hussein's low-morale and low-tech forces fighting according to outdated doctrine and tactics against a vastly superior enemy. Both Nikolaev and Nemtsov explicitly used the war to call attention to the inferiority of Russian forces and the necessity of their speedy and radical reform.[51]

During the first few years of the new millennium there were indications that the Duma Defense Committee might be able to improve the prospects of civil-military relations and of defense reform. Led by Nikolaev and a number of knowledgeable members on its roster—among them retired general Eduard Vorobyev and Alexei Arbatov—the committee made concerted efforts to increase the transparency of the budget process and to introduce legislation pertaining to defense reform. After the 2003 elections most of the outspoken DDC members with defense-related expertise were gone, however, and with them, the promise of an activist and skilled DDC. One expert suggests that the committee now acts like a military lobby trying to get the government to allocate more funds to the armed forces and, in exchange, gain some influence with the generals.[52]

Perhaps the most significant power that the Russian legislature still possesses vis-à-vis the armed forces, its license to formulate and oversee the defense budget, is gravely compromised for several reasons. Although the Duma is formally responsible for overseeing the budget (as well as the Ministry of Defense in general), it has no effective means at its disposal to study and investigate how disbursed funds are spent. There is no mechanism for legislators to carry out any sort of budget control or to acquire illuminating details about the expenditures proposed by the Defense Ministry. The Constitution does not permit parliamentary inquiries and thus further restricts the legislature's potential investigative role. The Duma can ask the Audit Chamber to look into how ministries spend their funds but this is infrequently done and even a damaging outcome seldom results in anyone being held accountable.[53] Members of the legislature who do not serve on the Defense Committee have virtually no access even to the inadequate and manipulated information that exists on how the ministry's budget is actually spent.

Changes implemented in the Duma's working rules after the 2003 elections have made matters worse yet and underscore the overall trend toward authoritarianism. One of these changes was to marginalize seasoned legislators in favor of those with demonstrated political loyalty to the Kremlin. For example, the new Budget Committee chairman, Yuri Vasilev, was not only new to the committee but new to the Duma itself. His lack of experience, compared with that of his predecessors as committee chairs, hints at the Putin administration's decision to reduce the Budget Committee's already limited influence and "ensure that control over budgetary decision-making remains exclusively in the executive branch."[54]

The second major role regarding the armed forces the legislature has retained after 1996 is its function to draft pertinent laws. Not surprisingly, there are several problems in this respect as well. For years legislators had argued that a law outlining civilian control over the armed forces was not necessary and, moreover, in adopting such a law "the parliament would be exceeding the limits of its constitutional authority" maintaining that "under the Constitution of the Russian Federation all military matters are the sole prerogative of the president and the government."[55] In terms of legislative work, under Yeltsin the Office of the President rejected parliamentary measures aimed at dividing responsibility between branches of government and proposed a law that consolidated oversight authority in the executive branch.[56] Since Yeltsin's exit from the political scene, the legislature has been far more reluctant to trouble the Kremlin with objections. Whatever legal regulations have been drafted or adopted are often replete with ambiguities or fail to determine basic questions.[57] New laws and regulations—such as the recent legislation on reducing the number of draft deferments and the period of conscription—are the result of initiatives from the executive branch not that of independent parliamentary deliberations.

The biggest problem is, however, that regulations are routinely ignored or violated, even by the president himself. Moreover, as in most authoritarian states, laws can be easily made and changed to suit the Kremlin's wishes. So, for example, the 1996 Defense Law was quickly amended in 2004 to rearrange institutional responsibilities between the Defense Ministry and the General Staff and their leaders in response to Kvashnin's consistent undermining of the ministry's authority. Still, those who anticipated that real defense reform would soon take off once the wings of the General Staff were clipped were disappointed because the amendment had not altered the principal reason that has allowed military elites to stall reform in the first place: civilian control over the armed forces is not balanced between the executive and the legislature in Russia. This quintessential condition of democratic civil-military relations has not been created and the status quo is unlikely to change in the foreseeable future. Thus the legislature's remaining two prerogatives of law-making and budget-passing have become less meaningful forms of oversight, owing to the general shift toward authoritarianism in Putin's Russia.

The departure of Yabloko and especially the Union of Rightist Forces (SPS) from the Duma following the 2003 elections foretold the further weakening in the legislature's ability and willingness to pressure the president on defense policy. No political formation had tried harder to move defense reform to the forefront of the government's agenda than the Nemtsov-led SPS. The party had organized dozens of meetings and demonstrations across the country and applied relentless pressure on politicians not to ignore the restructuring of the armed forces. Nemtsov clearly saw through the generals' opposition to reform and their manipulation of the president. In late 2001, for instance, he pointed out that "our generals deceived our president and slipped him a plan" that would further harm the prospects of defense reform.[58] The legislature no longer benefits from the active presence of numerous politicians who were not only tenaciously committed to defense reform but also were some of the country's few civilians knowledgeable about military-security issues. This is all the more troubling as the pool of independent civilian experts on defense matters so important for democratic civilian control is by and large missing in Russia. When NGOs proposed the formation of an expert group for civilian control over the armed forces, Deputy Defense Minister Lyubov Kudelina insisted that the "Chamber of Public Accounts, General Prosecutor's Office, and courts check them regularly. There are also inspectorates in the armed forces. Why do we need any other controllers?"[59] She "only" neglected to mention that none of these institutions were independent of the government.

Under Putin the legislature has turned into a pliant tool of the presidency. It is essentially a rubber stamp institution—not entirely unlike its pre-Gorbachev Soviet-era predecessor—without the power to force useful reforms through at any level if they are opposed by the executive branch. The United Russia Party thoroughly dominates proceedings. Its leader, Boris Gryzlov, is the Duma's Speaker who recently announced that in the next presidential election the URP will support "whichever candidate is proposed by President Putin."[60] In November 2005, by 370 votes to 18, the legislature approved a bill in its first reading that would drastically restrict the activities of the nearly 450,000 domestic and foreign nongovernmental organizations active in Russia, presumably in an effort to bolster national security. The second reading of the bill—characterized by Steven Solnick of the Ford Foundation's Moscow office as "a nasty piece of work"[61]—resulted in a vote of 376 to 10. As one expert lamented, the "Russian parliament is now little more than a Kremlin-controlled puppet show."[62]

PUTIN AND THE MILITARY

"Putin possesses few of Yeltsin's inhibitions against the unbridled use of executive power."[63] Even after Yeltsin's capture of superpresidential powers, his successor has managed to significantly expand presidential authority. In the fifteen years of its existence as a post-Soviet entity, Russia has become a centralized bureaucratic-authoritarian state. The presidential administration, the center of political power, wields influence similar to that once enjoyed by the Secretariat of the CPSU's Central Committee; the symbolism that it occupies the same complex of offices near the Kremlin on Staraya Ploshad is probably not lost on many.[64] During Putin's reign, prime ministers, their governments, regional governors, and local bureaucracies have become far less powerful than under his predecessor. For example, in the last several years the previously dual presidential and governmental oversight of the power ministries has been gradually replaced by the consolidation of presidential control.[65] According to a Russian expert, "politics in Russia today is court-driven and essentially Byzantine"; and the court is headed by the modern tsar, Vladimir Putin.[66]

The Russian president is a pragmatic bureaucrat whose temperament seems ideally suited to serve his main objective of strengthening the state. The pervasive "securitization" and "militarization" of government at the highest levels has been complemented by the appointments that many of Putin's former colleagues from the St. Petersburg city bureaucracy have secured in the state administration. In 2003, 21 percent of the Russian political elite came from his home region, a much higher percentage than in the case of any of his predecessors.[67] Given these individuals' statist and conservative attitudes and values, they have inevitably influenced domestic and foreign policies in a particular way. Putin has pursued a predictable and cautious personnel policy. Instead of impulsively hiring and replacing his subordinates like Yeltsin, he has chosen them with care and has been reluctant to fire them until clear evidence has compelled him to do so. He refereed the protracted internal strife between the Defense Ministry and the General Staff with remarkable restraint and intervened only in 2004 when Kvashnin's incessant recalcitrance had left him with no alternative. And, as I noted earlier, he nearly always compensates the high-ranking officers he does sack—for instance, Popov, Kvashnin, Troshev—with choice jobs in the state bureaucracy.

Under Yeltsin's watch the army had emerged as a "presidential institution."[68] Putin has further cemented this institutional identity. As Alexei Arbatov argued in a 2004 interview, given that the "president's power is unmatched," it was "entirely up to [him] whether true military reform takes place, or whether the military bureaucracy continues pretending that reforms are under way."[69] This, in other words, is what I argued at the outset: even though the essential direct cause for the absence of radical reform is the opposition of the military leadership, the ultimate reason in a superpresidential authoritarian regime as Russia's is, by definition, the chief executive. It bears reiterating that Putin came to power with the apparent resolution to radically transform the armed forces. Already in 1999, as acting president, he identified defense reform as a top priority. As time went on, however, his resolve has seemingly evaporated for numerous perfectly sensible reasons—the absence of real reformers on his team and his disinclination to enforce unpopular decisions on a key institutional support base, to mention just two—as I explained in the previous chapter. He has continued to pay lip-service to reform ever since. Depending on the occasion and the audience, at times he calls for its acceleration while at other times he proclaims that it has been, in fact, concluded.

Soon after taking office Putin repeatedly announced "wholesale" and "massive" reductions to the military establishment: 365,000 uniformed and 120,000 civilian personnel, by 2003. (In 2002, having made no progress, he postponed the deadline to 2005.) In the following year he declared that neither the government nor society supported the conscription system and promised the establishment of an all-professional army by 2010.[70] Both of these were crucial objectives that, if realized, could have led to what Russia truly needed: smaller but better armed forces. Not only have they not been implemented; in fact, both force reduction and the switch to a volunteer army have been explicitly abandoned. Beginning with late 2001 (following the 11 September terrorist attacks on the United States) Putin introduced a new theme into his speeches on military reform, in essence, retargeting the armed forces.[71] He has repeatedly urged the military to face future threats and set higher standards when recruiting professional personnel, although he seldom elaborates on the sort of incentives qualified individuals might need to embark on a military career. In any event, from this point on combating terrorism emerged as the fundamental task of the military (and security services). There are several inconsistencies in this regard, however, as in many other areas of Russian politics. The main contradiction, of course, is that Putin has failed to aggressively push the military to implement the necessary changes that would enable it to meet this new challenge. Moreover, he has also fervently supported developing a "global" army that needs to prepare for a major war against, as he recently put it, "Comrade Wolf, who goes ahead and eats whatever he wants, without listening to anyone else," (i.e., the United States).[72]

Putin has not had an easy time with defense reform. His apparent frustration with the issue has been shown by the conflicting signals he has given to the military leadership. In April 2003, for instance, he expressed his displeasure to the top brass and pleaded with them to speed up work on reform proposals and implementation.[73] He demanded that consultations between the Defense Ministry, the Finance Ministry, and other government agencies be wrapped up and previously agreed on timelines be observed. He also used major conferences at the Ministry of Defense to appeal to the officer corps to "take an active part in reforming the entire military organization of the state."[74] In a July 2005 Security Council meeting, for instance, he chided department heads and security agency chiefs for not having "managed to implement the agreed military reform programs."[75] Incidentally, this was two years after he and Defense Minister Ivanov declared the military reform "completed." Actually, as politicians like Boris Nemtsov suggested several years earlier, Putin had gradually realized that the generals resolutely opposed reforms and, perhaps, he had grown tired of fighting them.[76] One might argue that the president might rationalize that if his generals cannot deliver a conclusive victory in Chechnya how could he expect them to implement a reform they clearly do not want.

At other times, however, Putin applauded the army leadership and its "advancement of the defense reform." By early 2004 he had stopped mentioning both of the two major reform imperatives: further manpower reduction and the armed forces' full professionalization. Instead of insisting on tangible results of reform implementation and punishing the inappropriate conduct of some generals he found ways to appease them.[77] For instance, he brought back a number of Soviet-era symbols—something Yeltsin categorically refused to do—such as the old Soviet anthem (albeit with different words), resurrected the armed forces' emblem, the red star, and decorated retired military leaders popular among the top brass, such as the former defense minister and erstwhile coup plotter, Dmitri Yazov.

Similarly to his predecessor, Putin has made sure to entice the armed forces with promotions and other rewards just before elections. Prior to the 2004 presidential vote, for instance, he did his best to project a "tough-guy" image calculated to appeal to the military-security people as well as the general public. He made extravagant efforts to court the "'khaki' vote," going on a high-visibility tour of military exercises and installations. The president spent three days overseeing a military exercise near Murmansk, then traveled to a cosmodrome in northern Russia to witness the launch of a rocket carrying up a military satellite.[78] He has flown on supersonic bombers, submerged in nuclear submarines, sailed aboard numerous military vessels, and observed joint-force maneuvers, often while donning the uniform of the appropriate service. Needless to say, cameras are seldom absent from these events staged to show the president's closeness to the armed forces.

Professional military personnel—if not necessarily civilians—can also be counted on to appreciate his uncompromising attitude to crises. To them, Putin's approach to violent conflicts must look particularly appealing in comparison to that of Yeltsin and his prime ministers. It is hardly a leap of faith to presume that few *siloviki* were happy with the Chernomyrdin government's pleading with Chechen warlord Shamil Basaev after he and his men captured a hospital and took more than a thousand hostages in June 1995 in the town of Budennovsk in Stavropol region. Putin would have almost certainly ordered the special forces to annihilate rebels no matter the cost. In calamities such as the Moscow theater siege in 2002, the hostage crisis at the Beslan school in 2004, or the attack on Nalchik in 2005, the president's main objective was not saving civilian lives but liquidating all insurgents.[79]

Just as important, Putin has also managed to improve the remuneration of professional armed forces personnel even if not nearly all the announced wage increases have been instituted. Although real benefits for officers and soldiers have declined as a result of the cash-for-benefit scheme introduced in 2005, the massive poverty of officers characteristic of the late 1990s and early 2000s has been more or less eliminated. Moreover, in November 2005 the president announced—and in his May 2006 State of the Nation address reiterated—additional funding for military housing, pay raises totaling 67 percent in the next three years, and measures to increase veterans' pensions.[80] In short, although the conditions of officers are far from ideal, they have a lot less to complain about under Putin than they did under Yeltsin.

Another aspect of Putin's character that cannot but appeal to both the officers and the rank and file is his willingness to take responsibility for his actions. This attribute is particularly conspicuous when contrasted with the record of his predecessors—the weak-willed Gorbachev and the capricious Yeltsin—who repeatedly refused to accept blame for deploying the military.[81] At the same time, it is noteworthy that neither the *Kursk* disaster, nor the long-drawn-out Chechen conflict, nor the numerous other crises throughout his presidential tenure seem to have had any serious prolonged impact on his popularity. According to one November 2005 poll, 73 percent of Russians approved of his job performance, and he remained the country's most trusted politician by far—41 percent of respondents trusted him while the runner-up, Emergency Situations Minister Sergei Shoigu, enjoyed the confidence of only 14 percent of those asked.[82]

A July 2006 poll found that as many as 87 percent (with a margin of error of less or equal to 3.4 percent) of citizens trust him; the accompanying analysis concluded that the Russian president "enjoys almost limitless support."[83] In short, Putin has remained—by any objective measure—extremely popular in a political system that he has steered toward authoritarianism, a notion that I will try to explain in the book's last section.

Nevertheless, it is hard to disagree with Pavel Baev who contends that the "military-security [realm] is the area where Putin has his worst record of success while encountering the most damaging challenges to his leadership."[84] His reluctance to antagonize the military, however, is not a sufficient explanation for the absence of serious defense reform. The bottom line is that, for Putin, the incentives to transform the armed forces are far outweighed by the enormous risks, and, as Dmitri Furman of the Moscow-based Institute of Europe opined, the "simply insurmountable" difficulties that he would encounter.[85]

Conclusion

As I have argued in this book, the absence of substantial defense reform in Russia is a result of the institutional decay in civil-military relations. But, institutional decay is only an intervening variable because ultimately, in a superpresidential system like Russia's, the president is accountable for the failure of policy implementation. In this chapter I tried to support this contention by showing how Russian presidents—through their relationships with the armed forces, the power ministries, and the legislature—have apparently abandoned the objective of the military's radical transformation.

Both Yeltsin and Putin, albeit for different reasons, were most reluctant to push through defense reform against the objection of the armed forces leadership. To be sure, the generals' opposition was not the only reason for the presidents' unwillingness to stand by the reform. There are several important "mitigating factors"—the war in Chechnya, lack of consensus on how to approach reform, the absence of a vocal opposition after the 2003 legislative elections that would demand reform, and so on—that help us understand the presidents' reluctance to pursue this policy. At the end of the day, however, the fact remains that in the kind of authoritarian state that Russia has become in the past decade and a half, the executive branch could have implemented the sort of defense reform the country needs. Admittedly the political cost of that action would have likely been considerable but—given the coup-averse organizational culture of the army and Putin's improbably high popularity—probably not prohibitive.

The main reason why Russian presidents need to be concerned about the top brass' opposition to their policies has been a condition created by Yeltsin and Putin themselves, which is rooted in their establishment of a superpresidential system. One of the defining aspects of superpresidentialism is the restriction of legislative authority without which there can be no institutionally balanced control over the armed forces. Since both Yeltsin and Putin have equated civilian control over the military with presidential oversight, they denied themselves the potential benefit of an autonomous (that is, not beholden to the executive branch) parliament continually prodding, criticizing, and supervising the armed forces. Because the presidents have not shared the responsibility of managing the armed forces, they cannot shift the blame for the military's actions. They have not only failed to promote legal instruments that prohibit the political activism of military personnel (the second formative moment) but have actually encouraged the generals' political presence in concert with their own political interests, appointed military men to important political posts, and allowed continued military opposition to defense reform (the third formative moment). This sort of executive role, in turn, has fostered the institutional decay—the gradual erosion of institutional rules and norms—in Russian civil-military relations.

The bottom line is that as long as the armed forces are not held accountable by civilian authority, the prospects of substantial defense reform will remain minimal. Without the introduction of institutionally balanced civilian oversight and consistently applied enforcement mechanisms, it would be unwise to expect military elites to embrace the kind of defense reform their country needs. Russian political elites, as one expert has written, "insist on the generals' political loyalty in exchange for their minimal involvement in defense matters."[86] In the meantime, the country's institutional arrangements and networks of corporate interests practically guarantee the continuation of the status quo.

(((

CONCLUSION

The main focus of this book has been the absence of radical defense reform in Russia and the evolution of a peculiar sort of civil-military relations framework that explains it. In the larger sense, this study is about the reversal of Russia's post-Soviet democratization and, more specifically, about an important aspect of that process, military politics.

It is all too often forgotten, given the many examples of successful democratization experiences in Southern Europe, Latin America, and East-Central Europe in the relatively recent past, that democratization is not necessarily a one-way street that steadily and inevitably leads to fair governance. Neither is it an irreversible process. The transition to democracy is not always followed by democratic consolidation but, occasionally, by the breakdown of democracy and the return to authoritarianism. This second course of development is what we have witnessed in post-Soviet Russia. During the last decade, Russia's polity has been depicted in a variety of ways: "managed democracy," "presidential democracy," "controlled democracy," and so on.[1] Pinning different modifying labels onto "democracy," however, only obfuscates the reality of the Russian state's fundamental and increasingly authoritarian nature.

The contemporary Russian polity reminds me of an earthy Hungarian proverb according to which "fish stinks from its head" (*fejétől bűzlik a hal*) because the Russian state's antidemocratic nature is firmly rooted at its figurative head, the increasingly powerful executive. Since 1993 the Kremlin's occupants have managed to undo most of the advances the democratization process had accomplished in the preceding years, resulting in the gradual evolution of an increasingly brazen authoritarian state. As one seasoned expert recently wrote, "No serious observer can dispute the fact that Russia is no longer a 'managed democracy'; it is a bureaucratic authoritarian regime."[2] The "bureaucratic-authoritarian" label is easy enough to agree with and is a useful conceptual lens through which to view the Russian polity. "Putinocracy," a polity in which "all levers of governance are in the hands of one person" is another fitting if unconventional designation by an audacious Russian analyst.[3]

I begin this final section of the book by explaining why considering contemporary Russia an authoritarian state is appropriate and show how civil-military relations fit into the more general framework of the authoritarian polity. Although this is obviously a book about Russia, the issues I have discussed are highly relevant to those fortunate to live in democracies and have important implications for those formulating foreign policy. Therefore, I will devote the second part of this chapter to summarizing the reasons why citizens and policy makers in the United States and elsewhere should concern themselves with Russia's failed democratization in general, and haphazard defense reform and defective civil-military relations in particular.

The Failure of Democratization

Several scholars and journalists have ably analyzed and explained the breakdown of Russia's democratization experiment.[4] My aim here is merely to underscore the crucial milestones of this process and place civil-military relations in the larger context they delineate.

Until 1993 the flawed but independent Russian legislature had been the embodiment of an independent branch of political power that could counterbalance the growing power of the executive. In September–October 1993 all that had changed and the gradual decline of Russia's democratization experience had begun. In 2002, Lilia Shevtsova, one of the country's most insightful political scientists, described the Russian polity as semiauthoritarian, adding that "it falls short of pure authoritarianism so far—President Putin is unwilling to go too far at this point—both because he knows the state is too exhausted to quickly restore the Soviet regime" and because he, a rational person knew the implications of such an action.[5] Four years later one does not need to go out on a limb to put the "authoritarian" label on the Russian polity.

This contention is accentuated by developments in several major issue areas. Russia's human rights record remains appalling. Quite simply, fundamental human rights are not guaranteed in the country. Speech, assembly, and other universal rights are only free—as they once were in the Soviet Union—if they do not alarm the powers of the state. For example, individuals—like Igor Sutiagin—can be and have been sentenced to long prison terms for speaking with foreigners about sensitive subjects even though they possess no access to classified materials. The indiscriminate violence against civilians in Chechnya is the most obvious manifestation of this problem. As the human rights activist Sergei Kovalev sums up, "The authorities only talk about human rights with the media or foreign colleagues. Citizens are seen as instruments of the state."[6]

I have already discussed the distressing state of the media in chapter 1. Although there are still some sparks of independent life left in the print media, editors are quickly reminded that their hold on their jobs is tenuous even in the best of times. For instance, when the national daily *Izvestia* featured extensive coverage of the Beslan hostage crisis—including photographs of the injured and the dead—in September 2004, its editor, Raf Shakirov, was quickly fired.[7] Even though *Izvestia* was never an opposition paper, a slight deviation from the official line was enough to warrant state interference. In 2005, the popular television news anchor, Olga Romanova, was removed from her job for reporting a story about Defense Minister Sergei Ivanov's son, who killed an old woman in a traffic accident.[8]

Domestic calamities seem to have provided the Kremlin with justification to further strengthen its hold on the state. For example, after the *Kursk* accident media freedoms had notably decreased, while the tragedy at Beslan had seemingly compelled Moscow to take its overwhelming political dominance to a new level by revoking the voters' right to elect their regional governors directly and expanding the definition of a new law on extremism so far that it allows the authorities unchecked powers against its critics.[9] In fact, by then the autonomy of regions had already been slashed because on taking office one of Putin's first "reforms" was to establish seven supraregional districts and appoint his own supporters—mostly former army and KGB generals—as their leaders. These "viceroys," in turn, have done their best to undermine the authority of regional officials and subordinate them to the Kremlin.

The most important area of politics that clearly displays Russia's "slide toward autocracy," as James Goldgeier and Michael McFaul aptly termed this process,[10] has been the undermining of political influence of all political institutions independent of the presidency. The emasculation of the Russian parliament began in 1993.[11] The current legislature can hardly be regarded as an independent source of political power. Registration procedures for new parties have recently become more restrictive, just in case a political force might emerge to challenge the Kremlin. As in Soviet times, the judiciary applies the law selectively: those who for whatever reason fail to meet with the authorities' approval are seldom spared. The December 2005 law that drastically reduces the independence of nongovernmental organizations operating in Russia is merely the culmination of the Kremlin's decade-long harassment of one of the last remaining sources of institutional autonomy. The trend is unlikely to stop: in April 2006 the Duma debated a bill that would enable the Kremlin-appointed governors to take powers away from and subordinate to themselves mayors who are still directly elected.[12] According to a presidential aide, even the cabinet itself plays no crucial political role; instead, the most influential players on the stage of Russian politics are the *siloviki*.[13] Yet another major problem is the state's blatant disregard for property rights—if its interests so dictate. The cardinal sin of Mikhail Khodorkovsky, the former CEO of Russia's largest oil company, Yukos, was not that he amassed an improbably large fortune in a very short time—so did numerous other "oligarchs"—but that he dared to publicly criticize the president and financially support his challengers. Alternatively, it has also been suggested that the main reason for Khodorkovsky's imprisonment has actually been his intention to merge his company with ExxonMobil and the Russian firm, Sibneft, and thereby accumulate too many energy resources beyond the state's control.[14]

Unlike some other authoritarian rulers, Putin has not succeeded in raising the efficiency of the state, which remains extraordinarily corrupt. The 2005 study of Transparency International—a respected international think-tank specializing on corruption—found that Russia dropped to 126th place in the world between Niger and Sierra Leone.[15] The 2005 report of the democracy watchdog Freedom House concluded that Putin's antidemocratic policies had become more pronounced, and Russia had experienced the largest decline in democratic standards among all former Communist states. As a result Freedom House downgraded Russia from "partly free" to "not free" classification. Freedom House was especially critical of the executive branch's relentless campaign to concentrate all power in the Kremlin, the widely criticized unfair national and presidential elections, and the continued crackdown on independent organizations.[16] A distinguished Russian expert recently claimed that the Russian state has become "Soviet in both form and content."[17]

As long as a small but powerful elite monopolizes politics and effectively shuts out those that could challenge it, the public remains passive and content with material gains, information can be controlled, and the outside world does not care, there are unlikely to be major shifts in Russian politics. The Russian state's mistrust of democracy, its fear of the independent press and autonomous organizations, and its treatment of human beings as its own powerless subjects are, of course, nothing new. As Richard Pipes convincingly demonstrates in his insightful study of Russian political culture, conservatism is the dominant intellectual legacy of Russia, and its age-old leitmotif has been the conviction that Russians could prosper only under an autocratic regime.[18] Three different surveys conducted from 2003 to 2005 reveal that there is no stigma attached to Joseph Stalin in contemporary Russia and young Russians hold positive or ambivalent views of their country's worst modern dictator.[19]

Russia's history and its political culture are crucial to understanding the seemingly counterintuitive phenomena of its authoritarian drift and its leader's steady 70-plus-percent support—that no crisis or calamity seems able to dent—in virtually all opinion polls. It is not just the Russian state, it is also Russians themselves who are, at best, suspicious of democracy. As Pipes notes in a recent article, "There is a good deal of evidence that the antidemocratic, antilibertarian actions of the current administration are not being inflicted on the Russian people but are actually supported by them."[20] He goes on to show, with the help of a great deal of fresh public opinion data, that Russians' well-documented historical preference for strong and even "harsh" leaders has diminished little, that their trust of individuals outside of the family circle—the basis of Western civilization—is largely absent, and that they widely view democracy as a fraud. According to polls, 88 percent of respondents would choose order rather than freedom, only 11 percent "would be unwilling to surrender their freedoms of speech, press, or movement in exchange for stability," and 29 percent would be "quite prepared to give up their freedoms for nothing in return, because they attached no value to them."[21]

An illuminating way to think about the contemporary Russian polity is to view Putin as the successor to the tsars who has "re-instated Russia's traditional model of government: an autocratic state in which citizens are relieved of responsibility for politics and in which imaginary foreign enemies are invoked to forge an artificial unity."[22] "The defining element in present-day Russia is that the presidency, or rather the president, a modern tsar, is the only functioning institution" and the sole decision maker.[23] What happens after Putin's second term expires in 2008 is hard to predict but it is possible to make some informed guesses.

The bottom line is that in contemporary Russia whatever Putin wants is most likely to happen. There are several options. First, though he continues to maintain that he will leave office in 2008, this may not happen. Polls consistently show that 58–60 percent of Russians support a third term for him.[24] The constitution could be amended allowing a third or even subsequent presidential terms; the Duma would surely be accommodating and prepare the necessary legislation. Second, Putin may leave office but he might become prime minister and reconfigure political power-relations to ensure the marginalization of the presidency and the dominance of the head of government. Third, after a four-year hiatus Putin could return to the presidency in 2012. In any event, it is difficult to foresee him not playing an influential role in Russian politics.

It is important to realize that, even if he does stay around, Putin's domination of the Russian political scene may not necessarily be a bad thing—both for Russians and the world—given the less than promising alternatives. It was none other than Mikhail Khodorkovsky who recently observed—in a Siberian penal colony—that Putin "is probably not a liberal or a democrat, but he is more liberal and more democratic than 70 percent of the population."[25] Those who are considered his likely successors—deputy prime ministers Sergei Ivanov and Dmitri Medvedev—appear fully to share Putin's authoritarian impulses but might lack the political instincts that have allowed him to stabilize Russia.

DEMOCRATIZATION AND MILITARY POLITICS

Institutionally balanced civilian control of the armed forces is at the heart of democratic civil-military relations, which, in turn, is an indispensable component of a democracy. But, as Christopher Donnelly has noted, the Russian concept of *kontrol* refers to something very different than its Western counterpart insofar as it does not cover the government's capability to direct military and security-sector activity, only the legislature's ability to monitor both government policy and the compliance of military and security forces.[26] In fact, according to a Russian expert, "the very idea of civilian control seems alien, superfluous, and unacceptable" in Russia, even to members of the political, military, and academic elites, because no civilians ever headed the armed forces.[27] This, apparently, was one of the reasons for the evident lack of urgency in the Duma during the 1990s to set civilian control on legal democratic foundations even in the face of the growing political role of the armed forces and security services. Owing to the particular development of Russian civil-military relations—specifically the shifting balance of institutional responsibilities over the armed forces after 1993—one might argue that the capability and readiness of government leaders to exercise day-to-day control over the armed forces has diminished in the last fifteen years.

Some commentators have argued that under Yeltsin the legislature, and especially the Duma Defense Committee, had a good working relationship with the defense minister and his ministry.[28] This was a false impression, however, considering that even in the 1990s achieving actual civilian oversight was a low priority for the legislature that, in any case was forced to work with the very limited information it received from the Defense Ministry. The point is that the problem of civilian control might have become a fashionable topic among liberal politicians but it had never developed into a "state cause."[29] Furthermore, to achieve real parliamentary control would be difficult since the Russian Constitution does not grant the Duma oversight authority over executive branch structures.[30] In effect, the military has become a de facto presidential institution, a status cultivated by the top brass because it inherently denies any legislative interference into its affairs. Neither is there any mechanism to compel the government to provide details about the military budget to the legislature. Needless to say, it would be naïve to expect the president to seek constitutional reform that would strengthen the Duma's control over that of the government. In other words, the only political actors who could ensure that civil-military relations are reformed have no incentives to do so. Consequently, given the minimal role of parliament, the civilian control of the military—just like most other policy areas in contemporary Russia—is heavily dependent on one person, the president. The absence of democratic civil-military relations, on the one hand, poses a serious obstacle to the realization of democratic transition because it is a major component of that process while, on the other hand, it reflects the power relations that have doomed Russia's democratization prospects.

Having said all this, it is important to reiterate that the armed forces do not display any interest in replacing the government. It should be noted because it is often not fully recognized that even during the 1991 coup attempt Defense Minister Yazov was an unenthusiastic participant. A re-examination of his role in that affair a decade later concluded that he was "the single person whose actions did most to doom the coup to failure."[31] Equally important, the vast majority of the officer corps was against the army's political intervention and prevented the coup's success. The Russian military's opposition to violent political interference was most clearly shown in the 1990s. This was, after all, a period during which various political forces at different times had tried to coax the army into an active political role, when its privations had reached critical levels, and more generally, when its glorious past gave way to a thoroughly neglected, embarrassingly poor, and deeply demoralized present. In other words, the army's conditions amounted in many respects to a textbook case for a military coup.[32]

Looking back at the Russian military establishment in the post-Soviet era, one might find it surprising that it "has neither collapsed nor even rebelled against the government."[33] Taylor sees the military's organizational culture as the key to explaining this conundrum. Another one might be the lack of institutional cohesion in the armed forces, even within the upper echelons of the hierarchy. The numerous deep-seated cleavages in the officer corps—interservice rivalries, rank, age, assignment, among others—effectively preclude concerted action. Furthermore, though, to be sure, most officers support the president, view democratization with suspicion, and oppose defense reform, the officer corps as a whole does not have a shared position on these issues.

In 1995 Stephen Meyer wrote that in the context of the Russian military's institutional history and the still strong threads of professionalism in the officer corps it was useful to think of the army's politicization in terms of increased political awareness rather than political activism or intervention.[34] More than a decade later, I find myself only in partial agreement with him. Russian officers have certainly become more politically aware than they were during the Communist period for the reason that as the quintessential institutional beneficiaries of Soviet rule, they did not *need* to be concerned with politics. In the last fifteen years we have seen few incidents of overt political intervention by the armed forces. Nonetheless, as I argued in chapter 3, the military as an institution *has* become politically active and willing to stand up for its corporate interests in the political arena. In the military's defense it is important to recognize that the officers' political activism was not at their own initiative. Rather, it was incited by Gorbachev, stoked by Yeltsin, and reinforced by Putin.

The reform of the armed forces is closely connected, through the broader issue of civil-military relations, to the general state of Russian democratization. The politics of defense reform is at the core of Russia's domestic politics given the crucial role the military establishment has played throughout Russian history, including the more than seven decades of Communist rule during which the Soviet Union had built a great military empire.[35] Because the civilian control of the armed forces is a matter directly relevant to the executive, legislative, and judicial spheres, the interactions of these branches of government with the military had impacted all of these institutions. For instance, the clampdown on the free media reached a new stage following the *Kursk* disaster, the judiciary compromised whatever democratic standards it might have had by deciding, ex post facto, that the use of military units in the 1993 October storming of the "White House" was legitimate, and the legislature—even under Yeltsin—evaded its responsibility to write and pass a law of balanced and firm civilian control of the army.

One of the particular attributes of Soviet civil-military relations was the absence of civilian expertise in both the Defense Ministry and the General Staff. As Condoleezza Rice pointed out, this failure to create a civilian apparatus to advise the CPSU on security matters and to "check on," as it were, on military decision makers was not so much a feature of the totalitarian system but the success of Soviet army leaders to monopolize defense-related knowledge and thereby increase their influence.[36] In some post-Communist states, such as Romania and Poland, military academies opened their doors to civilians and/or mainstream universities and launched military-security-related programs in a clear effort to produce independent civilian defense specialists. In Russia, civilian expertise on military matters continues to be in very short supply because the existence of a pool of independent military-security experts directly contradicts the armed forces' institutional interests and there is no political actor that would change the status quo. The absence of such civilian knowledge—as Stepan's framework usefully highlighted—is an indication of the armed forces' political influence and a major defect in Russian civil-military relations.

In the beginning of this study I suggested that I anticipated neither a radical change in Russian civil-military relations nor the transformative defense reform the country needed in the foreseeable future. After all, the main argument of this book has been that ultimately it is Russia's power-ful executive branch, more precisely, the president, who is responsible for the military's political presence and the absence of substantial defense reform. Although forward leaps and reversals in the democratization pro-cess can occur—we have seen that in the case of Russia itself—one should not expect a turnaround in the Russia's thirteen-year authoritarian slide soon. Given that there is no major security threat to the country, there will be no compelling reason to drastically reform the military and, inevi-tably, to antagonize its leadership.

Finally, one ought to ask, what has been the military's impact on the failed democratization process and vice versa? The armed forces, meaning primarily its top echelons, had a very limited role in aiding democratiza-tion. The highlights, the events in which the armed forces played a positive role—but "positive" only in the sense that their role could have easily been much more negative than it turned out to be—were in 1991 and 1993 when the military was clearly reluctant to use its weapons for politi-cal ends. Far more important, however, is the military establishment's part in derailing the democratization process. Whenever possible, armed forces elites have fought tooth and nail policies and initiatives that pointed in the direction of democratization—from the appointment of a civilian defense minister to the legislature's feeble attempts to gain budgetary con-trol over military expenditures. In doing so the generals behaved as ratio-nal actors who pursued their own individual and institutional interests. A special feature of contemporary Russian authoritarianism is the preemi-nent role military and security professionals have been allowed to play in the state administration. Quite simply, under Putin military officers have acquired an unprecedented presence in the Russian polity.

The evolution of Russian civil-military relations has been a gradual pro-cess and the country's presidents—and especially Vladimir Putin—are re-sponsible for the particular direction it has taken. The bottom line is that civil-military relations in Russia suit the polity's authoritarian essence. The theoretical framework I outlined at the beginning of this study proved helpful in appreciating the changes in post-Soviet Russia's military politics. Colton and Stepan's contributions were useful in appraising the gradations of the officer corps' political involvement, their corporate interests, and ways in which they exerted their influence. As I expected, they were of little use in actually explaining the sustained deterioration of the rules and norms of civil-military relations as manifested by the passage of inappropriate or inadequate laws and regulations and by the top brass' insubordination, corruption, negligence, and lack of professionalism.

The institutionalist approach in general and the concept of institutional decay more particularly were quite valuable and help us discern the continuous modifications in the long-held norms of armed forces personnel. I also tried to show how the practical utility of the notion of path dependence and the concept of formative moments help us recognize how and why institutions change, in this case in a negative direction. These methods complemented each other and produced a more complete understanding of Russian civil-military relations. One of the keys to historical institutionalism is the awareness of the given institution's past. It is not surprising, therefore, that I found that familiarity with Russia's history—not just going back to the Communist period but reaching far beyond that—is essential to appreciating its political culture, without which the reasons for the failure of its democratization process would be hard to fully comprehend.

IMPLICATIONS TO THE UNITED STATES AND NATO

The way Russian civil-military relations unfold and defense reform progresses has direct implications to the national interests and foreign policies of the United States. This is so not only because civil-military relations comprise an important part of the overall democratization process. Russia possesses thousands of nuclear weapons and is the only country that at the moment can present a credible strategic threat to the United States. Moreover, since the early 1990s America and its Western allies have expended billions of dollars to ensure that Russia's aging nuclear stockpile is properly disposed of and safely kept, and have a stake in how those billions are spent. Moscow is also capable of disrupting or aiding projects of the North Atlantic Treaty Organization and has been a partner of sorts in the United States' "war on terror." In sum, Americans in general and especially security and foreign policy professionals should be seriously concerned with Russian military politics and defense reform. In this last section of the book, I shall briefly examine these issues and what they mean for the United States.

The Nuclear Dimension

The G-8, an elite group of prosperous democracies, now includes Russia which is neither prosperous nor democratic. This anomaly is largely explained by the fact that Moscow possesses thousands of strategic nuclear weapons, which remain the symbol of its importance in the international arena. In the post-Soviet period the weaknesses of its conventional forces have compelled the Russian government to place renewed emphasis on nuclear weapons—a sort of insurance policy for the country—to protect its interests.

Since 1991, when the USSR deployed 6,411 warheads on land-based ICBMs, 2,932 on submarines and 1,329 on strategic bombers, the size of Russia's nuclear arsenal has been cut in half as it implemented the Strategic Arms Reduction Treaty.[37] Between January 2000 and January 2005 alone, Moscow apparently reduced its nuclear strategic forces by 357 delivery vehicles and 1,740 warheads.[38] There is no doubt that Russia—along with the United States—has significantly slashed its nuclear arsenal to move away from Cold War-era overkill. Some nuclear weapon plants have been shut down and, more generally, the entire industry producing nuclear devices has been shrunk. In spite of some of the problems that remain, the Russian government has eliminated a significant amount of weapons-usable nuclear material. Moscow has also fulfilled its commitments under Article 6 of the Nuclear Non-Proliferation Treaty to repossess and destroy all nuclear weapons—approximately 4,000 warheads—stored in Soviet times in Ukraine and Kazakhstan. In the meantime, Defense Ministry publications occasionally "reassure" Russians that their country (and the United States) remains quite capable of destroying one another and the rest of human civilization.[39]

There are indications, however, that all is not well in the nuclear weapons sphere in Russia. Moscow's reluctance to give experts greater access to military sites impedes progress. In the past fifteen years the United States and other Western countries have given Russia billions of dollars for the purposes of destroying and safeguarding nuclear, chemical, and biological weapons of mass destruction. International agreements give American specialists right of entry to twenty-four nuclear installations and six nonnuclear sites in the country, but the limited access Russian authorities have granted Western weapons inspectors to nuclear facilities has seldom allowed the independent verification of the Kremlin's claims regarding its accomplishments. Western inspectors have not been admitted beyond the perimeters of numerous nuclear sites—which have been closed not only to foreigners but also to most domestic specialists—and they are granted no access to actual nuclear munitions either.[40] Russian press reports occasionally brand U.S. requests for inspection as American attempts "to establish control over Russian nuclear facilities."[41]

Chief of the General Staff Yuri Baluyevskii has repeatedly defended the access Russia permits foreign inspectors to its nuclear facilities.[42] In 2005 Atomic Energy Agency director Aleksandr Rumiantsev announced that Russia decided to refuse some of the financial aid the United States had offered to help secure Russian nuclear facilities because the situation had changed and these weapons were safely out of terrorists' reach.[43] Nonetheless, according to Russian experts, Moscow must obtain more foreign aid if it is to destroy all chemical weapons stockpiles by 2012, as agreed with the Organization for the Prohibition of Chemical Weapons in The Hague.[44] Although the Kremlin has increased the funds earmarked for the elimination of its chemical weapons (from $175 million in 2004 to $433 million in 2005), Russia has not advanced as expeditiously in this regard as has been expected. In June 2006 U.S. State Department officials announced that Moscow and Washington concluded a "seven-year extension of programs that provide U.S. money and expertise to secure and destroy Soviet-era caches of nuclear, chemical, and biological weapons."[45]

Another difficulty has been the fraudulent accounting of the funds Western governments have provided for Russia's denuclearization program, which cannot be said to be surprising in the larger context of the country's massive and widespread corruption. It has been widely alleged, for instance, that under former atomic energy minister Yevgenii Adamov millions of dollars simply disappeared in the 1990s. He was ousted by Putin in 2001 following an investigation into his ties to Russia's business community. In 2005 Adamov was arrested in Switzerland and extradited to Russia where he has since been held in jail.[46] In September 2006, Major General Vladimir Kiyaev was arrested on suspicion of large-scale fraud involving the nuclear industry in Krasnoyarsk Krai where one of the projects is funded by the U.S. Congress with $400 million.[47] Even some Russian researchers have urged the setting up of international oversight to account for the large amounts of foreign funds pledged to Russia for nuclear remediation projects.

The safety of Russian nuclear weapons remains an exceedingly important and controversial issue. Some experts insist that the lack of security around nuclear sites in Russia continues to be a much bigger threat than the environmental hazard posed by its nuclear arms. Staff members of the U.S. Senate Foreign Relations Committee recently argued that the issue was truly a race against time in trying to keep terrorists from getting nuclear materials from the former Soviet Union.[48] Defense Minister Ivanov indignantly dismisses such fears and maintains that Russian nuclear facilities are appropriately stored and guarded, and there has never been an attempt to compromise them.[49] His words may not fully reflect reality. A 1997 Nuclear Power Ministry document stated that more than five hundred tons of weapons-grade plutonium and uranium were stored in Russia in conditions that "do not conform to international safety standards." In 2001, General Igor Valynkin, chief of the armed forces' nuclear branch, told reporters that unnamed terrorists had made two attempts to penetrate Russian nuclear storage facilities.[50] In late 2005, however, Valynkin claimed that "theft or leakage of arms from our facilities is impossible."[51] Independent experts have noted that modern security and control systems have been installed—often paid for by Western funds—around civilian facilities, such as nuclear research institutes but not in military sites where "the security risk is greatest but where Russian authorities have not allowed a U.S. presence."[52] General Vladimir Verkhovtsev, chief of the Defense Ministry's Twelfth Directorate that "runs practically the whole reserve of nuclear ammunition" announced in September 2006 that systems guarding nuclear weapons were "currently being improved" and their modernization would be completed "within two–three years," suggesting that the security of nuclear weapons remains a serious, "live" issue.[53]

Threats to the safety of hazardous materials and to that of the environment often go hand in hand. Consider the Mayak Nuclear Waste Disposal Facility located just east of the Urals in Chelyabinsk Oblast, which is Russia's biggest reprocessor of spent nuclear fuel and is widely regarded as the site of some of the worst radioactive contamination on earth.[54] Mayak reportedly has been bankrupt since 2003 and has been a habitual violator of antidumping policies in nearby rivers. It has also been the scene of serious security threats in the past decade: a soldier was arrested while breaking into a warehouse, copper cabling has been stolen, aluminum rods have been discovered outside the plant, among other things. In February 2006 prosecutors brought charges against Mayak's management and in the following month sacked its general manager for ignoring the rules on handling hazardous substances—apparently "several dozen million cubic meters of liquid radioactive waste spilled into the Techa River"—and for "misusing public funds," usually a euphemism for large-scale embezzlement.[55]

Cooperation on nuclear issues between the United States and Russia has improved after the 11 September 2001, terrorist attacks. In June 2002 Washington withdrew from the 1972 Anti-Ballistic Missile Treaty—in accordance with treaty's provisions—to pursue a new missile-defense system. The Russian president downplayed fears about this action and declared that confrontation with NATO no longer was realistic. In any case, Russia's arms industry has developed new weapons in the last several years, including the mobile, off-road capable RS-12M1 Topol-M intercontinental ballistic missile with new generation warheads that apparently can penetrate any missile defense system. According to defense officials in Moscow, by 2025, when the U.S. plans to complete the deployment of its new missile defense, Russia's strategic nuclear forces will already have switched to weaponry capable of overcoming that defense.[56] Irritating items regarding nuclear proliferation issues remain between the two countries. One issue that has long troubled Washington and some of its allies has been Russia's willingness to transfer nuclear technology to and/or to maintain military ties with—not to mention to sell conventional weapons such as surface-to-air missiles to—states that Western governments consider sponsors of terrorism, such as Iran, North Korea, and Syria.[57]

NATO and Its Expansion

The enlargements of NATO have been among the most important events of international politics in the post–Cold War era.[58] One of the controversial aspects of the alliance's expansion was Russia's role or, rather the lack of it, in the process. Successive American administrations have insisted that enlargement was not directed against anyone and rejected the notion that it was an anti-Russian measure. Although the Kremlin acknowledged early on that it could not halt NATO's expansion, Moscow also made it abundantly clear that it did not support it. When talking about Russian views of NATO one should not fail to note that there is a distinct difference between the top brass' position on the alliance (full of suspicion and basically uniformly negative) and those of the political leadership (much more variable and dependent on political circumstances).

Perhaps the most important implication of NATO expansion to the concerns of this study is that it has harmed the prospects of democracy in Russia because it directly supported the stance of antidemocratic political forces there. NATO's enlargement also amounted to a breach of faith by

the West, after the assurances given to Gorbachev during the talks leading
to German reunification that it would not take place. Explaining the dan-
gers NATO expansion posed to his country Russian foreign minister Andrei Kozyrev declared in 1995 that "two things will kill the democratic
experiment here—a major economic catastrophe and NATO enlargement."[59] No significant segment of Russian political or military elites has
supported the Alliance's expansion. In 1997, the liberal reformer Anatolii
Chubais noted that this issue was the only one on which he agreed with
Communist leader Gennadii Zhuganov and nationalist maverick Vladimir Zhirinovsky.[60] Those who warned that relations between the United
States and Russia would worsen following the first expansion of the alliance were right. After 1997 Russian-American ties deteriorated, at least
partly owing to NATO's enlargement. Russia denounced NATO's war in
Kosovo and interfered in its operations after the cease-fire. The Alliance's
air campaign against Yugoslavia precipitated the most precarious turn in
Russian-Western relations since the early 1980s.[61]

Actually, the idea of Russian membership in the Alliance has surfaced
time and again beginning in 1994 when German defense minister Volker
Rühe and his colleague, William Perry, openly disagreed on this point
(Perry insisting that the issue was not closed).[62] In May 2000 NATO secretary general Lord George Robertson and a year later President George W.
Bush—in reference to President Putin's floating of the idea—said that
Moscow could one day join NATO though they avoided saying when that
might be.[63] Since the formation of the NATO-Russia Council in 2002, a
Russian ambassador has been invited to attend meetings and discuss issues of mutual concern. Diplomatic sources in Moscow have suggested
that while Russia wants to maintain good relations with the alliance, it
was not interested in membership in it. Russia's generals are even less
supportive. An article in the Russian Army's daily *Krasnaia Zvezda* maintained that "NATO [was] an American organization living on mostly
American money and implementing mostly American interests" and contended that, given Moscow's improving relations with European NATO
members, Washington should worry not about including Russia in the
alliance but keeping the Europeans in.[64] Even in the long run, Russia is
unlikely to become a full-fledged NATO member.

In spite of more cordial U.S.-Russian relations following the 11 September terrorist attacks, Moscow has remained skeptical at best about the
need and wisdom of further NATO enlargement, particularly expansion
that included republics of the former Soviet Union. Nonetheless, as

NATO was gearing up for the 2002 Prague Summit—during which it extended membership invitations to seven countries, including the three Baltic states—alliance leaders had done their best to assure Russia of their good intentions. Alexander Vershbow, the U.S. ambassador to Moscow, declared that Russia was "key to [NATO's] new agenda" while high-ranking NATO officials repeatedly sketched a bright future for NATO-Russia cooperation. President Bush did his own part by habitually referring to his colleague in the Kremlin as "my good friend Vladimir." Predictably, Russian military elites seemed less impressed by the love-fest between Washington and Moscow.[65] The reason Putin's opposition to enlargement has become less intense, however, might well have been his growing realization that with the addition of new members with extremely weak armies the Alliance was destined to become precisely "the sort of toothless political institution that Russia [had long] hoped for."[66]

NATO's eastward expansion has also served a convenient and logical justification for Russian military elites to continue to perceive the West as a potential enemy and to review Russia's conventional and nuclear strategy. The reality of NATO bases in a number of East European states and the former Soviet republics of the Baltics, not to mention the presence of American troops in the Kyrgyzstan and Uzbekistan, have provided a strong incentive for Moscow to adjust its own defense policies. Despite better relations with NATO, officials in Moscow, including Defense Minister Ivanov, continue to insist that the Alliance's military doctrine is "offensive" and a direct threat to Russia.[67] Nonetheless, Russian politicians frequently contradict themselves because they tailor their public statements to their audiences. Ivanov, for instance, soon after condemning the Alliance's purportedly offensive doctrine—when he was addressing a group of Russian generals—called for closer practical cooperation between Moscow and NATO in the fields of antiterrorism and regional security in front of Western journalists.[68] Speaking at the Council on Foreign Relations in New York, however, Ivanov called the "NATO-Russia relationship . . . undoubtedly one of the crucial contributions to both global and regional security."[69]

Although NATO-Russia relations are hardly unclouded, disagreements have not prevented the emergence of substantial cooperation in some respects. There have been a number of joint exercises and discussions of nuclear security and antiterrorism initiatives. Russia also readily cooperated with NATO in Afghanistan.[70] The NATO-Russia Council now has some twenty specialized groups concentrating on specific problems on a permanent basis. As so often happens, the proliferation of person-to-person contacts has led to more mutual trust and cooperation and, according to some experts, is slowly changing the anti-American mentality on the individual level. In recent years, Russia has also participated in large-scale military maneuvers with China and India, although an actual security pact between them may not be in the offing.[71]

Russian and American Interests

President Yeltsin was regarded in Moscow as someone too willing to toe the Western line. In the first couple of years of Putin's presidency, the military and security agencies were also occasionally disillusioned about what they saw as his "Gorbachevian" foreign policy and constant retreat in response to Western actions. This, according to Lilia Shevtsova, is one reason why the military has become even more vocal in politics, at times going as far as talking about "geostrategic suicide."[72] Nonetheless, during Putin's presidency the objective of regaining Russia's status as a great power has been pursued with vigor. Some experts suggest that his driving concern has always been the "restoration of Russian greatness" and the armed forces are clearly an essential component of that greatness.[73]

In an authoritarian state like Russia, foreign policy is not necessarily reflective of popular desires. Although Putin does not have to seek the approval of any real political opposition his foreign policy decisions are nevertheless constrained by the constituencies he does need to satisfy and the objectives he wants to achieve. Those constituencies are the security services, the armed forces, and the military-industrial complex, institutions that view the United States and the West less favorably than Russian society in general. At the same time, the kind of elevated international prestige that Putin and the *siloviki* covet and have successfully obtained— membership in the G8, the respect they are afforded as representatives of a major nuclear power, the invitations they receive to high-powered international conventions—remains entirely dependent on Western governments. Therefore, the unjustifiably elevated international status that Putin and Russian political elites do enjoy might be thought of as a sort of insurance policy (and, thus, justification) that they will refrain from taking steps that would lead to Russia become an international outcast and losing that status.

Even though the superficiality of Russia's democratic veneer has become increasingly apparent, it seems that as long as the Kremlin does not make terrible strategic mistakes and as long as Western statesmen are willing to play along with the charade of Russia's "managed democracy," Moscow may continue to bask in the prestige granted by the West. This is the reason that George Bush was Putin's favorite American presidential candidate in 2004. After all, Bush did not listen to congressmen and senators—most prominently the former presidential candidate, Senator John McCain—who wanted Russia excluded from the G-8. Moreover, the Kremlin probably calculated that John Kerry—and, historically, presidential candidates of the Democratic Party—would be more critical of Russia's human rights record and more mindful of the sham of its "democratization process."

At the risk of stating the obvious, some of the major problems between the United States and Russia remain because the United States is a western democracy and Russia is not. Promoting democracy domestically or abroad—especially if the location happens to be on Moscow's doorstep—is not considered to be in Russia's national interest. Among the former Soviet republics the Kremlin has preferred dictatorships and authoritarian states (e.g., Belarus, Kazakhstan, Tajikistan, Turkmenistan, Uzbekistan) and has responded to genuine democratization processes (Georgia, Kyrgyzstan, Ukraine) with heavy-handed intervention. In February 2006 Defense Minister Ivanov declared that Europe's last remaining tyrant, Aleksandr Lukashenko, was "the most popular candidate in Belarus," and if a democratization movement should emerge there Moscow "will react negatively, of course."[74] Putin also praised Lukashenko's "seeking constructive work with all sides" the day after Belarusian courts sentenced four prominent opposition leaders to prison terms to join others who had already been incarcerated.[75] Russia is even more opposed to the emergence of functioning democracies on its borders that might eventually want to join NATO—as Georgia and Ukraine have already indicated.[76] Another logical reason the Kremlin abhors the revolutions in neighboring states is that they jeopardize the viability of long-standing Russian military installations there.

In Central Asia, U.S. and Russian interests have collided more directly. After "losing" the Baltic states to the West, the Kremlin is determined not to see its position further weakened in its own neighborhood. It has become all too aware of Central Asia as its "historically rightful" sphere of interest and is loath to share, let alone relinquish, its hegemony. Accordingly, Moscow launched a comprehensive effort to bring Central Asia—where U.S. military units surfaced after 11 September 2001, and the beginning of the war against the Taliban in Afghanistan—under its control using military and economic instruments of power. In 2002 Russia established a six-member (Armenia, Belarus, Kazakhstan, Kyrgyzstan, Russia, and Tajikistan) military alliance, the Collective Security Treaty Organization (CSTO). Actually the CSTO is a renamed and updated version of the Commonwealth of Independent States' Collective Security Treaty, signed a decade ago. In a short time CTSO has become so active that one Russian analyst dubbed it "our own version of NATO."[77] Beginning with 2005, CSTO members started purchasing arms and military equipment from Russia on privileged terms. In October 2005 CSTO Secretary-General (and Colonel General of the Army) Nikolai Bordiuzha announced that a "large group of forces" would be created in Central Asia composed "not from battalions, but from regiments and divisions and, in the event of serious military conflict, it will defend CSTO members from all sides."[78] In the following month CSTO leaders decided to coordinate military training and to set up a working group "to monitor the situation" in Afghanistan.[79]

Russia maintains sixteen military bases and facilities abroad with approximately forty thousand servicemen and twenty-five thousand civilian employees.[80] They are currently stationed in Georgia, Kyrgyzstan, Transdniestria, Tajikistan, Ukraine (in the Sevastopol naval base which serves as the headquarters of Russia's Black Sea Fleet), and Uzbekistan. Bilateral agreements call for Moscow to withdraw its troops from Georgia by the end of 2007 and its sailors from Ukraine by 2017. Recent official statements suggest that Russia intends to keep its troops in Transdniestria "at least until 2020" and in Tajikistan for "another 10–15 years."[81] Of course, the Kremlin is not pleased about the presence of U.S. troops in the region and has repeatedly called for their pullout once the situation is stabilized in Afghanistan.

The United States established an airbase in Karshi-Khanabad, Uzbekistan, in 2001 to support American operations in Afghanistan.[82] Initially, Washington planned to lease the facility for twenty-five years and invested hundreds of millions of dollars in its improvement and maintenance. However, when the Uzbek government cracked down and killed as many twelve hundred peaceful protesters in Andijan in May 2005, Washington and the West saw a dictatorship at work while Russia saw demonstrators attempting to seize power. A senior Russian official praised the Uzbek government's bloody crackdown, saying that it "made proper conclusion and took proper steps which were absolutely correct."[83] After the U.S. government condemned the Uzbek regime and called for an international investigation, Islam Karimov, the Uzbek strongman, and his rubber-stamp parliament demanded the withdrawal of American forces from the country. The United States complied ahead of schedule and its place was taken—literally and figuratively—by Russian troops in early 2006, when Uzbekistan joined the CSTO.

Actually, Karimov had begun to worry about the U.S. forces in his country in March 2005 when Washington moved quickly to support the popular uprising in Kyrgyzstan that eventually unseated another tyrant, Askar Akaev.[84] Kyrgyzstan currently hosts both Russian *and* American troops on its territory, in bases only twenty miles apart. The U.S. presence there is irksome not only to Moscow but also to Beijing which has been interested in purchasing oilfields in neighboring Kazakhstan and has conducted joint military exercises with Kyrgyz forces. Although Russia withdrew its last border troops from Kyrgyzstan in 1998, five years later Bishkek authorized the opening of a Russian airbase in the Kyrgyz town of Kant.[85] Moscow made an unsuccessful attempt to interfere (true to form, on the dictator's behalf) in the 2005 Kyrgyz crisis using airplanes based at the Kant facility, but the fallout from this strategic blunder appears to have been moderate.[86]

The Folly of Appeasement

In late 2003 President George W. Bush declared Russia "a country in which democracy and freedom and rule of law thrive."[87] By this time, as Grigorii Yavlinski—an influential politician with the liberal Yabloko party—noted, Russia had "not [been] free" for a decade and the last vestiges of democratic institutions established after the collapse of communism had nearly vanished.[88] "Russian democracy" has become a cynical joke that seems not to have been recognized by some Western governments. One can understand the reasons for not wanting to unnecessarily antagonize Moscow, given some important mutual objectives—the fight against international terrorism, most obviously—and Western Europe's high-level of dependence on Russian energy. This is all the more important because, as Europeans were forced to realize in the winter of 2005–6, the Kremlin is not above using its gas deliveries for blackmail.[89]

Nevertheless, one cannot help but wonder why some Western leaders pretend that Russia is a functioning democracy? As a presidential candidate, George W. Bush called Moscow's brutality in Chechnya "unacceptable" and criticized the Clinton administration's indulgent attitude toward Russia. Can the terrorist attacks of 11 September and the subsequent low-level cooperation between the two countries really excuse official Washington's lack of apprehension regarding the breakdown of Russia's democratic experiment? What additional egregious assault does the Kremlin need to make on fundamental civic and human rights to finally push the United States, Britain, and other leading lights of the West to take a stand and stop appeasing and complimenting Moscow? When the remaining few courageous Russian journalists and scholars literally risk their lives to call the world's attention to Russia's drift toward autocracy, one is perplexed by the way some of their American colleagues applaud the "achievements" of Russian democracy and market reform.[90] How far is the West willing to go to compromise its own democratic standards by continuing this "friendship"?

Can democratic governments continue to be deceived by the statements of Russian politicians that are squarely contradicted by their actions? "Rest assured," Defense Minister Ivanov recently said to an audience at the Council on Foreign Relations in New York, "Russia [has] opted for the development of the democratic state, and adhering to the principles of a multipolar world."[91] Six months later, he termed the "attempt to democratize according to Western values is . . . a conscious provocation."[92] Should anyone take Putin seriously when he announces that "the main political-ideological task is the development of Russia as a free, democratic country" and that "without liberty and democracy there can be no order and no stability" when, in the very same April 2005 speech he describes the breakup of the Soviet Union as "the biggest geopolitical catastrophe of the twentieth century"?[93] Or, when, in a December 2004 public address he contended that the Russian media was as free as any other *and* suggested that the government make its work a bit less open for the media?[94]

Notwithstanding its frequent *declarations* of cooperation and partnership, the Kremlin's *actions* show that it has viewed Russian-American relations—not just in the former Soviet lands as we saw above, but around the globe—as a zero-sum game: whatever is bad for the United States must be good for Russia. There are many examples. A rift develops between the United States and some of its NATO allies following the 2003 invasion of Iraq; Moscow steps into the fray to forge closer ties with France and Germany. The United States—and the West—strongly objects to Iran's nuclear program; Russia insists on continuing to supply it, even though acquiring an unstable nuclear power on its own borders might not be the wisest policy. Hamas—an organization that openly repudiates Israel's right to exist and with whose leaders the United States refuses to bargain—wins the Palestinian elections; Russia is quick to hold talks with its leaders in Moscow. Venezuela's virulently anti-American president, Hugo Chávez, wants to rearm to "deter or repel any invasion by U.S. forces"; Russia is happy to oblige with a sale of 100,000 Kalashnikov rifles, a new Kalashnikov-producing factory, and 24 Sukhoi-30 fighter jets.[95]

In a recent article, Goldgeier and McFaul laid out a sensible proposal for a new U.S. foreign policy toward Russia.[96] They argue that the Bush administration should "slow Russia's democratic deterioration" via a deeper engagement both with the Russian government and Russian society. This is all the more important after the severe restrictions on NGOs became a law in January 2006.[97] Goldgeier and McFaul contend that

> what is most needed is a new version of the dual-track strategy President Ronald Reagan pursued after 1982: offering serious cooperation on strategic matters while at the same time standing up for America's democratic principles—principles President Bush has eloquently elaborated in discussing other parts of the world—and engaging directly with Russian society to help foster democratic development.[98]

Such a policy might include a new bilateral agreement pledging to discontinue research and development on nuclear weapons, making American assistance on the deactivation of existing Russian nuclear arms contingent on verifiable results, and discouraging Moscow's adverse influence on democratization movements in the former Soviet territories and elsewhere. The United States and its allies should be more assertive about Russia's human rights record and make Moscow's participation in international groups (such as the G-8) and conventions conditional on its implementation of democratic reforms. Pretending that Russia is progressing toward democracy even as it is moving in the opposite direction has served only the Kremlin's objectives while underscoring Western hypocrisy.

America has a vital interest in the evolution of a stable and democratic Russia. The deterioration of Moscow's conventional forces logically leads to its greater dependence on nuclear weapons, which, as recent accidents have shown, are not nearly as reliable as they should be.[99] This makes for a potentially very dangerous situation in a future crisis scenario. Some experts have suggested that the United States should step up efforts to increase military-to-military and military-to-civilian contacts with Russia, focusing on mid-level officers who might still be willing to entertain the notion that America is not Russia's sworn enemy. Nonetheless, this may not be an easy task. The two countries do not have the experience in military cooperation that would encourage trust between them. Levels of political trust have also been falling lately, in part due to much needed public statements about the shortcomings of Russian democratization by U.S. vice president Dick Cheney, Secretary of State Condoleezza Rice, and newly elected German chancellor Angela Merkel. Ultimately, as Alexei Arbatov recently noted, Washington and Russia "are still looking at each other as potential enemies" and "under these circumstances we cannot count on cooperation."[100] These perceptions will be hard to change as long as the substantially unreformed Russian military establishment continues to have an institutional interest in maintaining and perpetuating its Cold War attitudes.

The failure of Russian defense reform, as I argued in this book, reflects the type of civil-military relations that have emerged in an increasingly authoritarian state dominated by a virtually omnipotent president. To be sure, it would be unwise to presume that Russia could quickly develop civilian control and monitoring mechanisms similar to those that prevail in stable democracies. At the same time, it must be openly acknowledged that elemental democratic norms—such as the executive and legislative branches' shared obligation to oversee the armed forces—do not hold in any substantive form in Russian civil-military relations, and given overall political trends, a real change is unlikely to soon occur. Similarly, no one should have expected that Russia would have a consolidated democracy within a decade after the fall of the Soviet Union. But fundamental problems must not be papered over. It is time for Western governments to explicitly recognize that for more than a decade now Russia has been moving toward autocracy, not democracy, and adjust their policies appropriately.

((((

NOTES

Introduction

1. Jeffrey Tayler, "Russia Is Finished," *The Atlantic Monthly* 287:5 (May 2001): 51.

2. Michael McFaul, Nikolai Petrov, and Andrei Ryabov, *Between Dictatorship and Democracy: Russian Post-Communist Political Reform* (Washington, DC: Carnegie Endowment, 2004), 20.

3. *Structure and Change in Economic History* (New York: W. W. Norton, 1981), 201–2.

4. North cited in Paul DiMaggio and Walter Powell, introduction in DiMaggio and Powell, eds., *The New Institutionalism in Organizational Analysis* (Chicago: University of Chicago Press, 1991), 8.

5. Peter A. Hall, "The Movement from Keynesianism to Monetarism: Institutional Analysis and British Economic Policy in the 1970s," in Sven Steinmo, Kathleen Thelen, and Frank Longstreth, eds., *Structuring Politics: Historical Institutionalism in Comparative Analysis* (New York: Cambridge University Press, 1992), 96.

6. Robert H. Bates, R. P. de Figueiredo, Jr., and Barry R. Weingast, "The Politics of Interpretation: Rationality, Culture, and Transition," *Politics and Society* 26:4 (December 1998): 604–5.

7. Margaret Levi, "A Logic of Institutional Change," in Karen S. Cook and Margaret Levi, eds., *The Limits of Rationality* (Chicago: University of Chicago Press, 1990), 407.

8. North, *Institutions, Institutional Change, and Economic Performance* (New York: Cambridge University Press, 1990), 89.

9. Margaret Weir, "Ideas and the Politics of Bounded Innovation," in Steinmo, Thelen, and Longstreth, eds., *Structuring Politics*, 192.

194 NOTES TO INTRODUCTION

10. Paul Pierson, "When Effects Become Cause: Policy Feedback and Political Change," *World Politics* 45:4 (July 1993): 602. See also Kathleen Thelen, "Historical Institutionalism in Comparative Politics," *Annual Review of Political Science* 2 (June 1999): 369–404.

11. North, *Institutions, Institutional Change, and Economic Performance*, 100.

12. Paul Pierson, *Politics in Time: History, Institutions, and Social Analysis* (Princeton: Princeton University Press, 2004), 10.

13. Minxin Pei, "Racing Against Time: Institutional Decay and Renewal in China," in William A. Joseph, ed., *The China Briefing* (Armonk, NY: M. E. Sharpe, 1997), 27–28.

14. Neil J. Melvin, *Soviet Power and the Countryside : Policy Innovation and Institutional Decay* (New York : Palgrave, 2004), 25–26; see also 189–92.

15. Neil Devotta, *Blowback: Linguistic Nationalism, Institutional Decay, and Ethnic Conflict in Sri Lanka* (Stanford, CA: Stanford University Press, 2004), 16.

16. James Burk, "Theories of Democratic Civil-Military Relations," *Armed Forces and Society* 29:1 (fall 2002): 7.

17. See, for instance, John J. Johnson, ed., *The Role of the Military in Underdeveloped Countries* (Princeton: Princeton University Press, 1962); Edward Luttwak, *Coup d'État: A Practical Handbook* (Cambridge: Harvard University Press, 1968); and Donald L. Horowitz, *Coup Theories and Officers' Motives* (Princeton: Princeton University Press, 1980).

18. Timothy J. Colton, *Commissars, Commanders, and Civilian Authority: The Structure of Soviet Military Politics* (Cambridge: Harvard University Press, 1979), 231–49, esp. 234.

19. Alfred Stepan, *Rethinking Military Politics: Brazil and the Southern Cone* (Princeton: Princeton University Press, 1988), 92–97.

20. For a careful appraisal of these theoretical contributions, see Peter D. Feaver, "Civil-Military Relations," *Annual Review of Political Science* 2 (June 1999): 211–41.

21. Brian D. Taylor, *Politics and the Russian Army: Civil-Military Relations, 1689–2000* (New York: Cambridge University Press, 2003), 17.

22. Zoltan Barany, "Democratic Consolidation and the Military," *Comparative Politics* 30:1 (October 1997): 26–28.

23. See, for instance, Samuel P. Huntington, *The Third Wave: Democratization in the Late Twentieth Century* (Norman: University of Oklahoma Press, 1991), 232; and Valerie Bunce, "Rethinking Recent Democratization: Lessons from the Postcommunist Experience," *World Politics* 55:2 (January 2003): 175.

24. Thomas M. Nichols, *The Sacred Cause: Civil-Military Conflict over Soviet National Security, 1917–1992* (Ithaca, NY: Cornell University Press, 1993), 11–12.

25. See, for instance, Pavel K. Baev, *The Russian Army in a Time of Troubles* (London: Sage, 1996); Dale R. Herspring, *Russian Civil-Military Relations* (Bloomington: Indiana University Press, 1996); S. S. Solovyev and I. V. Obraztsov,

Rossiiskaia armia ot Afganistana do Chechnii (Moscow: Natsionalnii Institut imeni Yekaterini Velikoi, 1997); Robert V. Barylski, *The Soldier in Russian Politics: Duty, Dictatorship, and Democracy under Gorbachev and Yeltsin* (New Brunswick, NJ: Transaction, 1998); William E. Odom, *The Collapse of the Soviet Military* (New Haven: Yale University Press, 1998); P. Gazukin, *Rossiiskaia Armia na poroge XXI veka* (Moscow: Panorama, 1999); Françoise Daucé, *L'État, l'armée, et le citoyen en Russie post-soviétique* (Paris: Ed. L'Harmattan, 2001); P. Gazukin, *Stroitel'stvo i reformirovanie vooruzhennykh sil RF v 2000–2001 gg.* (Moscow: Panorama, 2001); Vladimir A. Zolotarev, *Voennaia bezopasnost' Gosudarstva Rossiiskogo* (Moscow: Kuchkovo pole, 2001); V. I. Dobrenkov, *Sotsiologia v Rossii: Voennaia sotsiologia* (Moscow: MUBIU, 2002); John Moran, *From Garrison State to Nation State: Political Power and the Russian Military under Gorbachev and Yeltsin* (Westport, CT: Praeger, 2002); Anne C. Aldis and Roger N. McDermott, eds., *Russian Military Reform, 1992–2002* (London: Frank Cass, 2003); Taylor, *Politics and the Russian Army*, esp. 206–320; Steven E. Miller and Dmitri Trenin, eds., *The Russian Military: Power and Policy* (Cambridge: MIT Press, 2004); and Aleksandr Golts, *Armia Rossii: 11 poteriannikh let* (Moscow: Zaharov, 2004).

26. See Thomas M. Nichols, *The Russian Presidency: Society and Politics in the Second Russian Republic* (London: Macmillan, 2001); Lilia Shevtsova, *Putin's Russia* (Washington, DC: Carnegie Endowment for International Peace, 2003); Richard Sakwa, *Putin: Russia's Choice* (London: Routledge, 2004); Peter Reddaway, *The Dynamics of Russian Politics: Putin's Reform of Federal-Regional Relations* (Lanham, MD: Rowman and Littlefield, 2005); and Timothy J. Colton and Cindy Skach, "The Russian Predicament," *Journal of Democracy* 16:3 (July 2005): 113–26.

27. *Webster's Ninth New Collegiate Dictionary* (Springfield, MA: Merriam-Webster, 1984), 990.

28. See, for instance, Edward N. Luttwak, *Strategy: The Logic of War and Peace* (Cambridge: Harvard University Press, 1987), 4.

29. See B. H. Liddell Hart, *Strategy* (New York: Praeger, 1954) 335.

30. Barry R. Posen, *The Sources of Military Doctrine* (Ithaca, NY: Cornell University Press, 1984), 7.

Chapter 1
The Tragedy and Symbolism of the *Kursk*

1. See Yuri Kliuev, "Sailor's Truth: Naval Exercises—How They Are Organized," *Izvestia*, 4 December 2001; and Ramsey Flynn, *Cry from the Deep: The Submarine Disaster that Riveted the World and Put the New Russia to the Ultimate Test* (New York: HarperCollins, 2004).

2. For more extensive technical data, see Bellona Report #2:96 by Thomas Nilsen, Igor Kudrik, and Alexandr Nikitin (http://spb.org.ru/bellona/ehome/russia/nfl/949a.htm). See also George Sviatov, "The Kursk's Loss Offers Lessons," *Proceedings of the United States Naval Institute* 129:6 (June 2003).

3. "Kursk: The Living Nightmare that Laid Bare Russia's Disarray," AFP (Moscow) August 9, 2001.

4. See Sergei Ivashko, "Relatives' Attempts to Resurrect Kursk Case Fails," http://www.gazeta.ru, 30 December 2002.

5. Numerous authors have made this connection between the two tragedies. See, for instance, Alla Yaroshinskaia, "A Putin Supporter Recants," *New York Times*, 14 August 2000; Georgi Bovt, "Russian Elite's Old Reflexes," *Izvestia*, 18 August 2000; Amy Knight, "Blame It on the Kremlin," *Globe and Mail*, 29 October 2002; and "Russia Marks Fifth Anniversary of Kursk Submarine Sinking," AFP (Moscow), 13 August 2005.

6. Anatolii Shvedov, "Resignations Take Place," *Izvestia*, 3 December 2001; and Alexander Golts, "Kursk Firings Should Not Be Military's Last," *Russia Journal*, 7–13 December 2001.

7. See Pavel Felgenhauer, "Cover-Up in Sub Tragedy," *Moscow Times*, 17 August 2000; and "The Chronicle of Tragedy" at http://www.mediaprom.ru/kursk/1/eng/xron...html.

8. See Viktor Baranets's interview with Kuroedov in *Komsomolskaia Pravda*, 22 November 2001, 8–9.

9. See the interview with Vice Admiral (Ret.) Yuri Senatskii in *Trud*, 22 August 2001; and *Novaya Gazeta*, 6–12 December 2001, 2.

10. Mark Kramer, "The Sinking of the Kursk," PONARS Policy Memo #145, 4 September 2000.

11. See Alexander Golts, "Military Reform Sinks Along with the Kursk," *Russia Journal*, 2 September 2000.

12. Vladimir Semiriaga, "The Cover Story," *Moskovskii Komsomolets*, 15 November 2001.

13. See, for instance, "Russia Blows Up Remains of Kursk to Protect Military Secrets," AFP (Moscow), 9 September 2002.

14. Clive Burleson, *Kursk Down!* (New York: Warner Books, 2002), 163.

15. "Kursk: The Living Nightmare that Laid Bare Russia's Disarray," AFP (Moscow), 9 August 2001.

16. See the interview with Manilov in *Krasnaia Zvezda*, 9 September 2000.

17. "Statement of Fatherland-All Russia Duma Faction Presented by Yevgenii Primakov," Federal News Service (Moscow), 23 August 2000, in Johnson's Russia List (henceforth JRL), 26 August 2000.

18. Cited in Radio Free Europe/Radio Liberty Newsline I (henceforth RFE/RL) 4:180 (18 September 2000).

19. AFP (Moscow), 15 September 2000; and Russia TV (Moscow), 7AM GMT, 15 September 2000 (BBC Monitoring).

20. Thomas Friedman, "A Russian Dinosaur," *New York Times*, 5 September 2000.

21. Cited in *Christian Science Monitor*, 22 August 2000.

22. See Boris Kagarlitsky, "Submarine Tragedy Breaches Curtain of Lies," in JRL #4486 (1 September 2000).

23. See, for instance, RFE/RL I, 4:164 (25 August 2000); Robert G. Kaiser, "Kursk Crew Sent No Signals after Sinking, Putin Says," *Washington Post*, 8 September 2000; Kramer, "The Sinking of the Kursk," 3; Alexei Smirnov, "Corruption Accompanies Raising of the Kursk," *Novye Izvestia*, 16 February 2002, 1–2.

24. See Vladimir Putin, *First Person: An Astonishingly Frank Self-Portrait by Russia's President* (New York: Public Affairs, 2000), Oleg Blotskii, *Vladimir Putin: Istoriia zhizn'i* (Moscow: Mezhdunarodnie otnoshenia, 2001); and Richard Sakwa, *Putin: Russia's Choice* (London: Routledge, 2003).

25. *Moskovskii Komsomolets*, 16 July 2001. See also, Lilia Shevtsova, "From Yeltsin to Putin: The Evolution of Presidential Power," in Archie Brown and Lilia Shevtsova, eds., *Gorbachev, Yeltsin, and Putin: Political Leadership in Russia's Transition* (Washington, DC: Carnegie Endowment for International Peace, 2001), 96–97.

26. See http://www.gazeta.ru, 21 August 2000.

27. Interfax (St. Petersburg), 15 September 2000.

28. Gorbachev continues to blame others for his handling of the crisis. See his "Turning Point at Chernobyl," *The Daily Times* (Pakistan), 17 April 2006.

29. See, for instance, his interview with CNN's Larry King in JRL, #4501 (9 September 2000).

30. Cited by Reuters (Moscow), 18 August 2000.

31. See Robert Moore, *A Time to Die: The Untold Story of the Kursk Tragedy* (New York: Crown, 2002), 247. See also Lilia Shevtsova, *Putin's Russia* (Washington, DC: Carnegie Endowment for International Peace, 2003), 115–18.

32. William E. Odom, *The Collapse of the Soviet Military* (New Haven: Yale University Press, 1998), 108–10.

33. See AP (Moscow), 23 August 2000; and AFP (Moscow), 13 September 2000.

34. Viacheslav Gudkov, "Northern Fleet Sails Out," *Kommersant*, 23 September 2002.

35. Yevgeniia Borisova, "Charities for the Kursk Sprout Up," *Moscow Times*, 23 August 2000.

36. "Kursk: The Living Nightmare that Laid Bare Russia's Disarray," AFP (Moscow), 9 August 2001.

37. Interview with General Valerii Manilov in *Krasnaia Zvezda*, 9 September 2000; and the interview with Admiral Eduard Baltin in *Nezavisimaia Gazeta*, 11 August 2001.

38. Catherine Merridale, "Cheated of Their Vodka and Cake," *New States-man*, 4 September 2000 in JRL, #4492 (5 September 2000). See also, Carlotta Gall and Thomas de Waal, *Chechnya: Calamity in the Caucasus* (New York: New York University Press, 1998), 14–17; and Anatol Lieven, *Chechnya: Tombstone of Russian Power* (New Haven: Yale University Press, 1998), 110–11.

39. Quoted in *Izvestia*, 28 August 2002.

40. See, for instance, Catherine Merridale, *Night of Stone: Death and Memory in Russia* (London: Granta Books, 2000).

41. See the interview with Admiral Senatskii in *The Guardian*, 17 September 2001.

42. *Vremia Novostei*, 22 August 2000.

43. See the interview in Interfax (Moscow), 12 June 2001.

44. Vladimir Malevannii, "The Investigation Is Ignoring the Law," *Nezavi-simoe Voennoe Obozrenie* #29, 10 August 2001, 2.

45. Burleson, *Kursk Down!*, 113.

46. See, for instance, "Russian Lawmaker Says Kursk Sank after Collision with British Sub," AFP (Moscow), 25 October 2000; *Zavtra* #48, November 2000, 1; "Polite NATO Wearies of Russia's Kursk Suspicions," Reuters (Brussels), 10 November 2000.

47. See Marina Tokareva's article, "Everyone Knows Why the Kursk Went Down," *Obshchaia Gazeta* #3, January 2001, 1; *Nezavisimaia Gazeta*, #12, January 2001. See also, *Rossiiskaia Gazeta*, 26 May 2001, 1.

48. See RFE/RL 4:164 (25 August 2000); the Kavkaz Tsentr document at www.kolumbus.fi/kavkaz/english/25_8.htm in JRL, #4480 (28 August 2000); and Interfax (Moscow), 29 August 2000 in JRL, #4484 (29 August 2000).

49. See Vadim Saranov's report in *Versiia*, 17–23 April 2001.

50. *Der Spiegel*, 16 October 2000; RFE/RL 4:215 (6 November 2000); and *Sunday Times* (London), 4 March 2001. For a Russian commentary on this hypothesis, see *Segodnia*, 6 March 2001, 2.

51. "Russian Navy Overrules Kursk Submarine Missile Strike," ITAR-TASS (Moscow), 5 March 2001.

52. See, for instance, *Magyar Nemzet*, 18 February 2002

53. See "Mutiny on the Kursk," *Versiia*, 10 April 2001, 3; and *Komsomolskaia Pravda*, 21 April 2001.

54. "Antigosudarstvennaia taina," *Rossiiskaia Gazeta*, 29 August 2002.

55. For more details about the fuel, see Moore, *A Time to Die*, 32–33.

56. See the interview with Dorogin in *Kommersant*, 27 July 2002; in JRL, #6385 (28 July 2002).

57. *Novaya Gazeta* #1, 10 January 2002; and *Vremia MN*, 13 August 2002.

58. See *Izvestia*, 3 December 2001; and *Nezavisimaia Gazeta*, 4 December 2001.

59. *The Guardian*, 9 August 2001.

60. *Rossiiskaia Gazeta*, 29 August 2002. It is noteworthy that investigators found many of the same problems following the 1989 sinking of the *Komsomolsk*, the last submarine disaster prior to the *Kursk*. See *Tribuna*, 7 April 2002.

61. Cited in *Christian Science Monitor*, 15 August 2000.

62. *Obshchaia Gazeta* #6, 7–13 February 2002.

63. See *Izvestia*, 3 July 2002; UPI (Moscow), 13 July 2002.

64. *Gazeta*, 3 December 2001; and Burleson, *Kursk Down!*, 22.

65. *Moskovskii Komsomolets*, 15 November 2001.

66. See, for instance, *Rossiiskaia Gazeta*, 29 August 2002.

67. See Moore, *A Time to Die*, 125–28.

68. Pavel Felgenhauer, "Military Unfit for New Toys," *Moscow Times*, 21 February 2002.

69. Cited in *Atlanta Journal Constitution*, 12 January 2001; in JRL, #5023 (12 January 2001).

70. See Iain Elliot, "The Kursk Disaster: Casualties of the Secret State," *Times Literary Supplement*, 1 August 2002.

71. See *New York Times*, 5 September 2000; and *Financial Times*, 5 September 2000.

72. See, for instance, NTV International (Moscow), 19:00 GMT, 12 December 2000 (BBC Monitoring in JRL, #4685, [13 December 2000]); and Moore, *A Time to Die*, 176–77.

73. Cited in "Candid Camera: Russia's Past Recaptured in Chilling Incident," *Times* (London), 24 August 2000.

74. *Moscow Times*, 2 September 2000.

75. *Novye Izvestia*, 31 July 2001.

76. Interfax (St. Petersburg), 15 September 2000.

77. Cited by RFE/RL 4:165 (28 August 2000).

78. Cited in *Moscow Times*, 2 September 2000.

79. See *The Sunday Times*, 3 March 2001; and *The Guardian*, 9 August 2001.

80. *NG-Stsenarii*, 15 November 2000, cited by Shevtsova, "From Yeltsin to Putin," 111.

81. RFE/RL 5:152 (13 August 2001). See also "Deep-Sea Fudge," *Economist*, 18 August 2001, 38–39.

82. AP (Murmansk), 27 October 2000. See also Reuters (Moscow), 26 August 2000; *Times* (London), 26 August 2000; and *Izvestia*, 28 August 2002.

83. AP (Moscow), 10 August 2002. See also *Moscow Times*, 23 August 2000.

84. *Izvestia*, 17 June 2002; and ITAR-TASS (Moscow), 5 December 2002. See also Pavel Baev, "The Russian Navy after the Kursk: Still Proud but with Poor Navigation," PONARS Policy Memo #215, January 2002, 4.

85. See RFE/RL 6:158 (22 August 2002); and *Moscow Times*, 5 September 2002.

86. See Yuri Zarakhovich, "Worse than the Kursk?" *Time Europe*, 15 September 2003.

87. See "Negligence Sinks Nuclear Sub," http://www.gazeta.ru, 1 September 2003; and "Coming Clean with Submarines," *The Russia Journal*, 1 September 2003.

88. RFE/RL 10:165 (7 September 2006) and 10:166 (8 September 2006).

89. See Cal McCrystal, "Four Horsemen of the Apparatchiks," *Financial Times*, 14 September 20002. For recent analyses of contemporary Russian media policy, see Masha Lipman and Michael McFaul, "Putin and the Media," in Dale Herspring, ed., *Putin's Russia* (Lanham, MD: Rowman and Littlefield, 2003), 63–84; and Yevgenia Albats, "Russian Media: A Dead Man Still Walking," Center for Public Integrity, 31 January 2005, available at www.publicintegrity.org/ga/report.aspx?aid=601.

90. Cited in RFE/RL 6:236 (18 December 2002).

91. See Seamus Martin, "Legacy of Former Soviet Union Infects New States," *Irish* Times, 22 December 2004. Shchekochikhin's symptoms were a more acute variety of the dioxin poisoning suffered by the then Ukrainian presidential candidate, Viktor Yushchenko in 2004.

92. Glasnost Defense Foundation data cited in Christopher Walker and Robert Orttung, "No News Is Bad News," *Wall Street Journal Europe*, 7 September 2006.

93. "Russia Low on World Press Freedom List," Ekho Moskvy radio (Moscow), 1300 GMT, 27 October 2004.

94. Human Rights Watch, *World Report 2005* (January 2005), at http://www.hrw.org; full text on Russia at http://hrw.org/we2k5/pdf/russia.pdf.

95. "Larry King Live" on CNN, aired 8 September 2000, 9PM EST, in JRL #4501.

96. "Vladimir Putin: Russian Army Has Already Started To Forget About Crisis," Rosbalt (Plesetsk) 18 February 2004.

97. "Putin: Russian Media as Free as Any Other," RIA Novosti (Moscow), 23 December 2004.

98. Michael McFaul in the *Sunday Times*, 27 August 2000.

99. See *Izvestia*, 11 July 2001.

100. David Satter, "A Low, Dishonest Decadence," *The National Interest* 72 (summer 2003): 122–23.

101. See Christian Caryl, "Death in Moscow: The Aftermath," *New York Review of Books*, 19 December 2002, 58–60.

102. "Russian Admiral Criticizes Appeal to NATO for Help in Rescuing Sub," Interfax (Moscow), 6 August 2005.

103. Vladimir Isachenkov, "Rescued Sailors Were Running Low on Oxygen," AP (Petropavlovsk-Kamchatky, Russia), 8 August 2005; and "Chaos, Secrecy Marked Rescue of Submarines: Russian Press," AFP (Moscow), 8 August 2005.

104. Nabi Abdullaev, "Has the Navy Learned the Lessons of the Kursk?" *Moscow Times*, 8 August 2005.

105. "Russia Marks Fifth Anniversary of Kursk Submarine Sinking," AFP (Moscow), 13 August 2005.

106. "A Real Leader Does Not Remain Silent," *Moscow Times*, 8 August 2005.

107. Ibid.

108. Quoted in RIA-Novosti, reported by RFE/RL 9:153 (15 August 2005).

109. "AS-28 and Cliches of the Cold War: We Were Lucky This Time," *Izvestia*, 9 August 2005.

110. Yuri Zakharovich, "Why No One Escaped from the Kursk," *Time* 159:22 (3 June 2002).

111. See also the penultimate chapter, "The Value of Human Life," in David Satter's *Darkness at Dawn: The Rise of the Russian Criminal State* (New Haven: Yale University Press, 2003), 198–221. For a fascinating examination of this concept, see Amnon Sella, *The Value of Human Life in Soviet Warfare* (London: Routledge, 1992).

Chapter 2
Assessing Decay

1. Leo Cooper, *The Political Economy of Soviet Military Power* (New York: St. Martin's Press, 1989), 39. See also A. S. Milovidov, *Voenno-teoreticheskoe nasledie V. I. Lenina i problemy sovremennoi voiny* (Moscow: Voenizdat, 1987).

2. V. D. Sokolovskii, *Soviet Military Strategy* (Englewood Cliffs, NJ: Prentice-Hall, 1963), originally published as *Voennaia Strategiia* (Moscow: Voennoe Izdatel'stvo Ministerstva Oborony SSSR, 1962).

3. See, for instance, Edward N. Luttwak, *The Grand Strategy of the Soviet Union* (New York: St. Martin's, 1983), 39.

4. See, for instance, M. A. Gareev, *M. V. Frunze: Voennii teoretik* (Moscow: Voennizdat, 1985), 242–43. For an excellent discussion of Soviet structural militarism and its legacies, see Steven Rosefielde, *Russia in the 21st Century: The Prodigal Superpower* (New York: Cambridge University Press, 2005), 33–57.

5. Mikhail Gorbachev, "Politicheskii doklad tsentral'novo komiteta KPSS XXVII s'yezdu kommunisticheskoi partii Sovetskogo Soiuza," *Pravda*, 26 February 1986.

6. Andrei A. Kokoshin, *Soviet Strategic Thought, 1917–1991* (Cambridge: MIT Press, 1998), 57. More generally, see Joseph S. Nye, Jr., "Nuclear Learning

and U.S.-Soviet Security Regimes, *International Organization* 41:3 (summer 1987): 371–402.

7. Nikolai V. Ogarkov, *Istoria uchit bditel'nosti* (Moscow: Voenizdat, 1985), 59.

8. See, for instance, V. Varennikov, "Na strazhe mira i bezopasnosti narodov," *Partiinaia zhizn'* 5 (March 1987): 12–13; and Yevgenii Primakov, "Novaya filosofia vneshnei politiki," *Pravda*, 7 July 1988.

9. Marina Kalashnikova, "All They Had to Do Was Give the Signal," *Kommersant Vlast'*, 29 March 2005, translated in Johnson's Russia List (JRL), #9111 (4 April 2005).

10. Sergei Karaganov, "New Military Doctrine Guarantees Russian Security," RIA Novosti (Moscow), 21 February 2000. See also, N. N. Efimov and V. S. Frolov, "V chem. Opasnost' geostrategii brzhezinskovo dlia rossii," *Voennaia mysl'* 5 (1999): 14–21.

11. Ogarkov, *Istoria uchit bditel'nosti*, 72.

12. See, for instance, Harriet Fast Scott and William F. Scott, *Soviet Military Doctrine: Continuity, Formulation, and Dissemination* (Boulder, CO: Westview Press, 1988), 255.

13. See, for instance, M. V. Frunze, *Izberannie proizvedenie* (Moscow: Voennizdat, 1950); and Edward N. Luttwak, *Strategy: The Logic of War and Peace* (Cambridge: Harvard University Press, 1987), 142–43, 152–54.

14. Richard Ned Lebow, "The Soviet Offensive in Europe," in Sean Lynn-Jones, Steven E. Miller, and Stephen Van Evera, eds., *Soviet Military Policy* (Cambridge: MIT Press, 1989), 320.

15. Raymond L. Garthoff, *Deterrence and the Revolution in Soviet Military Doctrine* (Washington, DC: Brooking Institution, 1990), 102–8. For a specific example, see Dmitri Yazov, *Na strazhe sotsializma i mira* (Moscow: Voenizdat, 1987), esp. 31–33.

16. Benjamin S. Lambeth, "A Generation Too Late: Civilian Analysis and Soviet Military Thinking," in Derek Leebaert and Timothy Dickinson, eds., *Soviet Strategy and Military Thinking* (New York: Cambridge University Press, 1992), 217–47.

17. Interview with Shaposhnikov on Radio Rossiia, 21 November 1993; cited in Benjamin S. Lambeth, *Russia's Air Power in Crisis* (Washington, DC: Smithsonian Institution Press, 1999), 37. For a general study on this first post–Cold War decade, see William D. Jackson, "Encircled Again: Russia's Military Assesses Threats in a Post-Soviet World," *Political Science Quarterly* 117:3 (fall 2002): 373–400.

18. Dvorkin quoted in Fred Weir, "Iraqi Defeat Jolts Russian Military," *Christian Science Monitor*, 16 April 2003. See also Alexei Arbatov, *The Transformation of Russian Military Doctrine: Lessons Learned from Kosovo and Chechnya* (Garmisch-Partenkirchen, Germany: George C. Marshall Center, 2000).

19. See, for instance, V. G. Reznichenko, "O voennoi doctrine rossiiskoi fede-ratsii," *Voennaia mysl'* 2 (1996): 9–10; and A. F. Klimenko, "Osobennost' novoi voennoi doktrini," *Voennaia mysl'* 3 (2000): 24–26.

20. Pavel Felgenhauer, "Military Cuts Illusory," *Moscow Time*, 30 August 2001.

21. For discussions of the importance of preparing for local wars, see V. M. Barynkin, "Lokal'nie voiny na sovremennom etape," *Voennaia mysl'* 6 (June 1994), 8–15; and S. Lavrenov, *Sovietskii soiuz v lokoal'nikh voinah i konfliktah* (Moscow: AST, 2005).

22. See, for instance, "General Staff Preparing for Global Nuclear War," Ros-Balt (Moscow), 3 October 2003; RFE/RL 7:189 (3 October 2003); and Alexei Nikolsky, "One War Is Not Enough," *Vedemosti*, 3 October 2003

23. "Defense Minister Encircled by Generals," *Novaya Gazeta*, 20–22 October 2003; and Matthew Bouldin, "The Ivanov Doctrine and Military Reform: Reasserting Stability in Russia," *Journal of Slavic Military Studies* 17:4 (December 2004): 619–41.

24. Cited in Lisa McAdams, "Downsizing of Russian Military Virtually Complete, Says Putin," Voice of America (Moscow), 7 November 2003.

25. "Expert Comments on CGS Baluyevskii's Strategic Situation Forecast," *Gazeta.ru*, 9 March 2005.

26. See Aleksandr Golts, "The Army of Defeat," *Novaya Gazeta*, 7–9 February 2005.

27. Alexei G. Arbatov, "Military Reform: From Crisis to Stagnation," in Steven E. Miller and Dmitri Trenin, eds., *The Russian Military: Power and Policy* (Cambridge: MIT Press, 2004), 105.

28. Trenin, "Conclusion: Gold Eagle, Red Star," in Miller and Trenin, eds., *The Russian Military*, 221.

29. Viktor Myasnikov, "The Red Army: Still the Scariest of Them All," *Nezavisimaia Gazeta*, 27 February 2006.

30. For some of the best U.S. and Russian work, see Steven Rosefielde, *False Science: Underestimating the Soviet Arms Buildup* (London: Transaction, 1982); Franklyn Holzman, "Soviet Military Spending: Assessing the Numbers Game," *International Security* 6:4 (spring 1982): 78–101, and "Politics and Guesswork: CIA and DIA Estimates of Soviet Military Spending," *International Security* 14:2 (fall 1989): 101–31; Lawrence Freeman, *U.S. Intelligence and the Soviet Strategic Threat* (Princeton: Princeton University Press, 1986); E. Gams and V. Makarenko, "Razmyshlenia o raskodakh oshestva na oboronu, voennom byudzhat i byu-dzhete ministerstve oborony," *Voprosy ekonomiki* 10 (October 1990): 149–53; Stanislav Menshikov, *Sovietskaia ekonomika: katastrofa ili katarsis* (Moscow: Inter-verso, 1990); James Steiner, "CIA Estimates of Soviet Military Spending,"

International Security 14:4 (spring 1990): 185–93; P. Gushvin, "Doveriia k statistike," *Vestnik statistiki* 9 (September 1992): 3–31; and Noel Firth and James Noren, *Soviet Defense Spending: A History of CIA Estimates, 1950–1990* (College Station: Texas A&M University Press, 1998).

31. All data in this paragraph come from Firth and Noren, *Soviet Defense Spending*, 130–31.

32. "Russia's In-the-Red Army," *Economist*, 2 August 1997, 37; and *SIPRI Yearbook 1995* (Oxford: Oxford University Press, 1995), 250–51.

33. See RFE/RL 3:200 (13 October 1999) and 3:201 (14 October 1999).

34. See, for instance, "Power Company Turns Off Lights at Russian Army Base," Reuters (Moscow), 12 September 2000; and Stanislav Menshikov, "Chubais Attacks Army and Remains Unscathed," *Moscow Tribune*, 1 February 2002.

35. "U.S. Victory Highlights Russian Weakness," AP (Moscow), 21 April 2003.

36. "Inflated Ranks, Tiny Budget, and Enduring Paranoia," *gazeta.ru*, 24 August 2004; and "Moscow Raises Spending for Defense," RFE/RL (Prague), 24 August 2004.

37. "Russian Defense Spending to Grow 27% in 2007," RIA Novosti (Moscow), 11 May 2006; and "Russia's 2007 Defense Bill to Exceed $11 Billion," RIA Novosti (Moscow), 31 August 2006.

38. "Russian Defense Minister Refutes Media Reports," *Mosnews.com*, 15 December 2005; and "Russia's Army to Become 70% Professional By 2008," RIA Novosti (Moscow), 22 February 2006.

39. "Russia's Defense Spending Declines Faster Than for Other Nations," Interfax-AVN (Moscow), 10 March 2006.

40. Oleg Vladykin, "Defense Budget: Secret Growth—Almost One-half of Military Spending May Be Hidden from the Taxpayers," *Moscow News*, 1 September 2006.

41. See, Ellen Jones and Fred W. Grupp, "Political Socialization in the Soviet Military," *Armed Forces and Society* 8:3 (spring 1982): 357–87, regarding ideological indoctrination in the Brezhnev era.

42. "Russian Army To Be Trimmed Down to 850,000 Troops," *Moskovskii Komsomolets*, 23 November 2000. Again, these numbers are not "written in stone"; many different estimates have been published. For instance, in September 2004 Ivanov said that in 1994 the army's manpower was 3.7 million (interview with Ivanov on NTV [Moscow], 6:20GMT, in BBC Monitoring featured in JRL #8363) while Alexei Arbatov claims that in 1991 there were only 2.7 million armed forces personnel in Russia (see his "Military Reform in Russia," *International Security* 22:4 [spring 1998], 98); a figure corroborated by *The Military Balance* (London: IISS, 1992), 92.

43. RFE/RL 10:58 (29 March 2006); and interview with Ivanov in *Izvestia*, 23 February 2005, cited in RFE/RL 9:36 (24 February 2005). See also the interviews with Chief of the General Staff Baluyevskii in *Krasnaia Zvezda*, 6 November 2004.

44. Aleksandr Golts, "The Social and Political Condition of the Russian Military," 77.

45. RFE/RL 10: 153 (21 August 2006); and "Russia's Population Down to 142.7 Million," at www.komersant.com, 23 February 2006, citing all Federal Statistics Service (Rosstat) data.

46. See Nicholas Eberstadt, "Russia, the Sick Man of Europe," *The Public Interest* 158 (winter 2005): 3–20; "Russian Population To Shrink by 30% to about 100 Million People by 2050," Interfax (Moscow), 27 March 2002; and "Demographic Crisis Poses Serious Danger to Russia's Future," *pravda.ru*, 24 November 24, 2005.

47. Otto Latsis, "Russia Faces Demographic Disaster," *Moscow News*, 7 September 2005.

48. Roman Kupchinsky, "Tackling Russia's Demographic Crisis," RFE/RL Russian Political Weekly, 6:11 (25 May 2006).

49. Murray Feshbach, contribution to JRL #8089 (26 February 2004).

50. Latsis, "Russia Faces Demographic Disaster."

51. "Putin Highlights Demographic Slump as Russia's Biggest Problem," RIA Novosti (Moscow), 10 May 2006; "Putin Tells His Security Council To Focus on Three Key Threats To Russia," ITAR-TASS (Moscow), 29 May 2006.

52. "About 90,000 Women Serve in Russian Armed Forces," ITAR-TASS (Moscow), 10 March 2005. See also Jennifer G. Mathers, "Women, Society, and the Military: Women Soldiers in Post-Soviet Russia," in Stephen L. Webber and Jennifer G. Mathers, eds., *Military and Society in Post-Soviet Russia* (Manchester: Manchester University Press, 2006), 207–27.

53. Pavel K. Baev, "Reforming the Russian Military: History and Trajectory," in Yuri Fedorov and Bertil Nygren, eds., *Russian Military Reform and Russia's New Security Environment* (Stockholm: Swedish National Defence College, 2003), 41–42.

54. "Generals Refuse to Leave Army," *Novye Izvestia*, 25 April 2002.

55. "Russia Spends on Defense Less Than Saudi Arabia," *Izvestia*, 30 May 2005.

56. Vladimir Voronov, "What Use Are Armed Forces Like These? A Requiem for the Military Reforms," *Novoe Vremia*, #32, August 2005.

57. "Military Unready to Face Threats, Says Putin," *Moscow Times*, 19 November 2003. The number of flight-hours increased little in a decade. See Grachev's statements in "Vooruzhennie sily Rossii—na strana zakona i konstitutsii," *Krasnaia zvezda*, 18 December 1992.

58. Viktor Litovkin, "Lack of Defense Spending Leads to Tragedies," RIA Novosti (Moscow), 29 September 2003; and Olga Oliker and Tanya Charlick-Paley, *Assessing Russia's Decline* (Santa Monica, CA: RAND, 2002), 72.

59. "Russia, USA on a Par as Regards Strategic Nuclear Forces—Defence Minister," Interfax-AVN (Moscow), 12 April 2005.

60. Cited in Aleksandr Golts, "The Final Excuses for Army Corruption," *The Russia Journal*, 7–13 June 2002. See also Vladimir Voronov, "The Secretive Armed Forces," *Novoe Vremia*, 39 (29 September 2002).

61. "The Victory Remains Ours," *Rossiiskaia Gazeta*, 4 May 2004; in JRL #9139, of the same day.

62. Roger McDermott, "Ivanov's Victory over Kvashnin May Open Pandora's Box," *Eurasia Daily Monitor* 1:40 (28 June 2004).

63. Sergei Ivanov, "Russia Must Be Strong," *Wall Street Journal*, 11 January 2006.

64. Aleksandr Golts, "Saber Rattling Sans Saber," *Moscow Times*, 17 January 2006.

65. For description and data on Soviet armaments, see *The Military Balance* (London: IISS, 1986), 36–46.

66. See *The Military Balance 2004–2005* (London: IISS, 2004), 104–10.

67. *Bulletin of Atomic Scientists* data cited in David Holley, "Russia Puts Emphasis on Nuclear Weapons," *Los Angeles Times*, 6 December 2000; and "Russia's Arsenal Has 927 Nuclear Delivery Systems," RIA Novosti (Moscow), 31 July 2006.

68. "Russia Will Spend 50% More on Weapons in 2006 than in 2005," Interfax-AVN (Moscow), 5 April 2006.

69. "Putin Highlights Strategic Forces," RIA Novosti (Moscow), 10 May 2006.

70. Beniamin Ginodman and Alexander Rotkin, "The Specter of the Soviet Army: Military Reforms in Russia Are Still Following the Soviet Pattern," *Newsweek Russia* 33 (101), 19–25 June 2006.

71. Ibid.

72. Myasnikov, "The Red Army"; and "Anatolii Tsyganok, "RF Armed Forces Are Unsuitable for 21st Century Warfare," *Nezavisimoe Voennoe Obozrenie*, 11 April 2006.

73. Tsyganok, "RF Armed Forces Are Unsuitable."

74. Article in *Krasnaia Zvezda* on 10 April 2006 summarized in RFE/RL 10:66 (10 April 2006).

75. RFE/RL 10: 168 (12 September 2006), citing a RIA Novosti Report.

76. "Demands for Military Reform," RIA Novosti (Moscow), 12 July 2005. See also Christopher J. Hill, "Russian Defense Spending," in *Russia's Uncertain Economic Future* (Washington, DC: U.S. Government Printing Office, 2002), 161–82.

77. RFE/RL 6:79 (26 April 2002) reporting on an article in *Trud*, 25 April 2002.

78. "Meet the Press," NBC TV, 17 March 2002. In a 1 March 2005 interview with *Izvestia*, Chief of the General Staff Baluyevskii confirmed Ivanov's point.

79. RIA Novosti (Moscow), 29 August 2002; and RFE/RL 6:167 (5 September 2002).

80. *Strana.ru* exposé of 28 July 2005 reported in RFE/RL 9:142 (29 July 2005).

81. Viktor Suvorov, *Inside the Soviet Army* (London: Granada, 1982), 408.

82. Yitzhak Tarasulo, "A Profile of the Soviet Soldier," *Armed Forces and Society* 11:2 (winter 1985): 225.

83. See, for instance, Stepan Il'in, *Moral'nii factor v sovremennykh voinakh* (Moscow: Voenizdat, 1979), 92–93.

84. See Ellen Jones, "Manning the Soviet Military," *International Security* 71 (summer 1982): 119; and S. Enders Wimbush and Alex Alexiev, *The Ethnic Factor in the Soviet Armed Forces* (Santa Monica, CA: RAND, 1982).

85. Tarasulo, "A Profile," 229; and Les Aspin, "The Soviet Soldier," *New York Times*, 8 June 1982.

86. *Krasnaia Zvezda*, 11 April 1990, cited in Roman Kupchinsky, "Crime and Corruption in the Russian Armed Forces," RFE/RL Crime and Corruption Watch 2:29 (22 August 2002).

87. Sergei Soloviov, "The Russian Officer Today: A Sociological Portrait," *Insight* 2:8; in JRL #6571, 25 November 2002.

88. "Chief of Russia's General Staff Speaks about Current Challenges," *Krasnaia Zvezda*, 6 November 2004.

89. "Sociologists Draw Image of Average Army Offcer," Interfax-AVN (Moscow), 28 June 2005.

90. Olga Timofeeva, "Russian Citizens Regard the Armed Forces with Respect and Pity," *Izvestia*, 22 February 2006.

91. "Russia's In-the-Red Army," *Economist*, 2 August 1997, 38; and "Most Russians Trust National Armed Forces," Interfax (Moscow), 3 February 2003.

92. "Senior Military Official: Russian Army Will Never Become Fully Professional," RosBalt (Saratov), 19 May 2003.

93. Viktor Myasnikov, "People and Army Alienated," *Nezavisimaia Gazeta*, 11 September 2005.

94. See, for instance, "Day at Sea Turns Sour for Putin," AFP (Moscow), 17 February 2004; "Navy Denies Two Failed Missile Launches," *gazeta.ru*, 18 February 2004; Pavel Felgenhauer, "It's a Wonderful Life on TV," *Moscow Times*, 2 March 2004; and Anna Politkovskaya, "Poisoned by Putin," *The Guardian*, 9 September 2004.

95. RFE/RL 6:164 (30 August 2002).

96. See "We Love the Army, But in a Strange Way," *Vremia Novostei*, 22 February 2002; "Most Russians Do Not Want Relatives To Serve in Army," RosBalt (Moscow), 24 February 2004; and Miasnikov, "The Red Army."

97. "Russians Unhappy with Their Generals," *gazeta.ru*, 28 April 2003.

98. Viktor Litovkin, "An Army without Patriots," *Russia Profile* 2:8 (October 2005): 11. Problems already began in the late 1980s; see Steven L. Solnick, *Stealing the State: Control and Collapse in Soviet Institutions* (Cambridge: Harvard University Press, 1998), 175–217.

99. Litovkin, "Army without Patriots." For similar data on the 2002–2004 conscription cycles, see Zarina Khisamova, "Spring Recruitment," *Ekspert* 17 (29 April 2002), 61–62; "Russian Army Puts Up Stiff Resistance to End of Draft," AFP (Moscow), 25 April 2003; and "Russian Army Fears Record-Low Draft," RFE/RL 8:187 (1 October 2004).

100. Oliker and Charlick-Paley, *Assessing Russia's Decline*, 64.

101. "Military Budget for 2003: One Step Forward—Two Steps Back," *Defense and Security* 115 (4 October 2004).

102. Ryszard Kapuściński, *Imperium* (New York: Knopf, 1994), 194.

103. Cited in RFE/RL 9:127 (8 July 2005). See also the analysis of Lukin's report on the Ministry of Defense in *Nezavisimaia Gazeta*, 1 July 2005, and for more general studies, Andrei Petukhov, *"Dedovshchina" v Armii i na Flote* (St. Petersburg: Morskaia Gazeta, 2000) and V. V. Savel'ev, *Kak vyzhit' v neustavnoi armii* (Rostov-on-Don: Feniks, 2003).

104. Naby Abdullaev, "Ivanov Says Hazing Not Army's Fault," *Moscow Times*, 16 February 2006.

105. "Aggressive Helplessness," *Vedemosti*, 16 February 2006. See also, "Hundreds Protest against Russian Minister after Hazing Accident," AFP (Moscow), 28 January 2006; and Konstantin Lantratov and Viktor Khramraev, "A Provisional Successor," *Kommersant*, 29 March 2006.

106. Cited in Claire Bigg, "Russia: Brutal Hazing Incident Rocks the Army," RFE/RL (Moscow), 27 January 2006.

107. RFE/RL 10:23 (7 February 2006); and "Public Chamber, Defense Ministry to Address Violence in the Army," ITAR-TASS (Moscow), 31 January 2006.

108. Steven Lee Myers, "Hazing Trial Bares Dark Side of Russia's Military," *New York Times*, 13 August 2006.

109. RFE/RL 10: 147 (11 August 2006), citing an Interfax report.

110. RFE/RL 5:200 (22 October 2001) citing *Tribuna*, 16 October 2001. See also Golts, "The Social and Political Condition of the Russian Military," in Miller and Trenin, eds., *The Russian Military*, 81; and *Segodnia*, 21 March 2001, cited in RFE/RL 5:59 (26 March 2001).

111. RFE/RL 9:238 (22 December 2005) citing a *Moscow Times* report.

112. RIA-Novosti (Novosibirsk) cited in RFE/RL 10:2 (2 February 2006).

113. "Estimates of 'Natural Wastage' in Russian Armed Forces Very Widely," *Izvestia*, 24 August 2000; "Death Rate High in Russian Army," BBC (Moscow) 13 September 2003; and "How Are the Mighty Fallen," *Economist*, 2 July 2005, 45.

114. See the posting on the Defense Ministry's website at *www.mil.ru*, 5 February 2006. For advice on surviving military service, see the unattributed article, "Instruction for a Salobon: How to Get through Army Service to Return Alive and Unharmed," *Trud*, 11 June 2006, translated in JRL, 2006-#135, 12 June 2006.

115. See Valentina Melnikova and Anna Lebedev, *Les petits soldats: Le combat des mères russes* (Paris: Bayard, 2001); Amy Caiazza, *Mothers and Soldiers: Gender, Citizenship, and Civil Society in Contemporary Russia* (London: Routledge, 2002), 101–54; and Valerie Zawilski, "Saving Russia's Sons: The Soldiers' Mothers and the Russian-Chechen Wars," in Webber and Mathers, eds., *Military and Society*, 228–40.

116. Cited in "Russian Conscripts' Defender Launches into Politics," AFP (Moscow), 14 November 2004. See also Oksana Yablokova, "Mothers Join the Party," *Transitions Online*, at *www.tol.cz*, 15 November 2005.

117. Nabi Abdullaev, "Ivanov Says Hazing Not Army's Fault," *Moscow Times*, 16 February 2006.

118. See *Nezavisimaia Gazeta*, 11 February 2002.

119. "Putin Urges Bill to Boost Pay in Army," UPI (Moscow), 18 March 2002.

120. Viktor Litovkin, "A Highly Resistant Strain," *Russia Profile*, 1 February 2006.

121. Alexei Alexandrov, "Ivanov's Budget," *Rossiiskie Vesti*, #31, 8 September 2005; and "Russia's Army To Become 70% Professional by 2008," RIA Novosti (Moscow), 21 February 2006.

122. Nikolai Poroskov, "Russian Military Lost More than Others in Benefits Elimination Program," *Vremia Novostei*, 18 January 2005.

123. "Sociologists Draw Image of Average Army Officer," Interfax-AVN (Moscow), 30 June 2005. See also M. Gorshkova and M. Kholmskaia, eds., *Srednii klass v sovremennom rossiiskom obshchestve* (Moscow: Rosspen, 2000).

124. "20 Per Cent of Russian Officers Ready to Resign Their Commission," *Russkii Kurir*, 3 March 2005, translated in CDI Russia Weekly, 4 March 2005; and Fred Weir, "Iraqi Defeat Jolts Russian Military," *Christian Science Monitor*, 16 April 2003. See also, Vadim Soloviov, "An Extremely Neglected Security Issue," *Nezavisimaia Gazeta*, 12 September 2002; and Pavel K. Baev, "The Plight of the Russian Military: Shallow Identity and Self-defeating Culture," *Armed Forces and Society* 29:1 (fall 2002): 129–46.

125. Interview with Ivanov on NTV, Moscow, 12 September 2004, 6:20 GMT, BBC Monitoring of the same day.

126. "20 Per Cent of Russian Officers."

127. See RFE/RL 10:58 (29 March 2006); and "Putin Highlights Strategic Forces."

128. RFE/RL 10:22 (6 February 2006), citing *The Moscow Times* and *lenta.ru*.

129. Ibid.

130. See the reports by ITAR-TASS and Interfax, cited in RFE/RL 9:113 (15 June 2005).

131. Cited in Dale R. Herspring, *Russian Civil-Military Relations* (Bloomington: Indiana University Press, 1996), 175; and Rensselaer W. Lee, "The Organized

Crime Morass in the Former Soviet Union," *Demokratizatsiya* 2:3 (summer 1994): 394, respectively.

132. See RFE/RL 1:129 (1 October 1997); and John P. Moran, *From Garrison State to Nation State* (Westport, CT: Praeger, 2002), 44.

133. RFE/RL 1:216 (15 November 1997). See also, Graham Turbiville, *Mafia in Uniform: The Criminalization of the Russian Armed Forces* (Ft. Leavenworth, KS: Foreign Military Studies Office, 1995); and Mark Galeotti, "Russia's Criminal Army," *Jane's Intelligence Review* 11:6 (June 1999): 8–10.

134. "Russian Army Plagued by Violence," AP (Moscow), 6 May 2003; "Russian Army Fraud," RFE/RL Crime and Corruption Watch 2:17 (3 May 2002); and RFE/RL 7:140 (25 July 2003).

135. Viktor Myasnikov, "Putin Attacks Chronic Commercialization of Russian Armed Forces," *Nezavisimaia Gazeta*, 11 November 2005.

136. Pavel Felgenhauer, "Billions Down the Drain," *Moscow Times*, 1 June 2004.

137. Bruce Porter, "The Military Abroad," in Timothy Colton and Thane Gustafson, eds., *Soldiers and the Soviet State: Civil-Military Relations from Brezhnev to Gorbachev* (Princeton: Princeton University Press, 1990), 292.

138. See Scott McMichael, *Stumbling Bear: Soviet Military Performance in Afghanistan* (London: Brassey's, 1991), 126; and Lester Grau, "The Soviet-Afghan War: A Superpower Mired in the Mountains," *Journal of Slavic Military Studies* 17:1 (March 2004): 129–51.

139. Three insightful analyses of these issues are Ninel' Strel'tsova, *Vozvrashenie iz Afganistana* (Moscow: Molodaia gvardia, 1990); Aleksandr Liakovskii, *Tragediia i doblest' Afgana* (Moscow: GPI Iskona, 1995); and Aleksandr Maiorov, *Pravda ob Afganskoi Voine* (Moscow: Prava cheloveka, 1996).

140. Boris V. Gromov, "Pravda vyshe sensatsii," *Sovietskaia Rossiia*, 15 November 1989.

141. See Mark Kramer, "Surprise! The Soviets Nearly Won the Afghan War," *Los Angeles Times*, 26 December 2004.

142. The Russian General Staff, *The Soviet-Afghan War: How a Superpower Fought and Lost*, trans. and eds. Lester Gray and Michael Gress (Lawrence: University Press of Kansas, 2002), 309. A sobering narrative and visual account of the war is O. Smirnov, *Nikto ne sozdan dlia voini* (Moscow: Molodaia gvardia, 1990).

143. *The Soviet-Afghan War*, 304.

144. Cited in Carlotta Gall and Thomas de Waal, *Chechnya: Calamity in the Caucasus* (New York: New York University Press, 1998), 161. For analyses of the political processes that led to the war, see John B. Dunlop, *Russia Confronts Chechnya* (New York: Cambridge University Press, 1998); and Matthew Evangelista, *The Chechen Wars* (Washington, DC: Brookings, 2002), 20–33.

145. See Edwin Bacon, "The Power Ministries," in Neil Robinson, ed., *Institutions and Political Change in Russia* (London: Macmillan, 2000), 137; and quoted in Benjamin S. Lambeth, "Russia's Wounded Military," *Foreign Affairs* 74:2 (March–April 1995): 89.

146. Robert Seely, *Russo-Chechen Conflict, 1800–2000* (London: Frank Cass, 2001), 241–26. See also Mark Kramer, "The Perils of Counterinsurgency: Russia's War in Chechnya," *International Security* 29:3 (winter 2004): 5–62.

147. Trenin and Malashenko, *Russia's Restless Frontier* (Washington, DC: Carnegie Endowment for International Peace, 2004), 106.

148. See S. S. Soloviov and I. V. Obraztsov, *Rossiiskaia armiia ot Afganistana do Chechnii* (Moscow: Natsional'ny institut im. Ekateriny Velikoi, 1997).

149. Pavel Baev, "The Russian Armed Forces: Failed Reform Attempts and Creeping Regionalization," in David Betz and John Löwenhardt, eds., *Army and State in Postcommunist Europe* (London: Frank Cass, 2001), 29; and "Sakharov Widow Says Chechen War Staged To Bring Putin to Power," AFP (Moscow), 27 January 2000.

150. Robert Bruce Ware, "Will Southern Russian Studies Go the Way of Sovietology?" *Journal of Slavic Military Studies* 16:4 (December 2003): 163–65. See also N. Grodnenskii, *Neokonchennaia voina: Istoria vooruzhennogo konflikta v Chechne* (Moscow: Charvest, 2004).

151. Michael McFaul, "Kremlin Man Fails the Test," *Sunday Times*, 27 August 2000. The strict restrictions on the media make the contributions of intrepid journalists, like Anna Politkovskaya, all the more invaluable. See her *Vtoraia chechenskaia* (Moscow: Zakharov, 2002) and, for the larger context, Bettina Renz, "Media-Military Relations in Post-Soviet Russia," in Webber and Mathers, eds., *Military and Society*, 61–79.

152. Trenin and Malashenko, *Russia's Restless Frontier*, 126. See also V. Tikhomirov, "Bor'ba za kavkaz," *Krasnaia zvezda*, 10 August 1993.

153. See Simon Saradzhyan, "Army Learned Few Lessons from Chechnya," *Moscow Times*, 15 December 2004. See also, A. Nikolaev, "Bol'shoi kavkaz-strategia Rossii," *Krasnaia zvezda*, 4 January 2001.

154. BBC Monitoring translation of an article from the weekly *Argumenty i Fakty*, 1 June 2004; in JRL #8240 (5 June 2004).

155. Trenin and Malashenko, *Russia's Restless Frontier*, 136. See also Tracey C. German and Christin Marschall, *Russia's Chechen War* (London: Routledge, 2003); and Valery Tishkov, *Chechnya: Life in a War-Torn Society* (Berkeley: University of California Press, 2004).

156. Vladimir Voronov, "The Secretive Armed Forces," *Novoe Vremia*, #39, 29 September 2002.

157. Aleksandr Golts, "Putin and the Chechen War: Together Forever," *Moscow Times*, 11 February 2004.

158. Remarks by Sergei Ivanov at the Council on Foreign Relations, New York, 13 January 2005. (Transcript in JRL #9026, 20 January 2005.)

159. See "Military Presence in Chechnya Is Increasing," *Nezavisimoe Voennoe Obozrenie*, #10, 18 March 2005; and Boris Kagarlitsky, "Who Did Lose Chechnya?" *Moscow Times*, 23 July 2002.

160. Vladimir Mukhin, "Chechnya: Defense Ministry Casualties," *Nezavisimaia Gazeta*, 22 August 2006; and Saradzhyan, "Army Learned Few Lessons." See also "Russian Defense Ministry Says Over 3,500 Soldiers Killed in Chechnya Since 1999," Interfax-AVN (Moscow), 26 February 2006.

161. "Death Toll in Russia's Chechnya Could Be 160,000," Reuters (Moscow), 15 August 2005.

162. Trenin and Malashenko, *Russia's Restless Frontier*, 156.

Chapter 3
Explaining the Military's Political Presence

1. See V. Boyarintsev, *Svinskaia demokratsia* (Moscow: Al'ternativa, 2005).

2. See Kathleen Thelen, "Historical Institutionalism in Comparative Politics," *Annual Review of Political Science* 2 (June 1999): 369–404.

3. For an outstanding study of this period, see Mark von Hagen, *Soldiers in the Proletarian Dictatorship: The Red Army and the Soviet Socialist State, 1917–1930* (Ithaca, NY: Cornell University Press, 1990). For different interpretations of the party-army nexus, see the chapters of Roman Kolkowicz, Timothy Colton, and William Odom in Dale R. Herspring and Ivan Volgyes, eds., *Civil-Military Relations in Communist Systems* (Boulder, CO: Westview Press, 1978), 9–75. See also Amos Perlmutter and William M. LeoGrande, "The Party in Uniform: Toward a Theory of Civil-Military Relations in Communist Political Systems," *American Political Science Review* 76:4 (December 1982): 778–90.

4. John Moran, *From Garrison State to Nation State: Political Power and the Russian Military under Gorbachev and Yeltsin* (Westport, CT: Praeger, 2002), 146.

5. Brian A. Davenport, "Ogarkov Ouster: The Development of Soviet Military Doctrine and Civil-Military Relations in the 1980s," *Journal of Strategic Studies* 14:2 (June 1991): 129–47.

6. Numerous experts have pointed out Gorbachev's aversion of taking responsibility for his controversial actions. See, for instance, Robert V. Barylski, *The Soldier in Russian Politics: Duty, Dictatorship, and Democracy under Gorbachev and Yeltsin* (New Brunswick, NJ: Transaction, 1998), 61–62; and Harold Elletson, *The General against the Kremlin: Alexander Lebed: Power and Illusion* (London: Little, Brown, 1998), 91–100. For a different interpretation, see Archie Brown's exceedingly sympathetic (to Gorbachev) treatment in *The Gorbachev Factor* (Oxford: Oxford University Press, 1995), 260–67, 280–83.

7. Lilia Shevtsova cited in John B. Dunlop, *The Rise of Russia and the Fall of the Soviet Empire* (Princeton: Princeton University Press, 1993), 96. For a more general study, see Murielle Delaporte and Thierry Malleret, *L'Armée rouge face à la perestroika* (Paris: Edition, 1990).

8. The magisterial account of this process is William E. Odom, *The Collapse of the Soviet Military* (New Haven: Yale University Press, 1998). See also, Dieter Kläy, *Perestrojka in der Sowjetarmee* (Zürich: Verlag der Fachvereine, 1993).

9. Edward Gibbon, *The Decline and Fall of the Roman Empire* (1776; reprint New York: Modern Library, 1957), 1:91.

10. See Thomas M. Nichols, *The Sacred Cause* (Ithaca, NY: Cornell University Press, 1993), 8.

11. Dmitri Trenin and Aleksei Malashenko, *Russia's Restless Frontier: The Chechnya Factor in Post-Soviet Russia* (Washington, DC: Carnegie Endowment for International Peace, 2004), 151.

12. See Article 19 of the "Statute on the Order of Performing Military Service," in *Russian Federation Legal Acts on Civil-Military Relations* (Moscow: Foundation for Political Centrism, 2003), 182. See also the 1997 Presidential Decree (#535) on securing the electoral rights of servicemen, cited in Irina Isakova, "The Evolution of Civil-Military Relations in Russia," in Andrew Cottey et al., eds., *Democratic Control of the Military in Postcommunist Europe* (London: Palgrave, 2002), 222–23.

13. Marybeth Peterson Ulrich, *Democratizing Communist Militaries* (Ann Arbor: University of Michigan Press, 1999), 9.

14. Ibid.

15. Sven Gunnar Simonsen, "Marching to a Different Drum? Political Orientations and Nationalism in Russia's Armed Forces," in David Betz and John Löwenhardt, eds., *Army and State in Postcommunist Europe* (London: Frank Cass, 2001), 45.

16. A fine account of these events is in Thomas M. Nichols, *The Russian Presidency* (London: Macmillan, 1999), 77–82.

17. "Dom Sovietov: s'ezd nachal rabotu," *Pravda*, 24 September 1993; and "Seeks Support of Military Units," Foreign Broadcast Information Service—Soviet Union, 27 September 1993, 27; both cited by ibid., 77.

18. For Yeltsin's own version of this incident, see Boris Yeltsin, *The View from the Kremlin* (London: HarperCollins, 1994), 271–83, and esp. 278–79.

19. See I. Kliamkin and L. Shevtsova, *Rezhim Borisa Vtoroga: Osobennosti postkommunicheskoi vlasti v Rossii* (Moscow: Carnegie Center, 1999), and Michael McFaul, *Russia's Unfinished Revolution: Political Change from Gorbachev to Putin* (Ithaca, NY: Cornell University Press, 2001), 207–9.

20. For more on Lopatin, see Odom, *The Collapse of the Soviet Military*, 184–85, 199–200.

21. See, for instance, Thomas M. Nichols, " 'An Electoral Mutiny?' Zhirinovsky and the Russian Armed Forces," *Armed Forces and Society* 21:3 (spring 1995): 328–29; and A. A. Konovalov, "The Changing Role of Military Factors," in Vladimir Baranovsky, ed., *Russia and Europe: The Emerging Security Agenda* (Oxford: Oxford University Press, 1997), 197.

22. Vladimir Serebriannikov and Yuri Deriugin, *Sotsiologia armii* (Moscow: ISPI RAN, 1996), 89. See also Geir Hønneland and Anne-Kristin Jørgensen, *Integration vs. Autonomy: Civil-Military Relations on the Kola Peninsula* (Aldershot, England: Ashgate, 1999), 63.

23. On this point, see George W. Breslauer, *Gorbachev and Yeltsin as Leaders* (New York: Cambridge University Press, 2002), 175.

24. Vladimir Ermolin, "Svoi interes u armii v zakonotvorchestve est,' " *Krasnaia Zvezda*, 24 August 1995; cited in Moran, *From Garrison State to Nation State*, 169.

25. See Timothy L. Thomas, "The Russian Military and the 1995 Duma Elections," *Journal of Slavic Military Studies* 9:3 (September 1996): 534–36; Andrey Korbut, "Voennikh vtyalivaiut v predvibornuyu gonky, *Nezavisimoe voyennoe obozrenie* (NVO), #41, 22–28 October 1999; and Vladimir Serebiannikov, "Voennie v zerkale vyborov," NVO, #29, 11–17 August 2000.

26. See Vladimir Ermolin, "Svoi interes"; and Jennifer G. Mathers, "Outside Politics? Civil-Military Relations during a Period of Reform," in Anne Aldis and Roger McDermott, eds., *Russian Military Reform, 1992–2002* (London: Frank Cass, 2003), 29–30.

27. Isakova, "The Evolution of Civil-Military Relations in Russia," 221.

28. See Aleksandr Golts, "The Social and Political Condition of the Russian Military," in Steven E. Miller and Dmitri Trenin, eds., *The Russian Military: Power and Policy* (Cambridge: MIT Press, 2004), 82; and Viktor Baranets, *El'tsin i Ego Generali: Zapiski Polkovnika Genshtaba* (Moscow: Sovershenno Sekretno, 1998), 40–45.

29. "Putin Expected to Pull Soldiers' Votes," *Moscow Times*, 16 December 1999. See also Dale R. Herspring, "Putin and the Armed Forces," in Herspring, ed., *Putin's Russia: Past Imperfect, Future Uncertain* (Lanham, MD: Rowman and Littlefield, 2003), 165–71.

30. Interfax (Moscow), 26 March 2000, citing General Nikolai Burgyba of the Defense Ministry's Education Department.

31. Isakova, "The Evolution of Civil-Military Relations," 221. See also Pavel K. Baev, "Putin's Court: How the Military Fits In," PONARS memo #153 (November 2000): 39.

32. Golts interviewed by Ekho Moskvy on 13 April 2005; the poll was published in *Nezavisimaia Gazeta* of the same day.

33. See Elletson, *The General against the Kremlin*, 96.

34. Troshev cited in "Top General Gives Advice to Troops Voting in Presidential Poll," AFP (Moscow), 17 March 2000. For more general treatments on electoral machinations in the military, see "Armiya golosovala po kommande: 'Volno!' " *Komsomolskaia Pravda*, 19 December 1995; and "Putin Expected to Pull Soldiers' Votes."

35. See, for instance, Golts, "The Social and Political Condition of the Russian Military," 82–87.

36. Carl A. Linden, *Khrushchev and the Soviet Leadership, 1957–1964* (Baltimore, MD: Johns Hopkins University Press, 1966), 43. See also William Taubman, *Khrushchev: The Man and His Era* (New York: W. W. Norton, 2003), 361–64.

37. For Ustinov's orthodox views on military and strategic affairs, see his "Strazh mirnogo truda, oplot vseobshchego mira," *Kommunist* 3 (February 1977); and *Otvesti ugrozu yadernoi voiny* (Moscow: Politizdat, 1982). Defense ministers Sergei Sokolov (1984–87) and Dmitri Yazov (1987–91) were candidate members of the Politburo.

38. For an excellent discussion of the "Afgantsy," see Mark Galeotti, *Afghanistan: The Soviet Union's Last War* (London: Frank Cass, 1995), 171–89. According to Lilia Shevtsova, during the Yeltsin era the "Afgantsy," in effect, became a "special military caste, occupying all the top leadership positions in the defense ministry." See Shevtsova, "Russia's Fragmented Armed Forces," in Larry Diamond and Marc F. Plattner, eds., *Civil-Military Relations and Democracy* (Baltimore, MD: Johns Hopkins University Press, 1996), 116.

39. See Timothy J. Colton and Michael McFaul, *Popular Choice and Managed Democracy: The Russian Elections of 1999 and 2000* (Washington, DC: Brookings Institution Press, 2003), 214. See also Mathers, "Outside Politics?" 30.

40. Cited in "U.S. Rejects Russian Request to Examine Subs," Reuters (Moscow), 16 September 2000.

41. See Wayne Allensworth, "Derzhavnost: Aleksandr Lebed's Vision for Russia," *Problems of Post-Communism* 45:2 (March/April 1998): 51–58; Elletson, *The General against the Kremlin*; and, for Yeltsin's view of Lebed's role in the elections, Yeltsin, *Midnight Diaries* (New York: Public Affairs, 2000), 36–37.

42. See Lebed's autobiography, *General Alexander Lebed: My Life and My Country* (Washington, DC: Regnery, 1997), 325–26.

43. Cited in David Remnick, "The War for the Kremlin," *The New Yorker*, 22 July 1996, 52.

44. For a useful portrayal of Rodionov, see Timothy L. Thomas and Lester W. Grau, "A Military Biography: Russian Minister of Defense Igor Rodionov," *Journal of Slavic Military Studies* 9:2 (June 1996): 443–52.

45. See Igor Rodionov, "Osnovnye Napravlenia Voennoi Reformy," *Nezavisimaia Gazeta*, 22 April 1996; and Golts, *Armia Rossii: 11 poteriannikh let* (Moscow: Zaharov, 2004), 40–48.

46. Trenin and Malashenko, *Russia's Restless Frontier,* 116.

47. See Andrey Korbut, "Voennikh vtilaviut v predvibornuyu gonku," *NVO,* 22–28 October 1999.

48. RosBalt (Moscow), 24 February 2002. See also the open letter condemning Putin in *Sovetskaia Rossiia* of the same day.

49. See Golts, *Armia Rossii,* 155–57; and Robert Seely, *Russo-Chechen Conflict, 1800–2000: A Deadly Embrace* (London: Frank Cass, 2001), 197. For a general discussion of the problems regarding the conduct of the first Chechen war, see A. V. Cherkasov, *Rossiia-Chechnia: Tsep' oshibok i prestuplenii* (Moscow: Zveniia, 1998).

50. Cited in *Pravda,* 26 June 1997. See commentaries in *Segodnia,* 25 June 1997 and 1 July 1997; and *Krasnaia Zvezda,* 27 June 1997. For a balanced biography of Rokhlin, see *Lev Rokhlin: Zhizn' i smert' generala* (Moscow: EKSMO, 1998).

51. See Sarah Mendelson, "Current Russian Views on US-Russian Security Relations and Military Reform," PONARS memo #25 (Harvard University, January 1998).

52. Aleksandr Golts, "Revolutsia v voennom dele nachalas," *Itogi* 28 (1997), 15, and "Iulskie tesisi tovarishcha Ilukhina," *Itogi* 29 (1998), 25.

53. Golts, "Iulskie tesisi," 25.

54. See Andrei Rogachevskii, "The Murder of General Rokhlin," *Europe-Asia Studies* 52:1 (January 2000): 95–110. Numerous conspiracy theories floated around in Moscow after Rokhlin's death particularly because, as Rogachevskii writes (on 104), it "would have suited almost everyone who knew him."

55. Brian D. Taylor, "Russia's Passive Army: Rethinking Military Coups," *Comparative Political Studies* 34:8 (August 2000): 941; and Colton and McFaul, *Popular Choice and Managed Democracy,* 159.

56. See, for instance, Olga Kryshtanovskaya and Stephen White, "Putin's Militocracy," *Post-Soviet Affairs* 19:4 (October–December 2003): 289–306. See also Trenin and Malashenko, *Russia's Restless Frontier,* 153; and Eugene Huskey, "Political Leadership and the Center-Periphery Struggle: Putin's Administrative Reforms," in Archie Brown and Lilia Shevtsova, eds., *Gorbachev, Putin, and Yeltsin: Political Leadership in Russia's Transition* (Washington, DC: Carnegie Endowment for International Peace, 2001), 123.

57. Interview with Shpak in *Tribuna,* 31 March 2004; cited in RFE/RL 8:60 (31 March 2004).

58. Stephen J. Blank, "Who's Minding the State? The Failure of Russian Security Policy," *Problems of Post-Communism* 45:2 (March/April 1998): 5.

59. Moran, *From Garrison to Nation-State,* 59.

60. See Vitaly V. Shlykov, "Does Russia Need a General Staff?" *European Security* 10:4 (winter 2001): 64–65.

61. Pavel Felgenhauer, "Hope Glimmers for Reform," *Moscow Times,* 29 March 2001.

62. See, for instance, Sergei Rogov, "Strategic Capitulation," *Nezavisimaia Gazeta*, 26 July 2000; and Andrei Piontkovsky, "Season of Discontent: Kvashnin and the Experts," *Russia Journal*, 19–25 August 2000.

63. For an excellent measure of Kvashnin, see Golts, *Armia Rossii*, 60–64.

64. See Troshev's memoirs, *Moia voina: Chechenskii dnevnik okopnogo generala* (Moscow: Zakharov, 2001).

65. As reported by http://www.polit.ru, 18 December 2002.

66. Pavel Felgenhauer, "Is Troshev Feeling Stressed?" *Moscow Times*, 7 June 2001. See also John Russell, "Terrorists, Bandits, Spooks, and Thieves: Russian Demonisation of the Chechens before and since 9/11," *Third World Quarterly* 26:1 (March 2005):109.

67. See Alexander Belkin, "Civil-Military Relations in Russia after 9-11," *European Security* 12:3–4 (September-December 2003): 1–19; and Trenin and Malashenko, *Russia's Restless Frontier*, 143.

68. John Lloyd, *Rebirth of a Nation: An Anatomy of Russia* (London: Michael Joseph, 1998), 117. See also Eva Busza, "State Dysfunctionality, Institutional Decay, and the Russian Military," in Valerie Sperling, ed., *Building the Russian State: Institutional Crisis and the Quest for Democratic Governance* (Boulder, CO: Westview Press, 2000), 113–36.

69. See Elletson, *The General against the Kremlin*, 165–74.

70. Stephen Foye, "Updating Russian Civil-Military Relations," *RFE/RL Research Report* 2:46 (19 Nov 1993): 48.

71. For different interpretations of the "Prishtina Dash," see Roy Medvedev, *Post-Soviet Russia: A Journey through the Yeltsin Era* (New York: Columbia University Press, 2000), 311; Yu. Morozov, V. Glushkov, and A. Sharavin, *Balkany segodnia i zavtra: Voenno-politicheskie aspekty mirotvorchestva* (Moscow: Center of Military-Strategic Studies of the General Staff, 2001), 250–56; Strobe Talbott, *The Russia Hand: A Memoir of Presidential Diplomacy* (New York: Random House, 2002), 332–49; Taylor, *Politics and the Russian Army*, 315–16; and Lilia Shevtsova, *Putin's Russia* (Washington, DC: Carnegie Endowment for International Peace, 2003)—who contends that Yeltsin himself might well have been left out of the loop—endnote 11, 285. In any case, the day after the "dash" Yeltsin promoted the leader of Russian paratroopers, Viktor Zavarzin, from Lieutenant General to Colonel General and instructed Defense Minister Sergeev to propose Zavarzin for a medal. See RFE/RL 3:131 (8 July 1999).

72. Shevtsova, *Putin's Russia*, 130; and Shlykov, "Does Russia Need a General Staff?" 46–47, 64.

73. Golts, "The Social and Political Condition of the Russian Military," 88–89; and Simon Saradzhyan, "Generals Tell Politicians: Hands Off," *Moscow Times*, 5 November 1999.

74. See B. Z. Doktorov, A. A. Oslon, and E. S. Petrenko, eds., *Epokha Yeltsina: Mnenia Rossiia* (Moscow: Fond "Obshchestvennoe mnenie," 2002), 129–35.

75. Karen Dawisha and Bruce Parrott, *Russia and the New States of Eurasia: The Politics of Upheaval* (New York: Cambridge University Press, 1994), 233.

76. For an excellent description of the activities—including illegal trade in military supplies—of Russian troops in Tajikistan, see Greg Austin and Alexei D. Muraviev, *The Armed Forces of Russia in Asia* (London: I. B. Tauris, 2000), 76.

77. See Leonid Ivashov, "Global'naia provkatsia," *Nezavisimaia gazeta*, 10 October 2001; Vladimir Soloviov, "Generals Joining Opposition to Kremlin," *Nezavisimaia gazeta*, 13 November 2001; and Andrei Artemov, "Zapad demonstriruet rossii novy formal sotrudnichestva," *Nezavisimaia gazeta*, 20 December 2001.

78. Golts, "The Social and Political Condition of the Russian Military," 88.

79. Taylor, *Politics and the Russian Army*, 318. See also, Zoltan Barany, "Controlling the Military: A Partial Success," *Journal of Democracy* 10:2 (April 1999): 54–56.

80. Stephen M. Meyer, "The Devolution of Russian Military Power," *Current History* 94: 594 (October 1995): 326.

81. Pavel K. Baev, *The Russian Army in a Time of Troubles* (London: Sage, 1996), 54.

82. Barylski, *The Soldier in Russian Politics*, 231.

83. Ibid., 361.

Chapter 4
The Elusive Defense Reform

1. "Russian Army: Reform Has Finished, Reforming Has Started," http://www.pravda.ru, 19 January 2004.

2. Cited by Viktor Litovkin in "Demands for Military Reform," RIA Novosti (Moscow), 12 July 2005.

3. Pavel Felgenhauer, "Military Cuts Illusory," *Moscow Times*, 30 August 2001.

4. See "Russian Armed Forces Are over One Million Men Strong Now," RIA Novosti (Moscow), 13 May 2003; and "Army More Than Halved Since 1992," Interfax (Moscow), 9 April 2003.

5. "As of January 1, 2005 Total Strength of Armed Forces Will Be 1,207,000," RIA Novosti (Moscow), 27 December 2004; interview with Defense Minister Ivanov in Interfax (Moscow), 2 January 2005; and *Izvestia* interview with Chief of the General Staff Baluyevskii, 1 March 2005.

6. Beniamin Ginorman and Alexander Rotkin, "The Specter of the Soviet Army," *Newsweek Russia* 33:101, 19–25 June 2006.

7. Interview with Baluyevskii in *Rossiiskaia Gazeta*, 1 November 2005.

8. Sergei Ivanov, "Russia's Geopolitical Priorities and Armed Forces," *Russia in Global Affairs*, 17 February 2004. See also "Chasty postoiannoi gotovnosti VS RF planiretsia perevesti na kontraktnuiu osnovu," http://www.strana.ru, 15 April 2003.

9. Nikita Petrov, "There Is No Threat, but We Do Need to Arm Ourselves," http://www.strana.ru, 29 April 2003. See also "Chief of Russia's General Staff Speaks About Current Challenges," *Krasnaia Zvezda*, 6 November 2004; and Aleksander Konovalov, "Defense Minister Rules Out Full Switch to Contract Military in Foreseeable Future," ITAR-TASS (Moscow), 2 February 2005.

10. "Putin Highlights Strategic Forces in State of the Nation," RIA Novosti (Moscow), 10 May 2006.

11. RFE/RL 10:58 (29 March 2006); and interview with Ivanov in *Izvestia*, 23 February 2005, cited in RFE/RL 9:36 (24 February 2005). Contrast these figures with Kvashnin's in "Russian Armed Forces Are Over One Million Men Strong Now, Chief-of-Staff Says," RIA Novosti (Moscow), 13 May 2003.

12. "Russia's Army to Become 70% Professional By 2008," RIA Novosti, 21 February 2006.

13. "Plan for Russian Contract Army Failing," BBC Monitoring of Ekho Moskvy radio, 07:00 GMT, 24 August 2006, in JRL 2006, #192.

14. RFE/RL 10: 157 (25 August 2006), citing an article in *Nezavisimaia ia Gazeta*, 24 August 2006.

15. "Plan for Russian Contract Army Failing."

16. Vladimir Putin, *First Person: An Astonishingly Frank Self-Portrait by Russia's President* (New York: Public Affairs, 2000), 42. See also Boris Reitschuster, *Wladimir Putin: Wohin steuert er Russland?* (Berlin: Rowohlt, 2004).

17. Cited by Richard F. Staar, "Russia's New Military Program," *Insight* 4:1 (25 January 2004), available at *http://perso.club-internet.fr/kozlowsk/ insight.html*. See also "Patriots Aren't What They Used To Be," *Novye Izvestia*, 23 November 2005.

18. See *Rossiiskaia Gazeta*, 12 March 2001; and "Russia Unveils 5-yr Plan for 'Patriotic Education'," Reuters (Moscow), 12 March 2001.

19. See the interview with station manager Sergei V. Savushkin in *Novaya Gazeta*, no. 25 (April 2005); and Steven Lee Myers, "Red Star over Russian Airwaves: Military TV Network," *New York Times*, 11 February 2005.

20. Irina Petrovskaya, "New TV Channel Inspires Chagrin, Not Pride," *Moscow Times*, 2 March 2005. See also David Gillespie, "Defense of the Realm: The 'New' Russian Patriotism on Screen," *Journal of Power Institutions in Post-Soviet Societies* 3 (2005), at www.pipss.org. and *Zvezda*'s website, www.tvzvezda.ru.

21. "How Are the Mighty Fallen," *Economist*, 2 July 2005, 46.

22. Defense Ministry head of personnel and training, General Nikolai Pankov quoted in *Kommersant-Daily*, 25 July 2006.

23. RFE/RL 10:108 (14 June 2006).

24. "Duma Votes To Slash Military Service in Russia," AFP (Moscow), 14 June 2006.

25. Russian news agencies cited in RFE/RL 9:61 (1 April 2005). See also "Too Few Come Forward to Staff Professional Russian Army," Interfax-AVN (Moscow), 7 October 2004.

26. Tatyana Kuznetsova, CSM's Moscow chairwoman cited in RFE/RL 8:11 (20 January 2004). These offices, Kuznetsova alleged, continued to charge up to $5,000 for complete draft deferments.

27. See the interview with Lyobov Kudelina, "Increased Defense Spending Won't Benefit the Army," *Izvestia*, 27 September 2000; in JRL #4545 of the next day.

28. See Alexei Arbatov and Petr Romashkin, "Biudzhet kak zerkalo voennoi reformy," *Nezavisimaia Gazeta*, 17 January 2003; "Cabinet To Make Public 2004 Military Budget Elements," RIA Novosti (Moscow), 12 November 2003; and "Inflated Ranks, Tiny Budget, and Enduring Paranoia" (interview with Alexei Arbatov), http://www.gazeta.ru, 24 August 2004.

29. Jeremy Bransten, "Moscow Raises Spending for Defense, Police, Secret Services," RFE/RL (Prague), 24 August 2004; and "Russia To Adopt New Militarized Budget," AFP (Moscow), 29 September 2004.

30. Oleg Vladkin, "Defense Budget: Secret Growth—Almost One-half of Military Spending May Be Hidden from the Taxpayers," *Moscow News*, 1 September 2006.

31. Pavel Zolotarev, "Three Sources—Three Components of Army Stagnation," *Nezavisimoe Voyennoe Obozrenie*, 5 January 2006.

32. For the Russian context, see David J. Betz, "No Place for a Civilian? Russian Defense Management from Yeltsin to Putin," *Armed Forces and Society* 28:3 (spring 2002): 481–504.

33. Cited in Viktor Baranets, *El'tsin i ego generalii: Zapiski polkovnika genshtaba* (Moscow: Sovershenno Sekretno, 1998), 249.

34. Cited in Michael Flynn, "Russia: Spy Mania," *Bulletin of the Atomic Scientists* 58:5 (September–October 2002): 16. See also Peter Baker, "Treason Trial for Russian Researcher Delayed Indefinitely," *Washington Post*, 25 December 2003; Grigorij Pasko, "Der Spion der keiner war: Der Fall Sutjagin ist nicht beendet," *Osteuropa* 55:1 (January 2005): 91–103; and Andrew Jack, *Inside Putin's Russia: Can There Be Reform without Democracy?* (Oxford: Oxford University Press, 2005), 17–18.

35. Ivashov interviewed in *Nezavisimaia Gazeta*, 18 December 2001.

36. Alfred Stepan, *Rethinking Military Politics: Brazil and the Southern Cone* (Princeton: Princeton University Press, 1988), 94–97.

37. Ekho Moskvy, 26 July 2005, cited by RFE/RL 9:140 (27 July 205).

38. For two assessments, see M. V. Alexeev and R. C. Sikorra, "Comparing Post-Cold War Military Conversion in the United States and Russia," *Contemporary Economic Policy* 16:4 (October 1998): 499–510; and H. Wiberg, "Technological Powers in Transition: Defense Conversion in Russia and the U.S., 1991–1995," *Journal of Peace Research* 36:5 (September 1999): 610–30.

39. Trenin at the book-launching event (for *The Russian Military: Power and Policy*) held at the Carnegie Endowment for International Peace in Washington, DC, 14 December 2004; CEIP transcript.

40. Leading generals and politicians (including Defense Minister Ivanov), have argued that the focus of the United States on international terrorism is partly a ploy to mask its expansionism. See, for instance, General Makhmut Gareiev, "Kakie vooruzhennie sily nuzhny Rossii?" *Otechestvennie Zapiski*, August 2002; cited in Alexander M. Golts and Tonya L. Putnam, "State Militarism and Its Legacies," *International Security* 29:2 (fall 2004): 129.

41. Arbatov, "Military Reform: From Crisis to Stagnation," in Steven E. Miller and Dmitri Trenin, eds., *The Russian Military: Power and Policy* (Cambridge: MIT Press, 2004), 106–16. For his earlier thoughts on the subject, see "Military Reform in Russia: Dilemmas, Obstacles, and Prospects," *International Security* 22:4 (spring 1998).

42. Arbatov, "Military Reform: From Crisis to Stagnation," 119.

43. Kim Murphy, "Russia Asserts Military Options," *Los Angeles Times*, 11 October 2003.

44. Cited in RFE/RL 9:142 (29 July 2005). See also Sergey Sevastyanov, "Russian Reforms: Implications for Regional Security Policy and the Military," in Judith Thornton and Charles E. Ziegler, eds., *Russia's Far East: A Region at Risk* (Seattle: University of Washington Press, 2002), 235–42.

45. RIA Novosti (Moscow), 5 September 2005; cited in RFE/RL 9:168 (6 September 2005).

46. "Putin Highlights Strategic Forces in State of the Nation," RIA Novosti (Moscow), 10 May 2006.

47. Viktor Myasnikov, "The Red Army: Still the Scariest of Them All," *Nezavisimaia Gazeta*, 27 February 2006.

48. See Arbatov, "Military Reform in Russia: Dilemmas, Obstacles, and Prospects," *International Security* 22:4 (spring 1998): 113–15.

49. Harold Elletson, *The General Against the Kremlin* (London: Little, Brown, 1998), 272.

50. Quoted in "Putin on Sunken Nuclear Submarine, Military Reform," Bloomberg (Moscow), 24 August 2000.

51. See Galia Golan, "Russia and the Iraq War: Was Putin's Policy a Failure?" *Communist and Post-Communist Studies* 37:4 (December 2004): 429–59.

52. See, for instance, "Professional Armed Forces May Not Appear In Russia in the Near Future," *Defense and Security* 118 (11 October 2002), WPS Media Monitoring Agency (http://wps.wm.ru)

53. Interview with Nemtsov, Ekho Moskvy Radio, 27 September 2002. The army's finance specialists seemed to have been ordered to generate prohibitively high conversion cost estimates. See Alexander Golts, "General Staff Strikes Back," *Russia Journal*, 1 February 2002.

54. "Aggressive Helplessness," *Vedomosti* (editorial), 16 February 2006. For a detailed study, see Rod Thornton, "Military Organizations and Change: The

'Professionalization' of the 76th Airborne Division," *Journal of Slavic Military Studies* 17:3 (September 2004): 449–74.

55. See G. A. Zhuganov, *Voennaia reforma: Otsenka ugroz natsional'noi bezopasnosti Rossii* (Moscow: Narodno-patrioticheskii Soiuz Rossii, 1997).

56. For an analysis of this party, see Henry Hale, "Yabloko and the Challenge of Building a Liberal Party in Russia," *Europe-Asia Studies* 56:7 (November 2004):993–1020.

57. For its plan, see www.svop.ru/live/materials.asp5m_id56974.

58. Aleksandr Bogatirev, "Nam nuzhna sovremennaia Armia," *Krasnaia Zvezda*, 17 April 2003.

59. Zarina Khisamova, "Spring Recruitment," *Ekspert*, 29 April 2002, 62. See also "Ministr Oboroni Rossii Sergei Ivanov: Nashu armiu usiliat dobrovolitsi iz SNG," *Komsomolskaia Pravda*, 2 April 2003; and "Russia Pledges to Follow Through on Delayed Military Reform," AFP (Moscow), 16 May 2003.

60. "Russia's Army to Become 70% Professional by 2008," RIA Novosti (Moscow), 21 February 2006; and RFE/RL 10:31 (17 February 2006).

61. Sergei Ivanov, "Russia Must Be Strong," *Wall Street Journal*, 11 January 2006.

62. Interview in *Krasnaia Zvezda*, 25 January 2006, cited in "Chief of General Staff on Changes in Russian Military Policy," RIA Novosti (Moscow), 27 January 2006.

63. Aleksandr Babakin and Viktor Myasnikov, "Quiet Military Coup: General Staff Thinks Up New Reform," *Nezavisimaia Gazeta*, 13 December 2005. For a useful historical perspective, see Aleksandr Golts, "An Army You Can't Change," *Moscow Times*, 20 December 2005.

64. "Aggressive Helplessness."

65. See, for instance, "Russians Unhappy with Their Generals," http://www.gazeta.ru, 28 April 2003; Theodore P. Gerber and Sarah E. Mendelson, "Strong Public Support for Military Reform in Russia," PONARS Policy Memo No. 288, May 2003; and Viktor Myasnikov, "People and Army Alienated," *Nezavisimaia Gazeta*, 11 September 2005.

66. Pavel K. Baev, "Reforming the Russian Military: History and Trajectory," in Yuri Fedorov and Bertil Nygren, eds., *Russian Military Reform and Russia's New Security Environment* (Stockholm: Swedish National Defence College, 2003), 38.

67. On the evolution of superpresidentialism, see Timothy J. Colton, "'Superpresidentialism' and Russia's Backward State," *Post-Soviet Affairs* 11:2 (April–June 1995): 144–49; and Scott Parrish, "Presidential Decree Authority in Russia, 1991–1995," in John M. Carey and Matthew Soberg Shugart, eds., *Executive Decree Authority* (New York: Cambridge University Press, 1998), 62–103.

68. Pavel Baev, "The Russian Army and Chechnya: Victory Instead of Reform?" in Stephen J. Cimbala, ed., *The Russian Military into the Twenty-First*

Century (London: Frank Cass, 2001), 75–96; and Alexander Golts, "Putin and the Chechen War: Together Forever," *Moscow Times*, 11 February 2004.

69. In a recent article Golts and Putnam also identified the military's institutional autonomy as a key explanatory variable. See their "State Militarism and Its Legacies," 123, 144–47.

70. This notion is recognized also by Steven Miller in his introduction, in Miller and Trenin, eds., *The Russian Military*, 31; and especially by Golts and Putnam, "State Militarism and Its Legacies," 141–55.

71. See, for instance, "Putin Praises Military for Selflessness, Courage," ITAR-TASS (Moscow), 23 February 2006. In spite of all its problems, the army remains one of the most trusted Russian institutions even if most Russians do not want their relatives to serve in it. See Alexei Levinson, "Neizbivni atribut," *Yezhenedelnii Zhurnal*, 17 September 2002; and Olga Timofeyeva's interview with Yuri Levada, "Russian Citizens Regard the Armed Forces with Respect and Pity," *Izvestia*, 22 February 2006.

72. See Pavel Felgenhauer, "General Staff in Command?" *Moscow Times*, 15 June 2004.

73. See Stephen Foye, "Updating Russian Civil-Military Relations," *RFE/RL Research Report* 2:46 (19 November 1993): 48; John Lloyd, *Rebirth of a Nation: An Anatomy of Russia* (London: Michael Joseph, 1998), 124; Zoltan Barany, "Politics and the Russian Armed Forces," in Zoltan Barany and Robert G. Moser, eds., *Russian Politics: Challenges of Democratization* (New York: Cambridge University Press, 2001), 191–92; and, more generally, Dmitri V. Trenin and Aleksei V. Malashenko, *Russia's Restless Frontier: The Chechnya Factor in Post-Soviet Russia* (Washington, DC: Carnegie Endowment for International Peace, 2004), 104.

74. For a good summary, see Alexei Arbatov, *The Transformation of Russian Military Doctrine: Lessons Learned from Kosovo and Chechnya* (Garmisch-Partenkirchen, Germany: George C. Marshall Center, 2000).

75. Simon Saradzhyan, "Putin Sacks 6 of Sergeev's Generals," *Moscow Times*, 1 August 2000.

76. Carolina Vendil, "The Russian Security Council," *European Security* 10:2 (summer 2001): 86.

77. See Mathers, "Outside Politics? Civil-Military Relations during a Period of Reform," in Anne Aldis and Roger McDermott, eds., *Russian Military Reform, 1992–2002* (London: Frank Cass, 2003), 25; and Baev, "Reforming the Russian Military," in Yuri Fedorov and Bertil Nygren, eds., *Russian Military Reform and Russia's New Security Environment* (Stockholm: Swedish National Defence College, 2003), 45.

78. See, for instance, Golts, "The Social and Political Condition," in Miller and Trenin, eds., *The Russian Military*, 91.

79. Litovkin, "Demands for Military Reform," RIA Novosti (Moscow), 12 July 2005.

80. "Kontseptsia national'noi bezopastnosti Rossiiskoi Federatsii," *Diplomaticheskii vestnik* 2 (February 2000): 3–13; and Alexander Golts, "Generals Cling to Cold War Past," *Bangkok Post*, 14 July 2003.

81. See "Defense Minister Encircled by Generals," *Novaya Gazeta*, 20–22 October 2003; and "Military Brains Ignoring Defence Minister," http://www.gazeta.ru, 26 January 2004.

82. Charles Gurin, "Observers Wonder How Ingushetia Gunmen Went Undetected," Eurasia Daily Monitor (Jamestown Foundation): 1:39 (June 25, 2004); Pavel Felgenhauer, "Kvashnin Won't Be Missed," *Moscow Times*, 20 July 2004; and "Heads Roll at Long Last," *Economist*, 24 July 2004, 48–49.

83. Golts, "Generals Cling to Cold War Past"; and Alexei Nikolski, "One War Is Not Enough!" *Vedomosti*, 3 October 2003.

84. See "Russian General Staff Official Takes Stock of Military Reform," BBC Monitoring of Channel 1 TV, Moscow, 19 October 2003. See also Baluyevskii, "Ends and Means: Chief of the General Staff on the Military Department's Strategies," *Rossiiskaia Gazeta*, 28 January 2005.

85. Interfax and RIA Novosti, 2 February 2005, reported in "Minister Admits Russia Will Always Need the Draft," RFE/RL 9:22 (3 February 2005); RFE/RL 10:54 (23 March 2006); "Russia Has No Choice but to Have a Large Army," Interfax-AVN (Moscow), 11 May 2006.

86. Golts, *Armia rossii: 11 poteriannikh let* (Moscow: Zaharov, 2004), 103.

87. Timothy J. Colton, *Commissars, Commanders, and Civilian Authority: The Structure of Soviet Military Politics* (Cambridge: Harvard University Press, 1979), 234.

88. Larry Diamond, *Developing Democracy: Toward Consolidation* (Baltimore, MD: Johns Hopkins University Press, 1999), 113.

Chapter 5
Civil-Military Relations and Superpresidentialism

1. See, for instance, Stephen M. Meyer, "How the Threat (and the Coup) Collapsed: The Politicization of the Soviet Military," *International Security* 16:3 (winter 1991/1992): 5–38; John W. R. Lepingwell, "Soviet Civil-Military Relations and the August Coup," *World Politics*, 44:4 (July 1992): 70–92; and V. Serebriannikov, *Zagadka perevorota: Kak razygryvali armeiskuiu kartu* (Moscow: Pravda Severa, 1992).

2. On this notion, see Timothy J. Colton, "Superpresidentialism and Russia's Backward State," *Post-Soviet Affairs* 11:2 (April–June 1995): 144–49; M. Steven Fish, "The Pitfalls of Russian Superpresidentialism," *Current History* 96:612 (1997): 326–30; and Igor Klyamkin and Lilia Shevtsova, *Rezhim Borisa Vtorogo*.

Osobennosti postkommunisticheskoi vlasti v Rossii (Moscow: Moscow Carnegie Center, 1999).

3. M. Steven Fish, "The Executive Deception: Superpresidentialism and the Degradation of Russian Politics," in Valerie Sperling, ed., *Building the Russian State: Institutional Crisis and the Quest for Democratic Governance* (Boulder, CO: Westview Press, 2000), 177–92, esp. 178–79.

4. M. Steven Fish, "The Dynamics of Democratic Erosion," in Richard D. Anderson, Jr., et al., *Postcommunism and the Theory of Democracy* (Princeton: Princeton University Press, 2001), 83–84.

5. Fish, "The Executive Deception," 178–79.

6. Timothy J. Colton and Cindy Skach, "The Russian Predicament," *Journal of Democracy* 16:3 (July 2005): 117–19.

7. Pavel K. Baev, "The Plight of the Russian Military: Shallow Identity and Self-Defeating Culture," *Armed Forces and Society* 29:1 (fall 2002): 133.

8. See Stephen Foye, "Updating Russian Civil-Military Relations," *RFE/RL Research Report*, 2 (19 November 1993): 48; and John Lloyd, *Rebirth of a Nation* (London: Michael Joseph, 1998), 124.

9. Yevgenii Primakov, *Vosem' mesiatsev plus* (Moscow, 2001), 93, cited in Dmitri Trenin and Aleksei Malashenko, *Russia's Restless Frontier: The Chechnya Factor in Post-Soviet Russia* (Washington, DC: Carnegie Endowment for International Peace, 2004), 109. See also Yeltsin's *Midnight Diaries* (New York: Public Affairs, 2000), 58–60.

10. Viktor Baranets, *Yeltsin i ego generali: Zapiski polkovnika genshtaba* (Moscow: Sovershenno Sekretno, 1997), 260–64; and Bertil Nygren, "Introduction," in Yuri Fedorov and Bertil Nygren, eds., *Russian Military Reform and Russia's New Security Environment* (Stockholm: Swedish National Defence College, 2003), 6.

11. Deborah Yarsike Ball, "The Pending Crisis in Russian Civil-Military Relations," Program on New Approaches to Russian Security (PONARS) Memo #4 (October 1997), 2–3.

12. ITAR-TASS (Murmansk), 21 August 1998.

13. For a profile of Stepashin, see Amy Knight, "Updating the Russian Who's Who," *New York Times*, 13 May 1999. For an account of the effect of the war in Kosovo on the Russian political and military establishments, see Deborah Yarsike Ball, "How Kosovo Empowers the Russian Military," PONARS Memo #61 (May 1999).

14. Geir Hønneland and Anne-Kristin Jørgensen, *Integration vs. Autonomy: Civil-Military Relations on the Kola Peninsula* (Brookfield, VT: Ashgate, 1999), 62.

15. Brian A. Davenport, "Civil-Military Relations in the Post-Soviet State: 'Loose Coupling' Uncoupled?" *Armed Forces and Society* 21:2 (winter 1995): 6. See also J. W. Derleth, "The Evolution of the Russian Polity: The Case of the

Security Council," *Communist and Post-Communist Studies* 29:1 (March 1996): 43–58.

16. Quoted by Marybeth Peterson Ulrich, *Democratizing Communist Militaries: The Cases of the Czech and Russian Armed Forces* (Ann Arbor: University of Michigan Press, 1999), 89.

17. Richard F. Staar, *The New Military in Russia: Ten Myths that Shape the Image* (Annapolis, MD: Naval Institute Press, 1996), 17.

18. David J. Betz, "No Place for a Civilian? Russian Defense Management from Yeltsin to Putin," *Armed Forces and Society* 28:3 (spring 2002): 495–96.

19. Aleksandr Golts, "Military Reform Sinks Along with the Kursk," *Russia Journal*, 2 September 2000.

20. "Russian Generals Dig in Heels over Defense Cuts," Jamestown Foundation Monitor, 11 October 2000.

21. "The Khaki-Colored Government" (interview with Kryshtanovskaya), *Nezavisimaia Gazeta*, 19 August 2003.

22. Cited in Carolina Vendil, "The Russian Security Council," *European Security* 10:2 (summer 2001): 86.

23. Pavel Zolotarev, "Three Sources—Three Components of Army Stagnation," *Nezavisimoe Voiennoe Obozrenie* (*NVO*), 5 January 2006.

24. "Putin Tells His Security Council to Focus on Three Key Threats to Russia," ITAR-TASS (Moscow), 29 May 2006.

25. Eva Busza, "Hard Times for the Russian State: State Dysfunctionality and the Russia Military," APSA convention paper, Boston, September 1998, 23. See also RFE/RL 2:148 (4 August 1998), citing a report in *Kommersant-Daily* of the same day.

26. Stephen J. Blank, *Russia's Armed Forces on the Brink of Reform* (Carlisle, PA: U.S. Army War College, 1998), 8.

27. Barylski, *The Soldier in Russian Politics*, 433. For comprehensive analyses, see Amy Knight, *Spies without Cloaks: The KGB's Successors* (Princeton: Princeton University Press, 1996); A. Savinkin and G. Hansen, eds., *Grazhdanskii kontrol' nad vooruzhennymi salmi* (Moscow: Russkii put', 1999); Maksim Glikin, *Militsia i bezpredel: Kto oni-oborotni v pogonakh ili nashi zashitniki* (Moscow: Tsentrpoligraf, 2000); and A. I. Kolpakidi and D. P. Prokhorov, *Imperia GRU* (Moscow: Olmapress, 2000).

28. *Komsomolskaia Pravda*, 29 August 1998; in JRL, #2339 (1 September 1998).

29. Stephen M. Meyer, "The Devolution of Russian Military Power," *Current History* 94: 594 (October 1995): 324.

30. Staar, *The New Military in Russia*, 70. For the conditions of Russian units in Chechnya see also Anatol Lieven, *Chechnya: Tombstone of Russian Power* (New Haven: Yale University Press, 1998).

31. Mark Galeotti, *The Age of Anxiety: Security and Politics in Soviet and Post-Soviet Russia* (London: Longman, 1995), 165–66. For another explanation of Barannikov's dismissal, see Roy Medvedev, *Kapitalizm v Rossii?* (Moscow: Prava cheloveka, 1998), 103.

32. Baev, *The Russian Army in a Time of Troubles* (London: Sage, 1996), 58. See also Sergei Parkhomenko, "Merlin's Tower," *Moscow News*, 28 April–4 May 1995.

33. RFE/RL 9:46 (10 March 2005), citing Interior Minister Rashid Nurgaliev's speech to the State Duma the day before.

34. See Lilia Shevtsova, "Russia's Fragmented Armed Forces," in Larry Diamond and Marc F. Plattner, eds., *Civil-Military Relations and Democracy* (Baltimore, MD: Johns Hopkins University Press, 1996), 119.

35. Galeotti, *The Age of Anxiety*, 166. See also Yuri Burtin, *Novy stroi: O nomenklaturnom kapitalizme* (Moscow: Seria Mezhdu Proshlim i Budushchim, 1995).

36. Simon Saradzhyan and Carl Schreck, "FSB Chief: NGOs a Cover for Spying," *Moscow Times*, 13 May 2005.

37. "Power to the Security and Law Enforcement People," *Russkii Fokus*, 24 May 2004. See also, Stephen White and Ian McAllister, "Putin and His Supporters," *Europe-Asia Studies* 55:3 (May 2003): 383–99; Anatolii Kostiukov, "Vlast' tsveta khaki," *Nezavisimaia Gazeta*, 19 August 2003; "Chekisty vo vlasti," *Novaya Gazeta*, 14 July 2003; and Olga Kryshtanovskaya, "The Commissars Have Returned," *Novaya Gazeta*, #63, 30 August 2004; Pavel Baev, "The Evolution of Putin's Regime: Inner Circles and Outer Walls," *Problems of Post-Communism* 51:6 (November–December 2004): 3–13.

38. Yuri Vasilev, "Glavnaia tema: Operativniki plokhie startegii," *Moskovskie novosti*, #26, 14 June 2003.

39. Baev, "The Evolution of Putin's Regime," 4; and personal communication with Jennifer Mathers of the University of Wales, August 2005.

40. Aleksandr Bovin, "Uniforms in Politics," *Nezavisimaia Gazeta*, 29 August 2003.

41. See, for instance, Yuri Golotiuk, "The Generals Have Been Told to Shape Up," *Vremia Novostei*, 24 July 2001; and "Putin Singles Out Border Guards for Praise," RFE/RL Russia Political Weekly 6:4 (9 February 2006).

42. "Russian 'Siloviki' Have Evolved Significantly in Past Few Years," *Argumenty i Fakty*, 23 March 2005. See also Lev Gudkov, "The Army as an Institutional Model," in Stephen L. Webber and Jennifer G. Mathers, eds., *Military and Society in Post-Soviet Russia* (Manchester: Manchester University Press, 2006), 48–52.

43. All quotations in this paragraph are from the *El País* interview with Ivanov, 11 July 2005; in JRL, #9198 (12 July 2005). For a brief analysis of Ivanov's home

institution, see Stella Suib, *Inside Russia's SVR: Foreign Intelligence Service* (Collingdale, PA: Diane, 2003).

44. Reports of *Vremia novostei*, 2 November 2004, and *Russkii kurir*, 28 October 2004, cited in RFE/RL 8:212 (9 November 2004).

45. In this paragraph I draw on Robert G. Moser, "Executive-Legislative Relations in Russia, 1991–1999," in Zoltan Barany and Robert G. Moser, eds., *Russian Politics: Challenges of Democratization* (New York: Cambridge University Press, 2001), 76–77. See also Thomas F. Remington, *The Russian Parliament: Institutional Evolution in a Transitional Regime* (New Haven: Yale University Press, 2001).

46. Galeotti, *The Age of Anxiety*, 159.

47. Ulrich, *Democratizing Communist Militaries*, 94–95.

48. I am grateful to Dale Herspring for this point.

49. "Russian General Critical of Military Reform," Interfax (Moscow), 7 February 2002.

50. Cited in RFE/RL 6:55 (22 March 2002).

51. See, for instance, Fred Weir, "Iraqi Defeat Jolts Russian Military," *Christian Science Monitor*, 16 April 2003; Vladimir Isachenkov, "U.S. Victory Highlights Russian Weakness," AP (Moscow), 21 April 2003; and the unusually frank discussion in the three-part series in *Krasnaia Zvezda*, 28 June and 7 and 18 July 2003.

52. Betz, "No Place for a Civilian?" 500.

53. See, for instance, Lyuba Pronina, "Duma Seeks Probe into Army Spending," *Moscow Times*, 19 February 2002.

54. Thomas Remington cited in "The Ever-Expanding Executive Branch," RFE/RL Russian Political Weekly 4:3 (29 January 2004).

55. Yuri A. Ivanov, "Legal, Political, and Budgetary Aspects of Civilian Control of the Military in Russia," in David Betz and John Löwenhardt, eds., *Army and State in Postcommunist Europe* (London: Frank Cass, 2001), 13.

56. Ulrich, *Democratizing Communist Militaries*, 81.

57. See A. G. Arbatov and E. L. Chernikov, eds., *Russian Federation Legal Acts on Civil-Military Relations: Collection of Documents* (Moscow: Foundation for Political Centrism, 2003).

58. "Russian Politician Accuses Military of Deceit over Professional Army," Interfax (Novosibirsk), 23 November 2001.

59. "Democracy Is No Good for the Military," *Defense and Security*, #140 (30 November 2001).

60. As reported in RFE/RL 9:9 (14 January 2005).

61. Solnick cited in Steven Lee Myers, "Bill to Increase Russia's Control over Charities Moves Ahead," *New York Times*, 22 December 2005.

62. Robin Shepherd, "Russia's Misplaced Pride Holds Back Its Democracy," *Financial Times*, 25 November 2005. See also the editorials, "Say Dosvidanye to

Democracy," *Wall Street Journal*, 24 November 2005; and "Putin's Power Grab," *Boston Globe*, 1 December 2005.

63. Colton and Skach, "The Russian Predicament," 120.

64. Pavel Felgenhauer, "Unbridled Dictatorial Drift," *Moscow Times*, 4 November 2003. See also V. Timchenko, *Putin i novaya Rossiia* (Rostov: Feniks, 2005).

65. In Irina Isakova, "The Evolution of Civil-Military Relations in Russia," in Andrew Cottey et al., eds., *Democratic Control of the Military in Postcommunist Europe* (London: Palgrave, 2002), 216.

66. Dmitri Trenin, "Reading Russia Right," Policy Brief #42, Carnegie Endowment for International Peace, October 2005, 2.

67. Interview with Russian sociologists on Ekho Moskvy Radio, 3 September 2003, 1008 GMT, BBC Monitoring, featured in JRL #7318 (9 September 2003). See also, Larisa Kaftan, "Russian Elite under Yeltsin and Putin," *Komsomolskaia Pravda*, 14 August 2003.

68. Baev, "The Plight of the Russian Military," 133.

69. "The Armed Forces in Deep Crisis: True Military Reforms Are Entirely Up To the President," *Novye Izvestia*, 6 April 2004.

70. Shevtsova, *Putin's Russia* (Washington, DC: Carnegie Endowment for International Peace, 2003), 131–32.

71. See "Zaiavlenie presidenta rossiskoi federatsii V. V. Putina," *Krasnaia zvezda*, 26 September 2001; "Putin Giving Military Broader Power," AP (Moscow), 28 October 2002; Vladimir Urban, "The Russian Military Gets a New Objective," *Novaya Gazeta*, 2 November 2002; Vadim Soloviov, "Russian General Staff's Answer to NATO," *NVO*, #2, January 2003; and Alexander Golts, "Military Reform in Russia and the Global War Against Terrorism," *Journal of Slavic Military Studies* 17:1 (March 2004): 29–41.

72. Cited in Ginodman and Rotkin, "The Specter of the Soviet Army: Military Reforms in Russia Are Still Following the Soviet Pattern," *Newsweek Russia* 33:101, 19–25 June 2006.

73. "Putin Displeased with Military Cooperation," TVS (Moscow), 1300 GMT, 24 April 2003, BBC Monitoring, in JRL, #7155 (26 April 2003). See also, "Putin Instructs Government to Speed Up Professional Army Plan," ITAR-TASS (Moscow), 12 May 2003; "Russia Pledges To Follow Through on Delayed Military Reform," AFP (Moscow), 16 May 2003; and RFE/RL 7:142 (29 July 2003).

74. Golotiuk, "The Generals Have Been Told to Shape Up"; and "Putin Appeals to Russian Officer Corps To Help Reform Army," ITAR-TASS (Moscow), 23 June 2003.

75. "Demands for Military Reform," RIA Novosti (Moscow), 12 July 2005.

76. Vladimir Isachenkov, "$11Bln Defense Budget Declassified," *Moscow Times*, 21 October 2002.

77. "Russian Reform: Mixed Signals," *Economist*, 29 May 2004, 54; and "Putin Praises Military for Selflessness, Courage," ITAR-TASS (Moscow), 22 February 2006. For a more optimistic assessment, see Dale R. Herspring, "Vladimir Putin and Military Reform in Russia," *European Security* 14:1 (March 2005): 137–55.

78. Richard Balmforth, "Eyeing Election, Putin Tours Military Manoeuvres," Reuters (Moscow), 18 February 2004; "Putin Seeks Votes from Suspicious Military," *Independent*, 8 March 2004; and Andrei Vladimirov, "Being Ready for 2008," *Itogi*, #34, 22 August 2005.

79. See, for instance, John B. Dunlop, *The 2002 Dubrovka and Beslan Hostage Crises: A Critique of Russian Counter-terrorism* (Stuttgart: ibidem-Verlag, 2006); and Amy Knight's thoughtful review, "The Kremlin Cover," *Times Literary Supplement*, 19 May 2006.

80. Vladimir Putin, "Stenograficheskii otchet o soveshchanii rukovodiashchego sostava Vooruzhennykh Sil," 9 November 2005 at http://president .kremlin.ru; and RFE/RL 9:212 (10 November 2005).

81. Betz, "No Place for a Civilian?" 138. See also, V. Yermolin, "Tbilisskii sindrom," *Krasnaia Zvezda*, 9 April 1991; and Mikhail Gorbachev, *Zhizn' i reformy*, vol. 1 (Moscow: Novosti, 1995), 385.

82. "73% of Russian Approve of Putin," Interfax (Moscow), 7 December 2005. According to another poll, conducted a few weeks before, 84 percent approved of his job performance. See "Putin's High Rating Confirmed By Polls," Interfax (Moscow), 18 November 2005.

83. "Russian Poll Indicates Putin Enjoys 'Almost Limitless' Support," ITAR-TASS (Moscow), 29 August 2006.

84. Pavel K. Baev, "Reforming the Russian Military: History and Trajectory," in Yuri Fedorov and Bertil Nygren, eds., *Russian Military Reform and Russia's New Security Environment* (Stockholm: Swedish National Defence College, 2003), 38.

85. Quoted in "Why Has Putin Failed to Tame the Bureaucracy?" RFE/RL Russian Political Weekly 3:13 (26 March 2003).

86. Dmitri V. Trenin, "Gold Eagle, Red Star," in Steven E. Miller and Trenin, eds., *The Russian Military: Power and Policy* (Cambridge: MIT Press, 2004), 225.

Conclusion

1. See David Collier and Steven Levitsky, "Democracy with Adjectives: Conceptual Innovation in Comparative Research," *World Politics* 49:3 (April 1997): 430–51.

2. Peter Rutland, "Russia: Democracy Dismantled," Jamestown Foundation Eurasia Daily Monitor, 10 January 2005.

3. This term and the definition is from Andrei Piontkovsky of Moscow's Center of Strategic Studies, in "A Unitary State with a Military Bureaucracy," *Nezavisimaia Gazeta*, 14 September 2004.

4. See, for instance, Peter Reddaway and Dmitri Glinsky, *The Tragedy of Russia's Reforms* (Washington, DC: U.S. Institute of Peace, 2001); Michael McFaul, Nikolai Petrov, and Andrei Ryabov, *Between Dictatorship and Democracy: Russian Post-Communist Political Reform* (Washington, D.C.: Carnegie Endowment for International Peace, 2004); Anna Politkovskaya, *Putin's Russia: Life in a Failing Democracy* (New York: Metropolitan, 2005); Andrew Wilson, *Virtual Politics: Faking Democracy in the Post-Soviet World* (New Haven: Yale University Press, 2006); M. Steven Fish, *Democracy Derailed* (New York: Cambridge University Press, 2005); and Richard Pipes, *Russian Conservatism and Its Critics: A Study in Political Culture* (New Haven: Yale University Press, 2006).

5. Cited in Elena Afanasieva, "The Imitator," *Novaya Gazeta*, #15, 4–6 March 2002. See also, V. Boiarintsev, *Svinskaia demokratsiia* (Moscow: Al'ternativa, 2005).

6. Cited in Andrew Jack, *Inside Putin's Russia: Can There Be Reform without Democracy?* (New York: Oxford University Press, 2006), 26–27.

7. Yevgenia Albats, "Russian Media: A Dead Man Still Walking," *Global Integrity*, 31 January 2005, available at www.publicintegrity.org/ga/report.aspx?aid=601.

8. Christopher Walker and Robert Orttung, "No News Is Bad News," *Wall Street Journal Europe*, 7 September 2006.

9. See, for instance, Uwe Klussmann, "Fuß auf dem Zünder: Moskau's Schlussforderungen aus dem Geiseldrama von Beslau," *Der Spiegel* #27, 4 July 2005, 94–95. Although since February 2005, when the law was passed, Putin had confirmed most of the incumbent governors in their posts, the point, of course, is that they are now beholden to him. See Kathryn Stoner-Weiss, "Russia: Authoritarianism without Authority," *Journal of Democracy* 17:1 (January 2006): 104–5; and Walker and Orttung, "No News Is Bad News."

10. James M. Goldgeier and Michael McFaul, "What To Do about Russia," *Policy Review*, no. 133 (October–November 2005).

11. Ibid.

12. RFE/RL 10:64 (6 April 2006) and RFE/RL 10:99 (1 June 2006), citing articles in *Izvestia* and *Moscow Times*.

13. Konstantin Smirnov, "A Frank Admission: The Cabinet Doesn't Play Any Significant Role in Russia," *Kommersant-Dengi*, #13, 4 April 2005; in JRL #9117 (11 April 2005).

14. Allen C. Lynch, *How Russia Is Not Ruled: Reflections on Russian Political Developments* (New York: Cambridge University Press, 2005), 14.

15. Yelena Panfilova, "Russia's Corruption Rating 'Critical,' " *Izvestia*, 19 October 2005.

16. "Nations in Transit," Freedom House, June 2005, see www.freedomhouse.org.

17. Nikolai Petrov in *Moscow Times*, 28 December 2004; cited by Rutland, "Russia: Democracy Dismantled."

18. Richard Pipes, *Russian Conservatism*. Three other original and historically informed explanations of Russia's political development are Tim McDaniel, *The Agony of the Russian Idea* (Princeton: Princeton University Press, 1996); Marshall T. Poe, *The Russian Moment in World History* (Princeton: Princeton University Press, 2003); and Lynch, *How Russia Is Not Ruled*.

19. See Sarah E. Mendelson and Theodore P. Gerber, "Failing the Stalin Test," *Foreign Affairs* 85:1 (January–February 2006): 2–8.

20. Richard, Pipes, "Flight from Freedom: What Russians Think and Want," *Foreign Affairs* 83:3 (May–June 2004): 9.

21. Ibid., 11.

22. Ibid., 15.

23. Dmitri Trenin, "Reading Russia Right," Policy Brief #42, Carnegie Endowment for International Peace, October 2005, 2. See also Richard Pipes, "On Democracy in Russia: It's Not a Pretty Picture," *New York Times*, 3 June 2004.

24. Dmitry Kamyshev and Viktor Khamraiev, "The Unconstitutional Majority," *Kommersant*, 8 June 2006; and RFE/RL 10:104, 8 June 2006. See also "A Third Term in Office," *Nezavisimaia Gazeta*, 9 June 2006; and "Russia's Putin Reiterates He Won't Run for Third Presidential Term," Prime-Tass (Shanghai), 16 June 2006, in JRL 2006-#139.

25. Cited in Stephen Kotkin, "Gasputin: All that Stands Between Democracy and Russia Is Russia," *The New Republic*, 29 May 2006, 33. See also Svetlana Babayeva, "The Burden of Power," *Moscow News*, 16 June 2006.

26. Christopher Donnelly, "Reshaping Russia's Armed Forces: Security Requirements and Institutional Responses," in Anne Aldis and Roger McDermott, eds., *Russian Military Reform 1992–2002* (London: Frank Cass, 2003), 305.

27. Yuri Ivanov, "Legal, Political, and Budgetary Aspects of Civilian Control of the Military in Russia," in David Betz and John Löwenhardt, eds., *Army and State in Postcommunist Europe* (London: Frank Cass, 2001), 11.

28. See Walter Parchomenko, "The State of Russia's Armed Forces and MilitaryReform," *Parameters: Quarterly of the U.S. Army War College* 29:4 (winter 1999–2000): 98–110.

29. Valerii Cheban, "Civilian Control over Power Structures Has Remained Virtual," *Nezavisimoe Voennoe Obozrenie*, 7 February 2003.

30. See Brian Taylor, "The Duma and Military Reform," PONARS memo #154 (November 2000): 45–47.

31. Reddaway and Glinsky, *The Tragedy of Russia's Reforms*, 211.

32. Zoltan Barany, "Controlling the Military: A Partial Success," *Journal of Democracy* 10:2 (April 1999): 54.

33. Dmitri Trenin, "Gold Eagle, Red Star," in Steven E. Miller and Dmitri Trenin, eds., *The Russian Military: Power and Policy* (Cambridge: MIT Press, 2004), 223.

34. Stephen Meyer, "The Devolution of Russian Military Power," *Current History* 94:594 (October 1995): 326.

35. Alexei G. Arbatov, "Military Reform in Russia: Dilemmas, Obstacles, and Prospects," *International Security* 22:4 (spring 1998): 83.

36. Condoleezza Rice, "The Party, the Military, and Decision Authority in the Soviet Union," *World Politics* 40:1 (October 1987): 65.

37. Rose Gottemoeller, "Nuclear Weapons in Current Russian Policy," in Miller and Trenin, eds., *The Russian Military*, 185. See also Thomas Graham, Jr. and Damien J. LaVera, *Cornerstones of Security: Arms Control Treaties in the Nuclear Era* (Seattle: University of Washington Press, 2003).

38. Andrei Loshchilin, "Over Five Years Russia Cuts Its Nuclear Strength by 1,740 Warheads," RIA Novosti (New York), 4 May 2005.

39. See, for instance, "After the Historic Summit in Moscow," *Nezavisimoe Voennoe Obozrenie*, #23, 12–18 July 2002. For a recent comprehensive assessment, see Alexei Arbatov and Vladimir Dvorkin, *Beyond Nuclear Deterrence: Transforming the U.S.-Russian Equation* (Washington, DC: Carnegie Endowment for International Peace, 2006).

40. See Tatyana Sinitsyna, "How Close Have American Inspectors Come to Russia's Nuclear Sites?" RIA Novosti (Moscow), 3 May 2005.

41. See Nikolai Poroskov, "RVSN Commander Solovtsov on Future Plans, Adamov, Cooperation with U.S." *Vremia Novostey*, 7 May 2005.

42. Interview with Baluyevskii in *Izvestia*, 1 March 2005.

43. RFE/RL 9:181 (23 September 2005).

44. Viktor Litovkin, "Russia Tries To Destroy Chemical Weapons on Time," RIA Novosti (Moscow), 9 August 2004.

45. RFE/RL 10:111 (19 June 2006), citing an article in the 16 June 2006 issue of *USA Today*.

46. Jason Cato, "Adamov Unlikely to Face U.S. Trial," *Pittsburgh Tribune-Review*, 22 April 2006; and Dmitry Starostin, "Russia's Ex-Nuclear Minister: 'It Was a Successful Arrest,'" *Moscow News*, 4 August 2006.

47. RFE/RL 10: 166 (8 September 2006), based on a report in *Nezavisimaia Gazeta* of the same day.

48. Philip Turner, "Former Soviet Nukes Still a Threat," UPI (Washington), 3 June 2005.

49. See for instance his remarks at the Council of Foreign Relations, New York, 13 January 2005 (CFR Transcript in JRL #9026 [20 January 2005]).

50. Pavel Felgenhauer, "Nuclear Security Is a Myth," *Moscow Times*, 10 August 2004.

51. "No Attempts to Enter Russia's Nuke Storage Facilities," *Interfax* (Moscow), 17 December 2005.

52. Felgenhauer, "Nuclear Security is a Myth."

53. Interview with Verkhovtsev in *Krasnaia Zvezda*, 5 September 2006, reported in "Nuclear Weapons Safeguarding Improved in Russia," ITAR-TASS (Moscow), 5 September 2006.

54. Turner, "Former Soviet Nukes Still a Threat."

55. Interfax dispatch reported in RFE/RL 10:36 (27 February 2006); and RFE/RL 10:48 (15 March 2006).

56. See, for instance, "New Russian Warhead," http://www.gazeta.ru, 2 November 2005.

57. See Pavel Felgenhauer, "Playing a Dangerous Game," *Moscow Times*, 14 December 2000; and Victor Yasmann, "What Is Behind Moscow's 'Iranian Game?' " RFE/RL Russian Political Weekly 6:1 (19 January 2006).

58. This section draws on Zoltan Barany, *The Future of NATO Expansion* (New York: Cambridge University Press, 2003).

59. Cited in Michael Mihalka, "Continued Resistance to NATO Expansion," *Transition* 1:14 (11 August 1995): 38. See also N. N. Beliakov and A. Iu. Moiseev, *Rasshierenie NATO na vostok: k miru ili voine?* (Moscow: Klub 'Realisty,' 1998).

60. Alexii K. Pushkov, "Don't Isolate Us: A Russian View of NATO Enlargement," *National Interest* 47 (spring 1997): 58–63. According to opinion polls "Nearly 90% of Russia's Political Elite Opposes NATO Enlargement," Rosbalt (Moscow), 29 April 2004.

61. Oksana Antonenko, "Russia, NATO, and European Security after Kosovo," *Survival* 41:4 (winter 1999–2000): 124, 140; and Dmitri Trenin, "Russia-NATO Relations: Time to Pick Up the Pieces," *NATO Review* 48 (spring/summer 2000): 19–22.

62. Igor Galichin, "NATO for Breakfast," *Segodnia*, 6 March 2000; and Tom Shanker, "Bonn Rebuffs US over NATO's Role for Russia," *Chicago Tribune*, 10 September 1994.

63. "Robertson Says Russia Could One Day Join NATO," Reuters (Moscow), 23 May 2000. See also Charles A. Kupchan, "Rethinking Europe," *National Interest* 56 (summer 1999): 73–80.

64. Yuri Pankov, "Why Russia Is Invited to NATO," *Krasnaia Zvezda*, 11 August 2001; and "Russia Wants Ties with NATO, But Not Membership," Interfax (Moscow), 9 August 2001.

65. See Olga Koleva's interviews with leading Russian generals in *Vremia Novostei*, 21 November 2002.

66. Sean Kay, "Heading Nowhere?" *International Herald Tribune*, 10 May 2002.

67. See, for instance, Sergei Ivanov, "Russia's Armed Forces and Geopolitical Priorities," http://www.polit.ru, 1 February 2004 in JRL, #8043 of the same date;

and "Intervention: U.S. Military Bases in Romania Will Complete the Circle," *Nezavisimaya Gazeta*, 8 December 2005.

68. Vladimir Soloviev, "Russia Wants To Be NATO Ally," *Kommersant*, 8 December 2005.

69. Ivanov's remarks to the CFR, 13 January 2005 (CFR transcript).

70. See the *Krasnaia Zvezda* interview with CGS Baluyevskii, 6 November 2004; Robert E. Hunter and Sergei M. Rogov, *Engaging Russia as Partner and Participant: The Next Stage of NATO-Russia Relations* (Santa Monica, CA: Rand, 2005); and Dmitry Trenin, "Russia's Security Integration with America and Europe," in Alexander J. Motyl, Blair A. Ruble, and Lilia Shevtsova, eds., *Russia's Engagement with the West: Transformation and Integration in the Twenty-First Century* (Armonk, NY: M. E. Sharpe, 2005), 281–94.

71. See Richard Fisher, "Puzzling War Games," *Wall Street Journal Asia*, 22 August 2005; and RFE/RL 9:161 (25 August 2005).

72. Shevtsova, *Putin's Russia* (Washington, DC: Carnegie Endowment for International Peace, 2003), 225.

73. See Jako Hedenskog, *Russia as a Great Power: Dimensions of Security under Putin* (London: Routledge, 2005).

74. Quoted by Interfax (Munich), dispatch reported in RFE/RL 10:22 (6 February 2006).

75. Steven Lee Myers, "Belarus: Putin Backs Leader," *New York Times*, 29 April 2006.

76. See Zoltan Barany, "NATO's Peaceful Advance," *Journal of Democracy* 15:1 (January 2004): 63–76, and "NATO's Post-Cold War Metamorphosis: From 16 to 26 and Counting," *International Studies Review* 8:1 (March 2006): 165–78.

77. Nikolai Poroskov, "Soldiers without Borders," *Vremia Novostei*, 11 August 2004. For more general studies on this issue, see Nicole Jackson, *Russian Foreign Policy and the CIS* (London: Routledge, 2003); and Lena Jonson, *Vladimir Putin and Central Asia: The Shaping of Russian Foreign Policy* (London: I. B. Tauris, 2004).

78. Cited in RFE/RL, 9:192 (12 October 2005). See also Alexei Nikolsky, "A Useful Failure," *Vedomosti*, 6 April 2005.

79. RFE/RL 9:223 (1 December 2005).

80. "Russia Has 16 Military Bases in Foreign Countries," Interfax-AVN (Moscow), 18 October 2005.

81. See RFE/RL 7:214 (12 November 2003) and 7:222 (25 November 2003); and "Former Soviet War Zones: The Hazards of a Long, Hard Freeze," *Economist*, 21 August 2004, 40–41.

82. See Vladimir Mukhin, "The Last Dash to the South," *Nezavisimaia Gazeta*, #164, 8 August 2005; and Vladimir Soloviov et al., "Changing the Guard," *Kommersant*, 24 November 2005.

83. C. J. Chivers, "Russia: Praise for Uzbek Crackdown," *New York Times*, 11 April 2006.

84. Nathan Hamm, "Farewell K2: Uzbekistan's American Fallout," at http://www.openDemocracy.net, 8 August 2005.

85. RFE/RL 7:181 (23 September 2003); and "Sometimes, Two's a Crowd," *Economist*, 1 November 2003.

86. Alexei Nikolsky, "A Useful Failure," *Vedomosti*, 6 April 2005. See also Scott Radnitz, "What Really Happened in Kyrgyzstan?" *Journal of Democracy* 17:2 (April 2006): 132–46.

87. "Putin Power," *Economist*, 11 October 2003.

88. Cited by Judith Ingram, "Group Says Russia Now at 'Not Free' Status," AP (Moscow), 20 December 2004. See also Pavel Felgenhauer, "Unbridled Dictatorial Drift," *Moscow Times*, 4 November 2003.

89. See, for instance, Alexander Motyl, "Ukraine vs Russia: The Politics of an Energy Crisis," at http://www.openDemocracy.net, 17 January 2006; and Ivan Krastev, "The Energy Route to Russian Democracy," at http://www. openDemocracy.net, 13 June 2006.

90. See, for instance, Anders Åslund, "Russia's Success Story," *Foreign Affairs* 73:5 (September–October 1994): 58–71, and *How Russia Became a Market Economy* (Washington, DC: Brookings Institution Press, 1995); Andrei Shleifer and Daniel Treisman, "A Normal Country," *Foreign Affairs* 83:2 (March–April 2004): 20–38; Andrei Shleifer, *A Normal Country: Russia after Communism* (Cambridge: Harvard University Press, 2005). Some much needed recent correctives are Steven Rosefielde, "Russia: An Abnormal Country," *European Journal of Comparative Economics* 2:1 (January 2005): 3–16; Stefan Hedlund, *Russian Path Dependence* (London: Routledge, 2005); and Peter Baker and Susan Glasser, *Kremlin Rising: Vladimir Putin's Russia and the End of Revolution* (New York: Scribner, 2005).

91. CFR Transcript, 13 January 2005.

92. Interview with Ivanov in the Spanish newspaper, *El País*, 11 July 2005; translated in Johnson's Russia List, #9198 (12 July 2005).

93. Cited in "Strengthening of Democracy Is Russia's Highest Priority: Putin," AFP (Moscow), 25 April 2005. See also Claire Bigg, "Was Soviet Collapse Last Century's Worst Geopolitical Catastrophe?" RFE/RL Russian Political Weekly 5:17 (2 May 2005); and Aleksei Chadaev, *Putin—ego ideologiia* (Moscow: Evropa, 2006).

94. "Putin: Russian Media As Free As Any Other," RIA Novosti (Moscow), 23 December 2004.

95. See RFE/RL 10:103 (7 June 2006); 10:110 (16 June 2006); 10:111 (19 June 2006); and 10:136 (27 July 2006).

96. Goldgeier and McFaul, "What To Do about Russia." For an earlier exposition, see their *Power and Purpose: U.S. Policy toward Russia after the Cold War* (Washington, DC: Brookings Institution Press, 2003).

97. Francesca Mereu, "Putin Quietly Signed NGO Bill Last Week," *Moscow Times*, 18 January 2006. See also, Yelena Rykovtseva, "Some Impermissible Absurdities," *Russia Profile* 3:1 (January–February 2006): 13.

98. Goldgeier and McFaul, "What To Do about Russia." See also, Beth A. Fischer, *The Reagan Reversal: Foreign Policy and the End of the Cold War* (Columbia, MO: University of Missouri Press, 2000); and Jack Matlock, *Reagan and Gorbachev: How the Cold War Ended* (New York: Random House, 2004).

99. See RFE/RL 8:32 (19 February 2004); "Military Rot Spreads to Russia's Nuclear Forces," AFP (Moscow), 19 February 2004; and Robert McMullin and Celeste Wallander, "Russian Insecurity Is Our Problem," *On the Agenda*, Center for Strategic and International Studies Newsletter, March 2004.

100. Arbatov cited by Anatolii Medetsky, "Report: Increase Nuclear Funding," *Moscow Times*, 24 May 2005. See also L. Mletsin, *Putin, Bush, i voina v Irake* (Moscow: Eksmo, 2005); and Dmitri Trenin, "Russia Leaves the West," *Foreign Affairs* 85:4 (July–August 2006): 87–96.

INDEX

Brezhnev, Leonid, 1, 45, 46, 48, 93, 121
Budanov, Yuri, 103
Budennovsk, 165
burial, of combat dead, 30–31
Burlakov, Matvei, 47, 68, 105–6
Burutin, Aleksandr, 59–60
Bush, George W., 184, 185, 187, 189, 190, 191

Carnegie Foundation, 123
Caucasus, 3, 114, 154
Ceauşescu, Nicolae, 154
Central Asia, 3, 51, 134, 187–89
Central and Eastern Europe, 141
Chaika, Yuri, 65
Chávez, Hugo, 191
Chechen Wars, 15, 30, 59, 66, 72–75, 76–77, 89, 91, 94, 96, 101–3, 107, 114, 134, 146, 147, 150, 153, 154, 164, 166, 167
Chechnya, 39, 90, 98, 103, 115, 131, 171, 190
Cheney, Dick, 192
Cherkesov, Viktor, 156
Chernobyl disaster, 20, 23, 29
Chernomyrdin, Viktor, 148, 152, 165
China (People's Republic of), 57, 97, 138, 186
Chobotov, Andrei, 156
Chubais, Anatolii, 148, 152, 184
Civic Union, 95
civilian control, 3, 5, 12, 17, 122, 149, 157–58, 160–61, 174–75, 192; of defense expenditures, 119–20, 122, 158–60; democratic, 3, 84, 119–20, 161; institutional arrangements of, 3, 4, 5, 83–84, 85–86, 93, 144–46, 149, 157–61, 167–68, 175, 192
civilian defense minister, 84, 120–21
civilian defense experts, 84, 86, 120–22, 161, 177
civil-military relations, 3, 79, 83, 99, 119–20, 140, 167–68, 175–76; and communism, 11–12; and democratization, 4, 11–12, 107, 142, 158–60, 192; decay of in Russia, 69, 104, 140; Russian, 3, 8–9, 106, 136–38, 142, 145–46, 176–77, 217 n71; Soviet, 7–8, 81–83, 109–10, 122,

144–46, 177; theories of, 10–12, 83–84, 108–10, 132, 141, 145, 178–79
Clausewitz, Carl von, 13
Clinton, Bill, 26, 190
Collective Security Treaty Organization (CSTO), 188–89
Colton, Timothy J., 10, 11, 134, 139, 141, 145–46, 178
combat readiness, 57–58, 114
Committee for State Security. See KGB
Committees of Soldiers' Mothers, 66, 118. See also Union of Soldiers' Mothers
Commonwealth of Independent States (CIS), 15, 48, 107, 108, 112, 131, 187–89
Communist Party of Russia (KPRF), 37, 97, 129
Communist Party of the Soviet Union (CPSU), 8, 12, 81, 84, 110, 116, 122, 145, 177; Central Committee of, 81, 162; Politburo of, 93, 151; Presidium of, 93; Twenty-seventh Congress of, 46
compensation, for combat deaths, 30, 31
Congress of People's Deputies, 86, 157
Constitution, 26, 84, 85, 118, 146, 150, 158, 159–60, 174, 175
Constitutional Court, 146, 157
contract service, 3, 55, 115, 124–25, 131
contract soldiers, 56, 73–74, 115
conscription, 4, 56, 65, 115, 117–18, 124–25, 130–31, 139–40, 147, 220 n26; public views of, 64; in Soviet era, 61;
conscripts, 55, 73; conditions for, 61–62, 64–66, 90–91; hazing of, 62, 64–66; quality of, 63–65
corruption, 9, 53, 65–66, 67–69, 90, 118, 124, 128–32, 138, 148, 181, 182, 220 n26
Council on Foreign Relations (New York), 74, 185, 190
Council for Foreign and Defense Policy (Moscow), 130
coup attempt of August 1991, 63, 82, 84, 95, 144–45, 176, 179
coups d'état, 10, 11, 79, 108, 109, 176
crime, 62, 64–66, 67–69
crisis management, 19–20, 23–31, 40–41, 42
Cuba, 107

Union of Rightist Forces (SPS), 26, 119, 127–29, 130, 161
United Kingdom. *See* Great Britain
United Russia, 119, 157, 162
United States, 3, 29, 32, 41, 46, 50, 51, 52, 53, 56, 123, 125, 129, 134, 139–40, 180–92; armed forces of, 51, 57, 75–76, 127, 179; bases of, in Central Asia, 188–89; defense spending of, 55; and Russia's nuclear program, 180–83
Unity, 129
U.S. Congress, 180
U.S.-Russian relations, 3–4, 32, 46, 107–8, 124–26, 134, 164, 180–92
U.S. Senate Foreign Relations Committee, 181–82
USS *Memphis*, 32, 33
USS *Toledo*, 32
Ustinov, Dmitri, 93, 121
Ustinov, Vladimir, 31–32, 33, 34, 67
Uzbekistan, 185, 187, 188–89

Valynkin, Igor, 182
Vedrine, Hubert, 3
Venezuela, 191
Verich, Gennadii, 24
Verkhovtsev, Vladimir, 182
Vershbow, Alexander, 185
Veselov, Yevgenii, 65
Vidaevo, 30, 36, 37
Vietnam, 107
Vilnius, 82
Volkogonov, Dmitri, 87
Voloshin, Aleksandr, 29
Vorobyev, Eduard, 107, 159

weapons development, 43, 59
weapons procurement, 54, 58–59, 125
weapons safety, 60
Weir, Margaret, 6
Western Europ, 189
"Western threat," 50–52, 75–76
women, 56, 131
Working Russia, 129

Yabloko, 39, 128, 130, 161, 189
Yastrzhembskii, Sergei, 103
Yavlinskii, Grigorii, 189
Yazov, Dmitri, 101, 144, 165, 176
Yeltsin, Boris, 1, 4, 9, 14, 28, 29, 53, 56, 68, 85, 94–99, 108, 120, 134, 137, 141, 143–57, 162, 165, 166, 177, 186; 1993 conflict with the legislature, 15, 83–85, 89, 143, 146–47, 152, 157–58; and civil-military relations, 85–86, 109–10,134–35, 217n71; committees, 148–52; and defense reform, 55–56, 84–85, 126–27, 146, 147–49, 152; and the military, 8–9, 17, 75, 84, 89–90, 104, 116, 146–50; and war in Chechnya, 71–72, 96, 98
Yugoslavia, 51, 106, 107–8, 149
Yukos, 172
Yushchenko, Viktor, 200n91

zero-sum game, Russia-U.S. relations as, 190–91
Zhirinovsky, Vladimir, 87–88, 184
Zhuganov, Gennadii, 37, 184
Zhukov, Georgi, 93
Zolotarev, Pavel, 120
Zvezda, 116–17